D0875738

DISCARDED

Yale Russian and East European Studies, 8

GOGOL

Victor Erlich

New Haven and London,
Yale University Press
1969

Published with assistance from the foundation
established in memory of Calvin Chapin of the
Class of 1788, Yale College.
Copyright © 1969 by Yale University.
All rights reserved. This book may not be
reproduced, in whole or in part, in any form
(except by reviewers for the public press),
without written permission from the publishers.
Library of Congress catalog card number: 76-81416
Standard book number: 300-0-1120-2
Designed by Helen Frisk Buzyna,
set in Times Roman type,
and printed in the United States of America by
The Carl Purington Rollins Printing-office
of the Yale University Press, New Haven, Conn.
Distributed in Great Britain, Europe, Asia, and
Africa by Yale University Press Ltd., London; in
Canada by McGill-Queen's University Press, Montreal; and
in Mexico by Centro Interamericano de Libros
Académicos, Mexico City.

891.78
G61ze

To Henry and Mark

71—11631

THE PUBLIC LIBRARY OF NASHVILLE & DAVIDSON COUNTY

APR 2 0 1971

Preface

The present book reflects my enduring fascination with its subject. It all started many years ago, when I had just turned seven. A well-chosen birthday gift—*Selected Works* by Nikolai Gogol—held me spellbound. Haunted by the eerie magic of Gogol's early Romantic tales, I chose to demonstrate my enthusiasm for the hefty volume by painstakingly copying it page by page. Eventually I was stopped in my tracks by an elder's amused query: "Why are you doing this?" Groping toward a pragmatic rationalization, I mumbled something to the effect that, should our house burn down, the precious book might perish. "So would your copy," sensibly retorted my relative.

In retrospect, my inconclusive labor of love seems a naïve attempt to incorporate a work one admires by reproducing it. Yet is not the urge to get inside an author who has meant a great deal to one among the mainsprings of literary criticism? If so, the book I have just completed is, in a sense, a belated enactment of a childish impulse. I can only hope that, in addition to satisfying its author's long-delayed need, this brief reexamination of Nikolaj Gogol will be of some interest to readers who have had occasion to puzzle over an immensely suggestive and still undeciphered writer.

To say this is not to imply that the substantial body of critical exegesis and biographical exploration which has grown around Gogol in the last 130 years or so fails to provide significant clues. Gogol scholarship is a gaudy mixture of obtuseness and irrelevance with brilliance and critical acumen. The dazzling forays into Gogol by such men of letters as

Andrej Belyj or Aleksej Remizov and the trenchant analyses by such literary historians as Dmitry Cizevsky, Boris Eikhenbaum, or V. V. Gippius are among the triumphs of Russian criticism. My indebtedness to these illuminations is acknowledged frequently—and gratefully—in the pages that follow.

While little of this material has as yet been made available to the English-speaking reader of Gogol, he has not lacked expert critical guidance. In addition to an excellent though necessarily brief section in D. S. Mirsky's *A History of Russian Literature,* a perceptive chapter in Donald Fanger's recent study of Romantic Realism, and suggestive and sensible comments by such American critics as Edmund Wilson or Philip Rahv, one ought to cite at least two books in English that have incontestable merit. V. Nabokov's *Nikolai Gogol* brilliantly recaptures and indeed recreates those aspects of Gogol that strike a responsive chord in the author of *Lolita.* V. Setchkarev's *Gogol* judiciously incorporates some of the more thoughtful recent interpretations. Yet these two approaches to Gogol seem to have the defects of their widely disparate virtues. Nabokov consistently ignores those dimensions of the Gogolian universe that he does not find congenial; Setchkarev, painstakingly comprehensive where Nabokov is willfully selective, shuns generalization and eschews synthesis. When all is said and done, yet another introduction to Gogol in English—less capricious than Nabokov's and more sharply focussed than Setchkarev's—might not be altogether redundant.

In the process of working on this volume I contracted various debts of gratitude which I would now like to acknowledge. I wish to thank the Guggenheim Foundation for having supported in the fall of 1964 the initial stage of my research—or rather my reimmersion—in Gogol, and Yale for having granted me a term's leave of absence at an early phase of my association with the university. I am grateful to students who participated in my recent seminar on Gogol: their lively response helped me test and articulate some of the notions embodied in this book. I think with special pleasure of one paper that emerged from the seminar: As will be indicated below, Michael Holquist's short study of Gogol and the

Romantic fairy tale made a tangible impact on my treatment of Gogol's Ukrainian period.

My work on *Gogol*, which proceeded by leaps and bounds, entered a hectic stage during the past summer and fall. I was trying to get the manuscript into final shape prior to my departure for Europe. This contingency placed a strenuous burden on my technical assistants, and I wish to thank Mrs. Lucille McKenna, Barbara Gottlieb, and Priscilla Hunt for having "come through" each time with dispatch and accuracy.

For better or worse, my wife is partly responsible for the existence of this book. When, several years ago, I was casting about for a new project, she steered me toward my first literary love. She has offered perceptive criticism of the emerging work and much-needed support during the somewhat trying periods when other commitments kept me away from the task.

My mother's contribution, though less recent, was no less essential. I had benefited in many ways from her profound knowledge of Russian literature, and more specifically from her enthusiastic and sophisticated appreciation of Gogol. Need I add that it was she who gave me *the* book?

V.E.

Paris
April 1969

Contents

The Grotesque Imagination

To say that Nikolaj Gogol is one of the most controversial major figures in Russian literature is to offer one of the few noncontroversial statements that can be legitimately made about this remarkable writer. Both during his lifetime and since his death, Gogol was often a center of what he himself called a "whirlwind of misunderstandings."[1] Though the scope of his achievement clearly is not at issue, we are still far from agreement as to the nature of his genius, the meaning of his bizarre art, and his still weirder life.

Every major aspect of the Gogol story seems to feature contradiction and invite perplexity. First there is the man, nearly as inept and self-destructive in "real life" as he was compelling in his writings, yet, on the eve of his death, coming perilously close to renouncing literature, his only source of strength, as dangerous and wicked. Then there is the writer, who, at the peak of his career, was hailed by the most influential literary critic of the day as a bold challenger of an oppressive and antiquated system, only to be denounced several years later by the same intelligentsia spokesman as an abject apologist for the Tsarist Establishment. There is the moralist, who, in his most sanguine moments, liked to cast himself in the role of a religious visionary but who, to Tolstoy, was merely a "small, fearful mind."[2] Finally, and perhaps most importantly, there is

1. Gogol, *Polnoe Sobranie Sochinenij* (Complete works) (Moscow, Izdatelstvo Akademii Nauk SSSR, 1952), *13*, 348.

2. Tolstoy, *Polnoe Sobranie Sochinenij* (Moscow, Khudozhestvennaja Literatura, 1936), *38*, 50. It is a tribute to the complexity and inconsistency of both

the artist, dubbed by the nineteenth-century social critics and their Soviet epigones the father of Realism in Russian literature yet to such a modern man of letters as Vladimir Nabokov a magnificently wacky prose poet, a compelling dramatizer of his private nightmares.

One hardly needs to insist that no single literary label could do justice to so elusive and baffling a phenomenon. Yet I submit that, in our inevitable attempts to pin down as best we can the nature of Gogol's imagination and the texture of his universe, we could do worse than invoke a concept which of late has loomed rather large in modern literary and art criticism, that of the grotesque. In fact, I would go as far as to suggest that few masters of world literature epitomize the grotesque imagination more fully or boldly than Nikolaj Gogol.

But, one may interpose at this point, is it legitimate to speak about the grotesque imagination as well as the grotesque manner? Or, to put it differently, can one treat the grotesque as a structure as well as an inherent quality, as a vision as well as a motif? I believe one can, and in this respect, as in some others, I am willing to follow the lead of an influential recent writer on the grotesque, the eminent German literary historian Wolfgang Kayser.

Kayser's *The Grotesque in Literature and Art*[3] offers a redefinition of the concept in terms broad enough to accommodate Hieronymus Bosch, Francisco Goya, and Salvador Dali, as well as E. T. A. Hoffmann, Edgar Allan Poe, Franz Kafka, and Christian Morgenstern. His wide-ranging, historical survey clearly suggests that the notion of the grotesque universe as one

great writers that some twenty years earlier, in the wake of his own moral crisis, Tolstoy could speak with admiration about the late Gogol's preaching and berate Russian public opinion for misconstruing his highly significant message as the raving of a madman (ibid., 26, 648-71).

3. (Bloomington, Indiana University Press, 1963), p. 224. Translated by Ulrich Weisstein from Kayser's *Das Groteske: Seine Gestaltung in Malerei und Dichtung.*

which plays havoc with normal distinctions and expectations is almost as old as the term "grotesque," derived ultimately from the Italian *grotta*. As early as the Renaissance *grottesco* meant

> not only something playfully gay and carelessly fantastic, but also something ominous and sinister in the face of a world totally different from the familiar one—a world in which the realm of inanimate things is no longer separated from those of plants, animals and human beings and where the laws of statics, symmetry and proportion are no longer valid.

Some two centuries later, a German man of letters, Wieland, focused more explicitly on the complex, contradiction-ridden emotional response to a grotesque work of art: "We smile at the deformations, but are appalled by the horrible and the monstrous elements as such." The basic feeling, however, "is one of surprise and terror, an agonizing fear in the presence of a world which breaks apart and remains inaccessible."[4]

This perplexity is not only a matter of losing intellectual control over the situation, but also, and perhaps more importantly, of a mounting emotional disorientation. In pausing before a famous triptych by that archetypal grotesque artist, Hieronymus Bosch, Kayser calls attention to the tenor of the right panel of the painting which represents hell: "One is struck by the silence with which the torments are inflicted. The victims themselves appear to be unaffected, an indifference that puzzles and frightens the observer. No emotions seem to have been expressed in the picture, neither fear of hell nor human compassion . . . The viewer is in no way instructed how to react to and how to interpret the picture."[5]

The same puzzling absence of a definable or appropriate affect, according to Kayser, characterizes some more recent instances of the grotesque. In discussing the bizarre *oeuvre* of

4. Ibid., p. 21, 31.
5. Ibid., p. 33.

Wilhelm Busch, a nineteenth-century German cartoonist and poet, he remarks that as soon as the discrepancy between the tenor of a work and the nature of its subject "exceeds the human measure and becomes inhuman, alienation ensues and we lose the ground from under our feet."[6]

"Alienation" (*Verfremdung*)—not as estrangement or emotional distancing from reality, but as sudden intrusion of the uncanny upon the seemingly familiar—is a major theme in Kayser's book: "The grotesque is a world rendered alien." At this point a significant distinction is offered: "Viewed from the outside, the world of the fairy tale could also be regarded as strange and alien, yet it is not a world rendered alien." The grotesque effect occurs when what seemed familiar and natural suddenly turned out to be strange and ominous. "It is *our* world that has been transformed,"[7] that has been unmasked as chaotic and absurd, vulnerable to the dark, demonic forces.

The twin themes of the absurd and the demonic recur predictably in Kayser's final attempts at definition: "The creations of the grotesque are a play with the absurd." The grotesque is "an attempt to invoke and subdue the demonic" not by denying it, but by bringing it to light. "The darkness has been sighted, the uncanny revealed, the incomprehensible articulated."[8]

An attempt to modify the Kayser thesis is found in *The Ludicrous Demon,*[9] a scholarly study of the grotesque in German post-Romantic prose by Lee Byron Jennings. The comic, Jennings argues, is not one of the variants of the grotesque but its inherent component. The "grotesque object

6. Ibid., p. 118.
7. Ibid., p. 184. I have permitted myself to tamper with the extant English rendition of Kayser's "die verfremdete Welt." Since "estrangement" suggests the emotional effect of a work of art upon the audience rather than the impact of a literary strategy upon the "world" portrayed in that work, I thought "world rendered alien" a closer equivalent of the original phrase than "an estranged world."
8. Ibid., p. 188. Again I allowed myself to modify the translation.
9. (Berkeley and Los Angeles, University of California Press, 1963), p. 214.

always displays a combination of fearsome and ludicrous qualities."[10] In other words, as Jennings' title implies, the grotesque
is the demonic rendered ludicrous.

Up to a point, Jennings' formula may be deemed a useful
antidote to Kayser's preoccupation with the uncanny and the
sinister. Yet, on balance, I find it rather confining. I am not as
convinced as Jennings seems to be that what Kayser had called
an "attempt to subdue the demonic" always succeeds, that our
fear of dark forces, which grotesque art allegedly seeks to allay,
is necessarily overcome or held at bay. "The disarming of the
demonic through humor"[11] is a phrase that is scarcely applicable to Hieronymus Bosch or, for that matter, to Franz Kafka.
While Jennings is right in suggesting that the grotesque tends to
construe the demonic as trivial, he might have paid more heed
to the reverse side of the coin, notably to the grotesque writers'
penchant for seeing the trivial as demonic.

We are ready, I believe, to return from our definitional
detour. Or have we been away at all? "Blurring the boundary
between the animal and the human," "playing havoc with
symmetry and the relative size of objects," "the demonic as
trivial," "the ground slipping from under our feet," "a play with
the absurd"—are not these remarkably accurate descriptions of
the strange universe which bears the signature of Nikolaj
Gogol?

In the pages that follow, I shall attempt to validate this query
by subjecting Gogol's major works to a close, if at times rather
brief, scrutiny. To be sure, the later masterpieces—*The Inspector General, Dead Souls,* and "The Overcoat"—will be treated
here as the principal test cases, as the most telling clues to the
nature of his art. Yet I propose to pay some attention to his
early and middle periods, so airily dismissed by Nabokov in his
provocative yet wantonly lopsided essay.[12] I shall do so, not for

10. Ibid., p. 10.
11. Ibid., p. 15.
12. *Nikolai Gogol,* (New York, New Directions, 1944), p. 172.

the sake of comprehensiveness—an objective which is not sought here—but in deference to the fundamental continuity and inner coherence of Gogol's literary endeavor. By the same token, while my principal concern will be with the writings, I shall shuttle intermittently between "life" and "work," between the man and the writer. The connection between the artist's biography and his creations is always a tenuous and complex matter, never more so than when the novelist under discussion is a master of stylization and indirection. Yet to ignore the impact of Gogol's ideological preoccupations upon his creative processes or to disregard the uncanny parallels between his bizarre personality and his craft would be to impoverish, indeed to distort, the subject of this book.

2

A Spellbinder Emerges

Nikolaj Gogol was born on March 20, 1809, in the little town of Sorochintsy, in the heart of the Ukraine which was to provide the setting of his early stories. He spent his childhood at the small ancestral estate under the aegis of his doting parents, Marja Ivanovna and Vasilij Afanasevich. At the age of twelve, he was sent to a boarding school, from which he was graduated in 1828. These are some of the incontrovertible facts bearing on Gogol's formative period. Much of the rest, including his genealogy, is murky, controversial, open to interpretation. In fact, in view of the future writer's proclivity for mystification, it seems singularly appropriate that his last name should have been, as it now appears, a product of an elaborate hoax. When Nikolaj was born, the family name was the hyphenated Gogol-Janovskij. Recent research[1] strongly suggests that Gogol's earliest certifiable ancestor was a Ukrainian village priest, Jan Jakovlevich Janovskij. It seems that the Gogol (or in the Ukrainian pronunciation, Hohol) element was injected by Janovskij's grandson and Nikolaj's paternal grandfather, Afanasij Janovskij who, as a result of his marriage to a girl from a wealthy Cossack family, became an owner of some landed property and of nearly three hundred serfs. Since Catherine the Great had just decreed that the right to own serfs was to be the exclusive privilege of the hereditary gentry, Afanasij, who

1. See especially Leon Stilman, "Nikolaj Gogol and Ostap Hohol," *Orbis Scriptus: Dmitrij Tschizewskij zum 70 Geburstag* (Munich, Wilhelm Fink Verlag, 1966), pp. 811-25.

apparently came from a long line of village priests, acquired a vested interest in upgrading his rather unspectacular genealogy. He claimed as his ancestor a seventeenth-century Cossack warrior, Ostap Hohol, who presumably had received a land grant from the King of Poland in recognition of important services rendered to the Crown.

While the elevation of Hohol into the ranks of Polish nobility seems to be a fact, the link between the Cossack colonel and the Janovskij family appears very dubious indeed to present-day Gogol scholars. According to Leon Stilman, "Grandfather Afanasij had added fiction to reality in coupling Gogol with Janovskij." If Stilman's view is correct, Afanasij's grandson Nikolaj, who eventually was to drop "Janovskij," eliminated from his hyphenated name the only element of reality. "The name of the seventeenth-century Cossack colonel now stood alone. It was the property of the writer, Nikolaj Vasil'-evich Gogol, and an essential part of his identity."[2] A further touch of irony is provided by the fact that "Ostap," the first name of Gogol's pseudo-ancestor, should have cropped up in his historical romance, "Taras Bulba,"[3] as that of the older son and right-hand man of the novel's chief protagonist, the burly Cossack chieftain who, in contradistinction to Ostap Hohol, was an implacable foe of the Poles.

Gogol's father, Vasilij Afanasévich, appears to have been an affable, gentle, and somewhat ineffectual squire, possessed of a moderate gift of gab and a flair for the theater. Before devoting himself to a rather unstrenuous task of managing his small estate as best he could, he served briefly as a postal clerk and subsequently drifted on several occasions into the role of majordomo at the manor of a wealthy and overbearing relative, the retired dignitary Troshchinskij. It seems that, in order to entertain his patron's numerous guests, he composed several spirited if undistinguished comedies with such titles as "The Simpleton" and "The Tricks of a Woman Outwitted by a

2. Ibid., p. 813.
3. See below, Chapter 4, pp. 52-54.

Soldier"—unpretentious slapstick affairs which drew heavily
on motifs and techniques of the Ukrainian puppet theater
(*vertep*) and which later proved of some interest to the author
of *The Inspector General*. Eventually Vasilij Gogol found his
role as court jester too demanding and hastened to exchange its
strains for the pastoral quiet of Vasil'evka and the company of
his beloved Marja Ivanovna. A sickly and somewhat hypo-
chondriacal man, he died in 1825, when Nikolaj had just
turned sixteen.

   Though Gogol's early interest in the theater and his literary
utilization of Ukrainian folklore clearly owed something to
Vasilij Afanasevich's amateurish efforts, the impact of this
mild-mannered man on his son should not be overestimated.
For his mother seems in fact, to have been the more significant,
if not necessarily the more interesting, parent. If nothing else,
Marja Gogol, who was only eighteen when Nikolaj was born,
was to survive her son. And she made her presence felt
throughout his entire life, whether directly as an addressee of
his letters, now affectionate, now overbearing, or indirectly as a
source of guilt or uneasiness during the periods of relative
neglect.

   The intensity of Gogol's emotional involvement with his
mother is so apparent that his biographers tend to agree on her
importance; yet they are wide apart in assessing her influence
and in diagnosing her personality. Though partisanship seems
to be oddly out of place in dealing with what clearly was a well-
intentioned and unremarkable woman, many writers have
insisted on becoming either her champions or her detractors.
No doubt, she has often been a mere foil. A critic fundamentally
unsympathetic to Gogol and distrustful of his motives would be
inclined to treat every misunderstanding between mother and
son as proof positive of the latter's selfishness, carelessness, or
ingratitude. Conversely, if the scholar's intent is to exonerate
Gogol at all costs, Marja Ivanovna's occasional complaints are
bound to be dismissed as unfair and unreasonable, if not
downright silly.

Both schools of thought seem to have overshot the mark. The kindly Sergej Aksakov may sound overgenerous when he credits Gogol's mother with an aesthetic sense and a touch of gentle humor, but he is essentially right, I believe, when he calls her a "kind, gentle, loving creature."[4] That she was a devoted and affectionate mother can hardly be doubted. But she must also have been a doting, overprotective, and overanxious one. Moreover, though not necessarily foolish, she appears pedestrian and incurably parochial. Her well-documented proclivity to attribute to her son not only the most unlikely literary achievements, but nearly every important technological advance made in his lifetime, including the inventions of the steamboat and the railroad, is testimony to both her inordinate faith in Nikolaj's genius and her naïveté.

Marja was generally devout, yet as her son once pointed out,[5] the piety she was eager to impart to her children was a matter of formal observance rather than internalized belief. Perhaps more importantly she was at least as superstitious as she was pious. In a revealing letter to his mother, written when he was twenty-four, Gogol avers that the only aspect of his early religious training which had a lasting impact on him was Marja Ivanovna's "scary" stories about the Last Judgment.[6] One suspects that she succeeded in conveying to her son her fear and distrust of the outside world, especially of that glittering den of iniquity, the city. It would be a characteristically modern exaggeration to place on the frail shoulders of Marja Gogol the entire blame for the well-known fact that in Gogol's religiosity fear was to loom larger than awe and the devil was to be a more compelling presence than God. Yet there is hardly any question that Gogol's deep-seated dread of the Evil One,

---

4. Sergej Aksakov, *Istorija moego znakomstva s Gogolem* (1854) (Moscow, Izdatelstvo Akademii Nauk SSSR, 1960), pp. 37-38.

5. Gogol, *Polnoe Sobranie Sochinenij* (Complete Works), *10* (1952), 282.

6. Ibid.

and, more broadly, his all-encompassing fear of life, received significant support from this befuddled, pretty ingenue propelled prematurely into marriage, childbearing, and widowhood. In spite of his mother's overprotectiveness, Nikolaj was allowed to leave the family nest at an early age. At nine, he was sent, along with his brother, to a boarding school at Poltava. Three years later, after his brother's death, he entered a newly established boarding school in Nezhin, a stagnant small town in the Poltava province. Here he was to remain, outside of summer vacations spent at Vasil'evka, until his graduation in 1828. By that time he was, or thought he was, ready to plunge into St. Petersburg.

As usual with Gogol, the eyewitness testimony as to what manner of boy he was in those years is less than conclusive. All biographers and contemporaries agree that his academic performance was unimpressive[7] through most of this eight-year period, that he was often taken to task by the school authorities for his laziness and sloppiness, that he had few friends at Nezhin and was regarded by his fellow students as average until his senior year when he made some impact as an actor, a director of amateur plays, and a budding poet. Beyond this, however, the recollections diverge sharply.

The affable Danilevskij, one of Gogol's few friends in Nezhin, who remained his intimate at least until the late 1830s, claims that on the whole, Gogol was rather well liked by his schoolmates, in spite of his sharp tongue and his fondness for practical jokes. According to Danilevskij, Gogol's relative loneliness in Nezhin was due to his own aloofness and secretiveness—which earned him, incidentally, the none too affectionate nickname of "mysterious dwarf"—and to his inner sense of

7. Recent investigations have partially disproved the assumption that Gogol was an indifferent and unmotivated student. On the basis of this data, Dmitry Cizevsky argues that Gogol could and did perform creditably whenever intellectually challenged by stimulating teachers (Dmitrij Tschizewskij, "Neues über Puschkin, Lermontov und Gogol," *Zeitschrift für Slavische Philologie,* [Heidelberg, 1955], *23*, 394-98).

superiority.[8] A very different picture emerges from a retrospective account by an aging St. Petersburg socialite and litterateur, Ljubich-Romanovich,[9] who claims that Gogol's entire stay in Nezhin was an ordeal: because of his gaucherie and slovenliness, especially his messy eating habits, he was the butt of malicious jokes. "He was constantly taunted and persistently spurned by the group." This irritating memoir, which breathes personal animus unmitigated by the passage of time and a coterie-like disdain for the uncouth and unprepossessing little provincial, ought to be taken with a grain of salt. But on the other hand, perhaps Danilevskij's genial testimony is just a bit too cheery.

In any case, there is scarcely any doubt that much of the time the young Gogol lived in a world of his own. Whether through his own choice or out of necessity, he kept his innermost thoughts and feelings largely to himself. Awkward, brooding, vulnerable, shuttling between melancholy and mischievous gaiety, he cut an odd figure. His own self-portrait—"Suspicious of everyone, I did not confide my secret thoughts to anyone, did nothing that could reveal the depth of my soul"[10]—is a characteristic overstatement. Gogol did confide in a few chosen ones, such as his older schoolmate, Vysockij, whom he deemed worthy of his trust. Another recipient of his "secret thoughts" was his maternal uncle, Pavel Kosjarovskij.

Judging from some of his confessions, the young Gogol's grand designs were as vague as they were lofty. Like many a sensitive and morbidly ambitious schoolboy, he dreamed about fame, about making an impact, about doing something memorable and useful. What makes his outpourings particularly revealing is not the hankering for glory, a common enough daydream, but its negative counterpart, the pervasive

8. Danilevskij as quoted by V. Shenrok in *Materialy dlja biografii Gogolja* (Moscow, 1892-97), *1*, 102.
9. "Gogol v nezhinskom licee", *Vestnik Evropy* (1895), pp. 548-60.
10. *Polnoe Sobranie Sochinenij, 10*, 112.

fear of anonymity, of obscurity, of "plant-like" passivity, which, amid the placid stagnation of the early nineteenth-century Ukrainian backwater, seemed a clear and present danger. "To be in the world," Nikolaj writes to his uncle, "and not to make one's existence register, that would be terrible!"[11] In a letter to Vysockij, written at the age of eighteen, he emotes, "How difficult it is to be buried in dead silence together with creatures of lowly obscurity! You know all our existers, all those who inhabit Nezhin. They squelch by their sheer pedestrian weight, by their petty smugness, the lofty vocation of man."[12] "Will my lofty designs be realized? Or will obscurity bury them in a gloomy cloud?"[13]

The urge to become somebody, to make an imprint, is clearly more apparent here than is a commitment to any particular path to fame, any specific career or vocation. To be sure, even at Nezhin, Gogol was already keenly interested in literature and the theater. Though hardly an assiduous student, he seems to have delved into belles lettres above and beyond the call of the curriculum, to have thrilled to Petrarch, Aristophanes, Schiller, Tieck, and, of course, Pushkin. Toward the end of his stay in Nezhin, along with a small band of budding litterateurs, he tried his hand at both verse and prose fiction. (The bulk of his ill-fated idyll, "Hanz Kuechelgarten," and a fragment of an aborted historical novel, seem to have been written in Nezhin.) "My first efforts," Gogol was to remark some twenty years later in "An Author's Confession" (1847), "were couched in a lyrical and serious vein. Neither I nor my schoolmates would have ever predicted that I was to become a comic and satirical writer."[14] Generally, Gogol's classmates turned out to be poor prophets: one of them is known to have said: "You may become a good poet, but you will never

11. Ibid., p. 111.
12. Ibid., p. 98.
13. Ibid., p. 112.
14. "Avtorskaja ispoved' " (An Author's Confession), *Polnoe*, 8 (1952), 438.

amount to anything as a prose writer."[15] Moreover, even though Gogol's early literary efforts achieved some recognition in his boarding school, they were adjudged inferior to those of another Nezhin boy, Kukolnik, who was to develop into a stodgy, third-rate playwright.

Yet while these undistinguished and partly uncharacteristic literary exercises appear, in retrospect, a significant step toward Gogol's maturer works, there is no indication that, during his Nezhin period, he ever felt committed or irresistibly drawn to literature as a vocation or a way of life, that his self-image was one of an aspiring writer. When, in the already-quoted letter to his uncle, he lifts the veil over his "lofty designs," literature is not even mentioned. The emphasis is on "serving the State," on a public administrative career:

> Perhaps it will be my luck to live out my whole life in St. Petersburg; this, at least, has long since been my goal. Since years past, in the years of uncomprehending childhood, I have burned with an inextinguishable zeal to make my life essential to the welfare of the State . . . In my mind I went through all the classes, all the governmental departments, and settled on the Department of Justice. I saw that . . . here I could be beneficial, that only here I could be truly useful to humanity.[16]

Somewhat earlier, he wrote to his mother:

> In sleep and during the waking hours . . . I dream about St. Petersburg and the service to the State . . . I have been happy until now, but if happiness is a matter of being content with one's condition, then my happiness will not be complete until I enter the service and acquire, so to say, a permanent station of my own." "I am testing my strength

---

15. Ljubich-Romanovich's testimony as quoted in Vikentij Veresaev, *Gogol v zhizni* (Moscow and Leningrad, Academia, 1933), p. 65.

16. *Polnoe Sobranie Sochinenij, 10,* 111.

before undertaking a great and noble task in behalf of my
Fatherland for the sake of my fellow countrymen . . . Next
year I shall enter the service of the State.[17]

The adolescent ponderousness of these outpourings should
not blind us to the possibility that the sentiments expressed
above were genuine. In "An Author's Confession," Gogol
insisted that the idea of service never abandoned him. The
statement is true. The phrases of the Nezhin schoolboy—"to
serve," "to be useful," "to do some good," "for the sake of my
countrymen"—reverberated through many a retrospective confession of the mature writer.

Later I shall comment further on what I might classify here
as a characteristically Gogolian incongruity—notably, the
spectacle of a dazzling prose poet, whose distinctive strength
lay in an imaginative manipulation of language, insisting on
seeing himself primarily as a moralist and student of human
nature and an indifferent stylist, and on justifying his literary
activity in terms of serving society or mankind. In this respect,
as in some others, Gogol's self-image as a man of letters was a
far cry from that of his great contemporary, Alexander Pushkin. Even while under the spell of the Romantic worship of art,
Gogol failed to emulate Pushkin's thorough unconcern with the
ultimate uses of the poetic craft: "the aim of poetry is poetry,"
he said once, in reply to a baffled inquiry about the purpose of
his narrative poem, "The Gypsies." Gogol could never be so
casual, so unself-conscious.

Not only is the young Gogol's civic-mindedness drastically
obtrusive; it is also tame, conformist, officious. The key term in
the letter is the "State" (*gosudarstvo*), rather than "mankind" or
"Fatherland." Once again, a parallel with Pushkin suggests
itself. Official Soviet interpreters notwithstanding, the great
poet was not a revolutionary firebrand. In fact, in his later
days, he came close to espousing a position that could be

17. Ibid., p. 83.

tenued liberal-conservative. Yet in his early political verse, in which he paid his due to the ardent libertarianism of the nascent Russian intelligentsia, the target of dedication is "Fatherland," a term which, in early nineteenth-century parlance, was closely wedded to "Liberty" and often inimical to autocracy. Quite appropriately, the finale of Pushkin's much-quoted epistle "To Chaadaev" anticipates the "dawn of captivating happiness" and the downfall of tyranny.

The young Gogol's patriotic zeal seems immune to such dangerous thoughts; its cast is static and ("a permanent station of my own") conservative. The State, the system, seems to be taken for granted, indeed embraced as the only framework within which constructive and beneficent activity can be carried on. There may be low-level abuses to be corrected, bureaucratic procedures to be improved, loyal subjects to be protected or assisted, but all this can be done only within the system, under the aegis of the wise central authority. Though it is entirely possible that the Nezhin schoolboy went out of his way to impress his right-mindedness upon his uncle, it seems fair to assume that to this ambitious young provincial, desperately anxious to escape small-town stagnation and anonymity, St. Petersburg appeared not only as an epitome of power and glamour but also as the repository of institutional wisdom.

His graduation from Nezhin in 1828 seems to have brought the daydream within the dreamer's reach. Several months later he was on his way. Followed by Marja Ivanovna's anxious prayers and extravagant hopes, armed with letters of recommendation from his once influential uncle, Troshchinskij, and accompanied by his classmate Danilevskij, Gogol left for St. Petersburg on December 15, 1828.

His great expectations were promptly and brutally dashed, "Oh how revolting was reality! What was it compared to the dream?"[18] These words of the romantic artist Piskarëv, in Gogol's Petersburg tale "Nevsky Prospekt," may well have

18. *The Collected Tales and Plays of Nikolai Gogol,* tr. Constance Garnett, ed. and rev. Leonard J. Kent (New York, Pantheon Books, 1964), p. 436.

epitomized his feelings upon entering the promised land. His first encounter with the capital was chilling, both literally and figuratively. A bad cold which he caught immediately upon arrival in St. Petersburg was, as were so many of his later ailments and symptoms, symbolic: the contrast between the cozy, warm, ego-boosting family nest and the frigid, impersonal, bureaucratic capital must have been nearly traumatic. Troshchinskij's letters failed to open a single strategic door. Whatever the retired dignitary's influence may have been in his day, it was now of little avail. The Establishment took precious little interest in the awkward, callow youth from Vasil'evka. The important position failed to materialize. The only station of his own which the system seemed ready to offer the ambitious provincial was a tedious clerkship "with the annual salary of a thousand rubles," as Gogol informed his mother, "that would barely pay for the apartment and meals . . . Staying all day at one's desk, copying the ancient babble and nonsense of the departmental supervisors . . . Is this what I am supposed to sell my health and my precious time for?"[19] "St. Petersburg shattered Gogol," said Andrej Belyj, a brilliant Russian Symbolist and a remarkable Gogolian, "and he got hold of irony as a mode of self-defense."[20] The point is well taken. Some twelve years later, Gogol was to debunk brilliantly the dehumanizing office routine in his short masterpiece, "The Overcoat." A little earlier, he was to strike back in "Nevsky Prospekt" at the frigid Capital, unmasking its glitter as false and evil and projecting the image of St. Petersburg as an eerie, uncanny, and treacherous city, an image which, through the good offices of Dostoevsky and Andrej Belyj was to reverberate well into twentieth-century Russian literature.

With the dream of a distinguished public career relegated to the dim future, Gogol's literary aspirations came to the fore. Among his personal effects, he had brought from Nezhin a

19. *Polnoe Sobranie Sochinenij, 10*, 143.
20. *Masterstvo Gogolja* (Moscow and Leningrad, Izdatelstyo khudozhestvennoj literatury, 1934), p. 186.

complete or nearly complete narrative poem bearing the somewhat misspelled German title "Hanz Kuechelgarten." In May
1829, this "idyll in scenes" was published, at the author's
expense, to be sure, under the assumed name of V. Alov. With
bated breath, the young poet waited for a sorely needed ego
boost.

Once again he was cruelly disappointed. The bulk of the metropolitan press greeted "Hanz Kuechelgarten" with resounding silence. There were only two reviews—both unequivocally
negative. The notice in the *Moscow Telegraph* was brief and
sarcastic; the *Northern Bee,* another leading journal, deplored
the appearance of the poem and blamed it on the young
author's arrogance and poor judgment: he should have known
better than to foist on the public a work so immature and so
inept.[21]

Gogol's reaction to this fiasco epitomizes and anticipates
what was to become his standard response to real or imaginary
failure. He bought up the extant copies of his hapless poem and
burned them in the first auto-da-fé of his strangely self-
destructive career. Then he promptly went abroad.[22]

The second review of "Hanz Kuechelgarten" appeared on
July 7, 1829. In early August, Gogol boarded a ship for
Lübeck and from there proceeded to the German spa of Travemünde. Toward the end of September, he was back in St.
Petersburg frantically looking for employment in the civil
service. In order to finance his sudden trip, he had appropriated a sum from his mother which was to have been an
installment on the Vasil'evka estate. Thus he owed her a good
story—a relatively acceptable explanation of an abrupt and
extravagant venture.

21. Paul Debreczeny, *Nikolay Gogol and His Contemporary Critics* (Phila-
delphia, American Philosophical Society, 1966), 56, part 3, 5.
22. The urge to flee the scene of humiliation was to become part of a characteristic Gogolian syndrome. Gogol's eloquent tribute, in Part One of *Dead
Souls,* to the "long, long road" hints broadly at the therapeutic value of traveling.

Whether in deference to his own wounded pride or to his mother's fond hopes, Gogol could not bring himself to tell the truth—notably to admit that he had had to do something drastic in order to come to terms with a debacle. What he did instead, in his much-quoted letter of June 24, 1829, was to treat Marja Ivanovna to what Nabokov calls "a purple patch of shameless fiction."[23] It appears that he had encountered a dazzling and "exalted" creature, nay, a "goddess lightly clothed in human passion," who plunged him into a "tempest of frenzy and terrific spiritual pain." Clearly, the only possible rescue from the unbearable anguish of love which could not have been reciprocated was a panicky flight: "She is too exalted, too exalted!"[24]

The bulk of Gogol's biographers treat that "exalted creature" as a figment of his fervid imagination. Vasilij Gippius, one of the most sagacious Gogolians, is not so sure. Though fully aware of Gogol's potential for mystification, he cautions his confreres against discounting automatically any statement of motives or intentions. Though I am generally in sympathy with Gippius' caveat I would, in this instance, tend to agree with the skeptics. True, Gogol's vaunted fear of women is rather beside the point here—after all, his story is one of an escape, of a voluntary withdrawal. But it does not seem plausible that Gogol, whose personal life in St. Petersburg was, to put it mildly, uneventful, would have concealed such a traumatic encounter from his friends and confidants, Danilevskij and Prokopovich. Still more suspect is the melodramatically literary quality of the alleged love object "whose shattering splendor impresses itself upon one's heart, whose eyes quickly pierce the soul."[25] Gogol's "goddess" sounds less like a glamorous St. Petersburg denizen than like the first in the series of those unbearably dazzling women who inhabit Gogol's fiction, or, for

23. *Nikolai Gogol,* p. 21.
24. *Polnoe Sobranie Sochinenij, 10,* 147, 148.
25. Ibid., p. 147.

that matter, like a slightly personalized counterpart of Alcinoë, the epitome of triumphant female beauty eulogized in his turgidly romantic essay, "A Woman" (1831). What finally impugns Gogol's credibility is that he offers too many disparate explanations of his departure from St. Petersburg. Having found himself in Travemünde, he tries to justify his presence in the spa by invoking an "abundant rash" which broke over his face and hands as the main reason for his trip to Germany. Nabokov describes the befuddled mother's reaction quite succinctly: "Putting two and two together—the mysterious passion and the mysterious rash—the good lady jumped to the conclusion that her son got entangled with some expensive courtesan and had caught a venereal disease."²⁶ The result was a panicky and reproachful letter which, in turn, elicited a stunned and indignant reply: "I read with horror your letter of September 6th."²⁷

I thought this much-reported incident worth recounting, not merely for its anecdotal value, but because it dramatizes so neatly the self-defeating quality of Gogol's Machiavellianism. However unpalatable the truth, the "shameless fiction" proved even more disturbing; the elaborate maneuver backfired.

Some fifteen years later, a sensitive but not always incisive contemporary, Pavel Annenkov, who knew Gogol quite intimately during his *Dead Souls* period, commented with some admiration on Gogol's shrewdness, on his ability to use people for his purposes.²⁸ In the light of all available evidence, this ambivalent tribute would have to be seriously modified. That Gogol was a keen and not overly charitable observer, that he had, at least intermittently, a remarkable insight into human folly, amply documented both by his writings and by some of his correspondence, that he was not above manipulating people

26. *Nikolai Gogol*, p. 23.
27. *Polnoe Sobranie Sochinenij, 10,* 157.
28. "N. V. Gogol v Rime letom, 1841 g.," *Gogol v vospominanijakh sovremennikov* (Moscow and Leningrad, Gosizdat, 1952), p. 250.

and capitalizing on their weaknesses, is all too plausible. (Gogol admitted to a pragmatic view of friendship in a revealing letter to Sergej Aksakov.[29]) Yet it is also part of the record that some of these manipulations were less than successful. The blatant misjudgments, the aborted schemes, the repeated failures to gauge properly the effects of one's actions, suggest that at times Gogol's grip on reality was not too reliable. Perhaps Annenkov confused deviousness with shrewdness.

We might even question whether "Hanz Kuechelgarten" was a legitimate occasion for so much embarrassment and shamefaced double-talk. Was this poem quite so worthless as the two reviewers proclaimed it to be? There is no question but that Gogol's abortive debut is an immature and derivative performance. Vasilij Gippius correctly observes that the weakest aspect of Gogol's youthful poem is its verse.[30] The young author proved equally inept at handling two classical Russian meters—the rhymed iambic tetrameter and the blank iambic pentameter. Some of the lines are all too apparent and feeble echoes of Pushkin's *Evgenij Onegin*. The imagery of the idyll, however, is not devoid of interest. The metaphor-studded and highly emotive descriptive sequences, couched in the Sentimentalist vein, point directly toward the dithyrambic nature poetry of Gogol's legitimate debut, *Evenings on a Farm near Dikanka*. More broadly, the idyll's claim on our attention lies not in what it is, but in what it foreshadows. In spite of its glaring inadequacy, "Hanz Kuechelgarten" is not simply a freak or a totally false start. Though the setting of the poem and its clumsily German title clearly owe a great deal to the eighteenth-century German pastoral "Luise" by Johann Hermann Voss, the theme of the vague longing for a distant fame which obtrudes itself into the idyll is one that loomed large in Gogol's life and work.

As the curtain goes up over the peaceful German village of Luenensdorf, the two protagonists, the young dreamer, Hanz,

29. *Polnoe Sobranie Sochinenij, 8,* 416.
30. *Gogol* (Leningrad, Mysl, 1924), p. 23.

and his lovely neighbor, "angel bright" Luise, grow into adoles-
cence under the benign gaze of their elders, against the mellow
backdrop of conventional rural scenery. Hanz and Luise
clearly are slated for each other. It is everybody's expectation
that, before long, they will marry and will live happily ever
after. Luise is ready. Hanz loves her dearly, yet he is troubled,
confused, torn. He is not prepared to commit himself to idyllic,
uneventful happiness. Vaguely stirred by the masters of the
ages, from Aristophanes to Schiller, alerted to the challenges
and temptations of the wide, wide world—above all, to the
claims of Beauty and Glory—he daydreams about Greece. The
self-reference here is all too apparent. Though the Nezhin
schoolboy's grand designs were at least, on the face of it, less
aesthetically motivated than Hanz's "Sehnsucht," some of the
latter's gloomy meditations strike what should be by now a
familiar note: "Should I perish here without finding a loftier
purpose? Should I fall victim to obscurity and be dead to the
world while still alive? . . . How can my heart, filled with glory,
be satisfied with nothingness? Not to reach toward the beauty
of the world—not to make my existence count?"[31]

For a while, the wanderlust takes over. Hanz stealthily
leaves the village and embarks on a pilgrimage to Greece. He is
cruelly disappointed. The Greece of the ancients is no more.
The coarse, grubby present overlays and mocks the past glo-
ries. The aesthetic ideal proves—or appears?—a phantom, an
optical illusion which is now blamed on the "restless wiles of
the evil spirit." Guiltily, Hanz retraces his steps in order to
recapture what seems the only reality, the warmth of the family
nest, the here-and-now of Luise's pure love and devotion. On
the face of it, the idyllic is fully vindicated. Or is it? Even as the
wedding bells are ringing, the bridegroom's troubled counte-
nance—his visible nostalgia for the dream he has lost—seems
to inject a dissonant note into the rural festivities.

Whether as a matter of general confusion or of deliberate

31. *Polnoe Sobranie Sochinenij, 1* (1940), 78-79.

ambiguity, the nature and implications of Hanz's disenchantment are never made quite clear. Is it an indictment of the
dream or of the dreamer? Has the goal of Hanz's journey
actually proved deceptive, or is it rather that this particular
pilgrim was too tame to meet the challenges of the arduous
journey? To put it differently, is the dream illusory or merely
elusive? Did the confrontation with reality unmask the ideal, or
did it simply suggest that the "given" is necessarily grubby,
coarse, nauseating, and conversely, that anything worthy of
admiration and enthusiasm is inevitably beyond one's reach?

Be that as it may, Gogol's naïve pastoral seems to embody,
however clumsily, the conflict that was to become his major
theme—the tension between *Gemütlichkeit* and wanderlust, or,
to put it more negatively, between the fear of life and the fear
of death-in-life. More immediately, Hanz's ambivalence was an
inadequate transposition of the dilemma of his creator who, on
the eve of his big plunge, must have wondered anxiously
whether it was possible to conquer the world without being
conquered by it, to achieve success in the metropolis while
retaining the pristine purity of Vasil'evka.

Whatever the wider implications of Gogol's ill-starred entry
into the literary world, the abrupt German escapade absorbed
the first shock of the defeat. The self-administered therapy
seems to have worked. Whether invigorated by the journey, or
egged on by the sense of guilt over the mortgage money so
cavalierly appropriated, Gogol resumed his job hunting in St.
Petersburg with a zeal that had been conspicuously lacking
and, one might add, with a relative lack of discrimination. His
first civil service job—a minor position at the Imperial Chan-
cery—was secured through the intercession of the notorious
Faddej Bulharyn, a prolific and unsavory litterateur whose
connection with the Tsarist secret police was the talk of the
town. (It was, incidentally, the same Bulharyn who had panned
"Hanz Kuechelgarten" and was soon to become one of the
most consistent detractors of Gogol's writings.) So painful was
the financial squeeze that the meager rewards of stultifying

drudgery could no longer be spurned. Yet, needless to say, Gogol's heart was not in his job.

As the shock of the "Hanz Kuechelgarten" fiasco wore off, Gogol's literary aspirations reasserted themselves. This time the medium was narrative prose and the setting the land of Gogol's childhood rather than the pallid, conventionally sentimental Germany of his adolescent reading. Soon the humiliation of a premature exposure was to be forgotten in the flush of his successful debut with a gaudy, spirited batch of Ukrainian goblin tales that proclaimed to the Russian public a new and distinctive literary force.

This flurry of literary activity received a significant boost from immensely gratifying and valuable personal contacts Gogol made in the early part of 1831. At long last, the provincial had emerged from his obscurity to enter the ranks of the capital's glittering literary elite. The turning point was the encounter with Baron Delvig, a highly cultivated minor poet and discriminating critic-editor, whose almanac, *The Northern Flowers,* published one of Gogol's first attempts at prose fiction, a rather lurid chapter from a historical novel, over the strikingly self-effacing signature OOO. Through Delvig, a respected member of the Pushkin cenacle, Gogol met the affable Vasilij Zhukovskij, the precursor of Russian Romanticism, who was to become one of Gogol's most influential literary protectors, the critic and educator Pëtr Pletnëv, "mainly remembered," as Nabokov puts it, "for Pushkin's dedicating to him *Evgenij Onegin,*"[32] and, last but certainly not least, Alexander Pushkin himself.

It seemed that the Petersburg literati were intrigued rather than charmed. They found Gogol a bit odd, diffident, and signally lacking in social graces. The reaction of Alexandra Rosset-Smirnova, an attractive and quick-witted socialite, a friend of Pushkin and Zhukovskij, who later was to become one of Gogol's closest confidantes, seems representative: "Il m'a

32. *Nikolai Gogol,* p. 28.

paru gauche, timide et triste," she declares in her memoirs. "Pushkine," she remarks later," a de suite apprivoisé le khokh- ol [Ukrainian] recalcitrant. . . . Ils [Zhukovskij and Push- kin] ont tout taquiné Gogol sur sa timidité et sa sauvagerie."[33] Clearly the teasing was friendly and affectionate. These gifted and shrewd men must have sensed under a rather unprepossess- ing exterior something not merely odd but truly unusual and thus worth cultivating and encouraging.

In the long run, it was Zhukovskij rather than Pushkin who took an active personal interest in Nikolaj Gogol. Gogol's friendship with Pushkin seems to have been overadvertised. Gogol himself may be partly responsible for the now contested notion that the two great men of letters were intimates: in his letters to his mother, he was not above overstating his social successes in the capital. Also, it is fair to assume that, on occasions, he mistook Pushkin's naturally friendly and open manner for personalized warmth and cordiality. Actually, it is difficult to visualize an intimacy between men so thoroughly different—the gay, volatile, spontaneous, extrovert Pushkin, and the brooding, secretive, and sly Gogol. The correspon- dence between the two masters does nothing to dispel these doubts. The somewhat teasing, playful, mildly ironical tone of Pushkin's letters to Gogol seems to have been designed, in part, to keep the younger man at arm's length. Gogol, no doubt, would have welcomed a warmer tone, yet, lacking encourage- ment, he responded in kind. His correspondence with Pushkin is respectful, restrained, at times nearly impersonal.

When all is said and done, the much-touted friendship was primarily a literary one. Even here, legend seems to magnify reality. The often-quoted sentence from Gogol's lament over Pushkin's death—"I undertook nothing without his advice. I did not write a line without seeing his face before me"[34]—need not be taken literally. Yet it seems undeniable that Pushkin

33. Shenrok, pp. 320, 323.
34. *Polnoe Sobranie Sochinenij, 9,* (1952), 111.

played a significant part in Gogol's literary career. As will be shown below, his generous praise of *Evenings on a Farm near Dikanka* helped to launch Gogol on his way. Furthermore, if we are to believe Gogol, both *The Inspector General* and *Dead Souls* owe their basic designs to Pushkin's fertile suggestions.[35] Moreover, to Gogol, through all his vicissitudes, Pushkin was to remain the poet par excellence—the very embodiment of the spirit of poetry, a creator whose dedication to art and beauty was a standard by which to measure one's own often troubled and ambivalent commitment to the aesthetic ideal.

If being taken up by the legislators of the capital's taste gave Gogol's literary ambitions a new lease on life, his turn to the Ukrainian locale was motivated in part by nostalgia and in part by shrewd recognition of the growing market for the exotic "local color." To judge by his 1830-31 letters, he was determined to capitalize on this regionalist fad, part and parcel of the Romantic ambience, eager to dazzle the urbanites by the borrowed dash and color of what Andrej Belyj called the "singing and dancing Ukraine." In fact, this notion first occurred to him shortly after his arrival in St. Petersburg. On April 30, 1829, he wrote to his mother:

> Please send me two of father's Ukrainian comedies, 'The Sheep Dog' and 'Roman and Parasha'. Here everybody is so interested in things Ukrainian that I'll try to see if one of them could not be staged here . . . I feel that nothing should be neglected, everything should be made use of. If one thing fails, one should try another, and then another.[36]

Some two years later he pleaded with his "dear sister" to send him posthaste "in letters or small packages" whatever information on Ukrainian songs and tales and on "clothes worn in the olden days" she could lay her hands on.[37]

35. See below, Chapters 6, 7.
36. *Polnoe Sobranie Sochinenij, 10*, 142.
37. Ibid., pp. 208-09.

The haphazard frenzy of these requests militates strongly against the notion that Gogol was steeped in Ukrainian folklore. Indeed, it is a tribute to the magic of his prose and, in a degree, to his residual affinity for the rhythms and tonalities of Ukrainian balladry that, as late as 1861, serious scholars such as Panteleimon Kulish[38] and Mikhail Maksimovich[39] could wrangle about the ethnographic accuracy of *Evenings on a Farm near Dikanka*. Interestingly enough, it fell to Dostoevsky then to point out the singular inapplicability of this criterion to what he aptly called Gogol's "demonic vaudeville."

38. Cf. *Osnova* (St. Petersburg, 1861), Nos. 4, 5, 9.
39. *Den'* (St. Petersburg, 1861), Nos. 3, 5, 7, 9.

3

A Demonic Vaudeville

The first volume of *Evenings on the Farm near Dikanka* appeared in September 1831. It comprised "The Sorochintsy Fair," "St. John's Eve," "The May Night, or the Drowned Maiden," and "The Lost Letter." May 1832 saw the publication of the second part of the cycle, which featured "A Christmas Eve," "A Terrible Vengeance," "The Enchanted Spot," and "Ivan Fedorovich Shponka and His Aunt."

The title of the collection hinted broadly at the regional, "folksy" flavor of the narratives. Presumably the tales were "selected" by the beekeeper, Rudy Panko of Dikanka, a rustic old-timer who chose to present to a literate metropolitan audience some of the more entertaining yarns spun by voluble storytellers during long winter evenings at his farm near Dikanka. This time Gogol was sufficiently confident to drop the pen name "Alov" and reveal his identity, but he still seemed to need a buffer between himself and his public in the form of a fictitious editor or narrator.

The liveliness of the critics' response to the *Evenings* did much to offset the ignominy of Gogol's earlier effort and to propel him out of the hated anonymity into the limelight he craved. Not that the responses were uniformly favorable. If Faddej Bulharyn, who had panned "Hanz Kuechelgarten," found some merit in Rudy Panko's tales, Polevoj, another detractor of Gogol's hapless idyll and a prolific critic and publicist, remained adamant. Yet what mattered to Gogol most was Pushkin's often cited accolade: "An astounding book!

Here is fun for you, authentic fun of the frankest kind without anything maudlin or prim about it! . . . And moreover, what poetry, what delicacy of sentiment in certain passages!"[1] In his *Nikolai Gogol,* Nabokov terms Pushkin's praise exaggerated although not altogether inexplicable. "Almost nothing of any real worth (except Pushkin's own prose)," he notes, "was being published in the way of Russian fiction." As far as Nabokov is concerned, the "charm and fun [of *Evenings*] have singularly faded since then." He speaks disdainfully of the "juvenilia of the false humorist Gogol," of the "operatic romance and stale farce," and steadfastly refuses either to be entertained by the fun or frightened by the horror of Gogol's Ukrainian tales (pp. 30-32).

It seems to me that in querying Pushkin's notion of fun, Nabokov is not only unduly harsh but also rather uncharacteristically literal minded. To be sure, few modern readers will find these picturesque goblin tales irresistibly funny. Granted, too, that what passes for comedy in *Evenings*—with the significant exception of "Ivan Fedorovich Shponka and His Aunt"—rests more often than not on unabashedly farcical, slapstick effects drawn from the traditional repertory of the Ukrainian puppet theater. Gogol scholars[2] long recognized many protagonists in *Evenings,* especially in the opening story, "The Sorochintsy Fair" (for example, the shrewish wife, the cunning gypsy, the gullible peasant, the dashing Cossack), as stock characters in the *vertep.* But the gaiety which so delighted Pushkin is not solely or primarily a matter of the book's capacity to induce belly-laughs. The great poet may well have been hinting at qualities other than the admittedly crude farce—the dash and color of Breughel–like village pageants in

1. In his review of the second edition of *Evenings* (1836), Pushkin offers a more restrained estimate of the volume as he takes note of some "stylistic flaws and implausible plots" which he was glad to overlook four years earlier. He was not sorry to have gone overboard: in *Mirgorod* and *Arabesques* the "author has justified our confidence" (see *Pushkin-Kritik* [Moscow, Izdatelstvo khudozhestvennoj literatury, 1950], pp. 479-80).

2. See especially Gippius, *Gogol,* pp. 30-31.

"The Sorochintsy Fair" and "The Christmas Eve," the youthful exuberance of the lads and lassies in "The May Night," and the vaguely exhilarating sense of the fluidity of existential boundaries, the magical sense of freedom from contingency, the freedom of the fairy tale.

For in the topsy-turvy world of Gogol's Ukrainian tales anything or almost anything can and does happen. Time and again, laws of nature are whimsically kicked about as fundamental distinctions between the human and the subhuman, the whole and the part, the animate and the inanimate are disregarded. As a recent student of Gogol, J. M. Holquist, has put it, "[In] the universe of Gogol's early tales, the wall which separates the world of men and the world of the spirits has many chinks in it and articles from the one sphere keep floating through into another, as when a letter which appears to a young Cossack, Levko, in his dream can show up the next day at the meeting of the village council."[3] Abrupt, unmotivated metamorphosis is the leitmotif of *Evenings*. Evil stepmothers turn into black cats and then into sinister-looking mermaids ("The May Night"), devils become pigs ("The Sorochintsy Fair"), middle-aged village belles double as part-time witches ("A Christmas Eve").

Needless to say, the agency for these transformations is provided by black magic, more broadly, by the supernatural machinery of the Ukrainian folktale. Yet, as already suggested, the folkloristic authenticity of Gogol's first cycle should not be overestimated. The heady brew which confronts us here owes at least as much to the fantastic tales of the German Romantics, Ludwig Tieck and E. T. A. Hoffmann, as to the hastily collected bits of regional lore. To put it differently, the genre of *Evenings,* is a mode of literary stylization rather than of parochial naïveté, a variant of what the German literary historians have dubbed the *Kunstmärchen* - the artistic fairy tale.

3. "The Devil in Mufti: The *Märchenwelt* in Gogol's Short Stories," *PMLA, —82* (October 1967), 355.

In her provocative book, *The Romantic Fairy Tale: Seeds of Surrealism,* Marianne Thalmann argues persuasively that the Kunstmärchen makes use of the trappings and stock devices of the folk tale in order to convey a rather sophisticated notion that there are more things on heaven and earth than were dreamt of in the Rationalist philosophy. The artistic fairy tale thus becomes a vehicle for a multidimensional view of reality, for a fictional universe where contradictions and incongruities can occur without any psychological motivation.[4] The traditional formulas of the folk fairy tale serve here as *sui generis* alibis for the implausibility of the plot, for the intermittent obtrusion of the marvelous and the uncanny in a setting that, in some of its particulars, is not altogether different from a reality which the reader can recognize as his own.

The folk fairy tale signals the ontological remoteness of its world by the archaic flavor of its preambles ("once upon a time") and by vague references to an unidentified "certain kingdom." In the Kunstmärchen, this distancing effect is reduced to a minimum. Hoffmann's whimsical story, "The Golden Pot," where witches and singing golden snakes coexist precariously with stodgy German civil servants, bears the subtitle, "A Contemporary Fairy Tale." Similarly, the bulk of Gogol's Ukrainian tales are set in the recent past, a past still accessible to the oldest members of the Dikanka community. "A Christmas Eve" features Catherine the Great. The events recounted in "The Lost Letter" and "An Enchanted Spot" presumably happened to the narrator's grandfather. The same quality of relative proximity and specificity characterizes the locale of *Evenings.* Granted that the fare served up by the garrulous beekeeper, Rudy Panko, was an exotic one to a St. Petersburg dweller and that the Ukraine of Gogol's early stories is less a geographical reality than a "literary device" (Holquist), an idealized never–never land. The fact remains that, on the

4. *The Romantic Fairy Tale: Seeds of Surrealism* (Ann Arbor, University of Michigan Press, 1964).

face of it, the scene of *Evenings* was part of the Russian Empire, a region which Gogol's readers could locate on the map.

The opening passage of "A Christmas Eve" characteristically combines the cozy neighborliness of a village gossip with the stock figures of the fairy tale. After featuring "the witch on the broomstick who rose up in the air with the smoke" from a hot chimney, the narrator treats us to the following:

> If the assessor of Sorochintsy, in his cap edged with lambskin and cut like a Turk's, in his dark blue overcoat lined with black astrakhan, had driven by at that moment with his three hired horses and the fiendishly braided whip with which it was his habit to urge on the coachman, he would certainly have noticed her for there is not a witch in the world who could elude the eyes of the Sorochintsy assessor.[5]

This blend of the fantastic with the quotidian, rendered in copious, indeed extravagant detail, was to become Gogol's trademark. Here it seems part and parcel of that multidimensional quality which Marianne Thalmann associates with the world of the Kunstmärchen. Actually, in speaking about *Evenings,* the key term should be duality rather than multiplicity. In the finale of the opening story, "The Sorochintsy Fair," the gay and gaudy exuberance of the wedding feast subsides into authorial wistfulness and melancholy:

> In the distance there was still the sound of dancing feet, something like the far-away murmur of the sea, and soon all was stillness and emptiness. Is it not thus that joy, lovely and fleeting guest, flies from us? In vain the last and solitary note tries to express gaiety. . . . Sad is the lot of one left behind, heavy and sorrowful is his heart and nothing can help him![6]

5. *The Collected Tales and Plays of Nikolai Gogol,* pp. 92-93.
6. Ibid., pp. 22-23.

Some sixteen years later, in his already-quoted retrospective statement,[7] Gogol was to insist that the chief motive behind the rollicking tales of *Evenings* was the author's desire to cheer himself up, to snap out of his congenital "melancholia." Should the sudden lapse into sadness at the end of "The Sorochintsy Fair" be viewed as a breakdown of the willed euphoria? Or should one rather regard the sudden shift of tone in the last paragraph as the characteristically Gogolian device to be employed to greater effect in such narratives as "The Tale of How Ivan Ivanovich Quarreled with Ivan Nikoforovich," or "The Madman's Diary"? In any case, this alternation of conflicting moods, when seen within the context of *Evenings,* seems a paradigm of the fundamental duality of theme and manner which dominates the cycle, of its uneasy hovering between the comical and the sinister or, as Gippius has put it, between "demonology" and "farce."[8]

These two strains converge or interpenetrate in tales where deviltry is lighthearted and mischievous rather than ominous. In "The Sorochintsy Fair," the resourceful gypsy takes advantage of a tall tale about a runaway devil who haunts the fair under the guise of a pig in order to further the marital plans of a young suitor. Amid the confusion and panic caused by an uncannily effective impersonation of the Evil One, the shrewish stepmother loses control over events and reluctantly concurs in the wedding that rowdily crowns the story. In "A Christmas Eve," the devil is not the subject, but a perpetrator of a practical joke. In this, Gogol's "jolliest" tale, it proves relatively easy to subdue and outwit the malicious prankster, in fact, to turn him into an unwilling tool of a good cause. In the early phase of the narrative, the fiend amuses himself rather harmlessly by stealing the moon and thus plunging the whole village, getting ready for the festivities, into a burlesque turmoil. Yet as

7. "Avtorskaja ispoved' " (An Author's Confession), *Polnoe Sobranie Sochinenij* (Complete Works), *8* (1952), 439.

8. *Gogol,* p. 25.

the story progresses, he is dislodged from his controlling position and reduced to a subservient role. The pious and sturdy
blacksmith, Vakula, has patiently wooed a snooty village belle,
Oksana. To effectively frustrate her suitor, this Ukrainian Barbara Allen had recourse to a fairy tale princess strategy—that
of an immensely difficult assignment. The smitten blacksmith
was requested to prove his devotion and prowess by bringing
his lady love a pair of golden slippers from the wardrobe of the
Empress Catherine the Great. The requirement seemed perfectly safe. Yet nothing is really safe, for nothing is truly
impossible, in the world of the fairy tale. The single-minded
lover grabs the devil by his tail, leaps on his back and forces the
recalcitrant troublemaker to carry him posthaste to St. Petersburg. He is promptly received by the Empress—probably the
most fantastic incident in the story—who, touched by his
gauche sincerity, produces the coveted object. The proud
beauty has no choice but to yield to her resourceful admirer.
Virtue and determination have triumphed over mischief; in
fact, they have managed to put the mischief-making powers of
the fiend to good use.

A happy ending and the devil shown as a petty trickster
easily subdued by prayer and cunning of the virtuous are the
trademarks of narratives which rely most heavily on the folk
tale or the folk theater. By the same token, in tales whose
inspiration is literary rather than folkloristic, the demonic is no
laughing matter. In "St. John's Eve," a poor farm hand, Petrus,
whose poverty prevents him from marrying his beloved
Pedorka, enters into a compact with the sinister Basavryuk, the
local emissary of the fiend. In order to secure a fortune that
would enable him to mollify Pedorka's rich peasant father, he
murders, at the forest witch's behest, a six-year-old child who
turns out to be his love's baby brother. Two sacks of gold, thus
acquired, break the old man's resistance. But the happiness of
the young couple is short-lived. Petrus' remorse is temporarily
submerged by amnesia. He is plagued by intermittent fits of
depression. The appearance of the forest witch on the anniver-

sary of the crime brings back the repressed bloody deed. Petrus and his gold go up in flames. Pedorka flees to a convent.

A number of scholars, including Gippius, Vsevelod Setchkarev, Frederick C. Driessen,[9] have called attention to parallels between "St. John's Eve" and the equally gruesome "Liebeszauber" by the German Romantic, Ludwig Tieck, which could well have been available to Gogol by 1830. (The Russian translation of "Liebeszauber" appeared in 1827.) In Tieck's story, the girl, in love with the protagonist, Emil, sets out to cast a spell on the young man. A witch who is called in insists on a human sacrifice. The victim is a small child, once again the young lady's brother. In addition to the motif of shedding innocent blood, "Liebeszauber" shares with Gogol's tale the themes of amnesia and an explosive reappearance of the submerged trauma. Emil, who witnessed from his window the immolation of the child, regains his memory on the wedding day. Overcome by revulsion and despair, he kills his bride and commits suicide.

Perhaps more significant than the apparent indebtedness to the German Romantic tale of horror, is the affinity between this lurid bit of Gogol's "false juvenilia" and some of his later narratives. The notion of lust as a tool of the fiend, as a path to perdition and self-destruction, was to become one of Gogol's pervasive, indeed obsessive themes. It was Petrus' love for Pedorka that delivered him into the devil's hands and made him commit the heinous crime to be paid for with his death. The image of a man in love going up in flames, a *sui generis* realization of the hackneyed metaphor, "I am consumed by love," was to recur in Gogol's most effective horror story. In "Viy," the huntsman, Nikita, turns into a heap of ashes after being ridden by the Master's beautiful daughter who, needless to say, is a witch.[10]

9. Ibid., p. 32 n. 16; Setchkarev, *Gogol: His Life and Works,* tr. Robert Kramer (New York University Press, 1965), p. 119; Driessen, *Gogol as a Short-Story Writer* (The Hague, Mouton and Co., 1965), pp. 76-85.

10. See below, Chapter 4, pp. 63-65.

The theme of crime and punishment which dominates "St. John's Eve" is sounded more mellifluously and yet still more grimly in Gogol's first extended tale of horror, "A Terrible Vengeance." In this richly textured narrative, redolent, as Mirsky aptly put it, of Cossack ballads and German Romanticism[11] and set in the remote past of the Ukrainian heroic oral tradition, evil reigns supreme. Neither the hero's knightly valor nor his good wife's radiant virtue can stand up against the resourcefulness and the ubiquity of the dark forces as epitomized by the sorcerer, the protagonist's sinister father-in-law. This melodramatically drawn villain, who in some episodes bears a distinct resemblance to such evildoers in Hoffmann as Trabacchio ("Ignaz Denner"), is a walking abomination. A traitor to the Cossack cause, he collaborates with the infidels, be they Turks or Poles. It is a measure of his fall from grace that he does not even enjoy good Cossack food. He harbors an incestuous passion for his lovely daughter, Katerina. He shoots and kills his valiant son-in-law, stabs the bereaved widow, and then compounds his unspeakable crime by the wanton murder of a holy hermit.

The vengeance wreaked upon the fiend is every bit as terrible as his misdeeds. As he flees the scene of his crimes, he encounters the avenging figure of a giant horseman on the top of a Carpathian mountain.

The [horseman's] wild laugh echoed through the mountains like a clap of thunder . . . [he] stretched out his mighty hands, seized the sorcerer and lifted him into the air. The sorcerer died instantly and he opened his eyes after his death. He rolled his dead eyes from side to side and saw dead men rising up from Kiev, from Galicia and the Carpathian mountains, exactly like him. The horseman laughed once more and dropped the sorcerer down a precipice and all the

11. *A History of Russian Literature* (New York, Knopf, 1949), p. 150.

corpses leaped into the precipice and fastened their teeth in the dead man's flesh.[12]

Poetic justice? Hardly. The elaborately ghoulish retribution seems to convey the sense of a world in which the processes of divine justice have been subverted by the very fiendishness which they seek to contain. The extravagant crescendo of horror projected against the backdrop of an ominously jagged landscape, where Carpathian peaks and precipices serve as an equivalent of Gothic castles and dungeons, twists the cosmos into a grotesque, Bosch-like nightmare.

"A Terrible Vengeance," the most ambitious literary effort of the young Gogol, has been variously judged a major success or at least a partial failure. My own feeling upon rereading the story is that it is remarkably effective, and at times masterful, in its own terms, but scarcely terrifying. Is it because the melodramatic proliferation of atrocities "surpasses the human measure" (Kayser)[13] and hinders a "normal" emotional response? Or is it, to put it a bit differently, because the grimness of the vengeance is both extravagant and unrelieved? Perhaps. Yet it occurs to me that the emotional effect of these bloodcurdling sequences might paradoxically be undercut by what Dmitry Cizevsky rightly hailed as the most significant achievement of "The Terrible Vengeance," its style.[14] The horror seems to be distanced and kept at bay by the elaborate verbal texture—a language so highly organized, so richly orchestrated, saturated with "alliteration, assonance, repetition, inversion, hyperbole and metaphor"[15] that it is possibly the most extravagant and blatant instance of poetic prose in Russian narrative fiction.

12. *Collected Tales and Plays,* p. 169.
13. *The Grotesque in Literature and Art,* p. 118
14. Tschizewskij, *Russische Literaturgeschichte des 19 Jahrhunderts* (Die Romantik), (Munich, Eidos Verlag, 1964), *1*, 102.
15. Setchkarev, p. 111.

Lovely is the Dnieper in tranquil weather, when freely
and smoothly its waters glide through forest and mountains.
Not a sound, not a ripple is stirring. You look and cannot
tell whether its majestic expanse moves or does not move;
and it might be of molten crystal and like a blue road made
of mirrors, immeasurably broad, endlessly long, twining
and twisting about the green world . . . Rarely a bird flies to
the middle of the river. Glorious it is! No river like it in the
world! . . . When dark blue storm clouds pile in masses over
the sky, the dark forest totters to its roots, the oaks creek,
and the lightning slashing through the storm clouds suddenly
lights up the whole world—terrible then is the Dnieper.[16]

The sonorous eloquence of this much anthologized eulogy,
its pervasive rhythms which so often verge on metrical regular-
ity, its rapturous and implausible hyperboles ("Rarely a bird
flies to the middle of the river"), are the earmarks of the
"higher" of the two styles which precariously coexist in *Evenings*. For in the hybrid universe of Gogol's *Kunstmärchen*, the
duality of tone and matter, the shuttling between the eerie and
the droll, is compounded by the alternation of two contrasting
styles, or more exactly, two discordant voices—the chatter of
the "folk" and the "high-pitched rhetoric" (Mirsky) of quivering romantic lyricism. The former strain is represented by the
friendly beekeeper, Rudy Panko, and his garrulous crew. As
Setchkarev has noted in his useful volume (pp. 118-19), the
"homely conversational tone" of the jovial beekeeper's prefaces
is reminiscent of the prologues to Sir Walter Scott's *Tales of my
Landlord* attributed to that chatty old-timer Jedediah Chish-
botham. Yet, whatever the source of Gogol's inspiration, the
technique of latching on to a narrator clearly distinct from and
inferior to the author, of mediating the story, or much of it,
through a set of verbal mannerisms which clearly betray the

16. *Collected Tales and Plays,* pp. 160-61.
17. *A History of Russian Literature,* p. 149.

speaker's lowly social status and the restricted range of his awareness, was to become one of Gogol's favorite strategies. Moreover, the procedure adopted in Rudy Panko's "naive" monologues is a rather elaborate one. Instead of a folk-narrator mediating between the author and his audience, we are introduced in the rambling prefaces to three protagonists—the beekeeper himself, who acts as a moderator or an M.C.; his most valued story-teller, the earthy sexton, Foma Grigorievich, whose gift of gab is highly praised and whose attire is rather irrelevantly eulogized; and his rival, a pretentious young man in a pea-green coat. It is not necessary to see the latter antipodes as the bearers of two contrasting voices in *Evenings* and assume, with the Dutch Gogol scholar, Frederick Driessen,[18] that the more lyrical narratives, such as "The May Night," were told by the precious young gentleman. What matters here is that this painstaking stage setting which plays up the contrast between the earthy and the extravagant speech, forcibly calls the readers' attention to the problem of the narrator or the narrative mode as that of a choice between different stylistic options.

As one moves from the preludes to the stories themselves, the claim to ethnic earthiness proves at least partly misleading. The Rudy Panko-like narrator obtrudes himself upon the scene only intermittently. Four stories—"St. John's Eve," "The Lost Letter" and "An Enchanted Spot" attributed to Foma Grigorievich, and "Ivan Fedorovich Shponka and His Aunt," told presumably by another habitué of the beekeeper's conclaves—maintain quite consistently the rambling manner of a lowbrow storyteller, complete with long-winded digressions, head shaking and neighborly winks at the audience. Some of this coziness, as already indicated, infiltrates "A Christmas Eve," a story which has no such attribution, yet whose ambience is more folkloristic than literary. Yet, in the lyrically operatic "The May Night," in "The Terrible Ven-

18. *Gogol as a Short-Story Writer,* pp. 70-71.

geance," and in the opening passage of "The Sorochintsy Fair,"
the folksy clowning is displaced by rhapsody, by rapture and
awe before the beauties of the vastly idealized, indeed mythi-
cized Ukrainian landscape.

How intoxicating, how magnificent is a summer day in the
Ukraine, how luxuriously warm the hours when midday
glitters in stillness and sultry heat and the blue, fathomless
ocean covering the plain like a dome seems to be slumbering, bathed in languor, clasping the fair earth and holding it
close in its ethereal embrace! ("The Sorochintsy Fair")[19]

Do you know the Ukrainian night? No, you do not know the
Ukrainian night! Look at it: the moon looks out from the
center of the sky; the immense dome of heaven stretches
further, more inconceivably immense than ever; it glows and
breathes; the earth is all bathed in a silvery glow, and the
exquisite air is refreshing and warm and full of languor, and
an ocean of fragrance is stirring . . . Divine night!
Enchanted night! And suddenly it all springs to life—the
woods, the pond, the stones, the glorious clamor of the
Ukrainian nightingale bursts upon the night, and one fancies
the moon itself is listening in mid-heaven."[20]

To call these passages descriptive clearly would be misleading. An early Soviet critic, Valerjan Pereverzev, author of an
interesting, if crudely one-sided study of Gogol, stated the
matter succinctly when he said, "Gogol does not describe
nature; he emotes about it."[21] Many of Gogol's contemporaries, and some of his more recent critics, have deplored the
dearth of sensory detail, the vagueness and occasional incoherence of epithets and similes. Admittedly, some of the sequences

19. *Collected Tales and Plays*, p. 8.
20. Ibid., p. 55.
21. *Tvorchestvo Dostoevskogo* (Moscow, Sovremennye problemy, 1912), p.
15.

lack any discernible pictorial logic. Thus, it is not easy to see how the "blue fathomless ocean" can at the same time "cover the plain like a dome and hold the fair earth close in its ethereal embrace." But to concede this is not necessarily to agree with those who judge these "inflated" passages an overall failure. A verdict such as this is scarcely meaningful without an assessment of the aesthetic intent and function of Gogol's nature poetry. With their blatantly personifying metaphors, their rhetorical sweep, their tendency to substitute emotionally loaded epithets for descriptive detail, Gogol's "fantasies on the theme of nature" (Setchkarev) are an extreme instance of the Romantic descriptive style. The intent here clearly is not to conjure up a vivid picture, but to express an attitude, to convey a mood, an ambience, by means of "musical" devices, intonational crescendos, leitmotifs, rich, obtrusive euphony. In this endeavor, I submit, the author of *Evenings* is much more successful than he is in achieving vividness or intellectual coherence, which are scarcely at issue here.

Moreover, some Gogol scholars notwithstanding, his rhapsodies are hardly a foreign body in the hybrid universe of *Evenings*. For one thing, the contrast between the high-pitched lyricism of these effusions and the earthy tomfoolery of the rustic old-timers is part of the incongruity which is built into the structure of the cycle. For another, the lyrical set-pieces provide a singularly appropriate backdrop for, or accompaniment to, the fairy tale-like proceedings, a vehicle for dematerializing nature and inducing an entranced state of mind receptive to magic and eager for a miracle. The dream-like "silvery glow" of the Ukrainian night, the "glorious clamor of the Ukrainian nightingale," these are the sounds and colors of Gogol's regional Kunstmärchen.

A striking instance of this urge to metamorphose nature is a remarkable sequence in "A Terrible Vengeance," which I find more compelling than the already quoted and widely anthologized ode to the Dnieper:

Sweet it is to look from mid-Dnieper to the lofty mountains, to the broad meadows, to the green forests! Those
mountains are not mountains; they end in peaks below as
above, and both under and above them lie the high heavens.
Those forests on the hills are not forests; they are the hair
that covers the shaggy head of the wood demon. Down
below he washes his beard in the water, and under his beard
and over his head lie high heavens. Those meadows are not
meadows; they are a green girdle encircling the round sky,
and above and below a moon hovers over them.[22]

One of the remarkable things about this string of negative
similes is that it epitomizes the process which so often is at
work in the Dikanka cycle—that of mobilizing motifs and
techniques of Slavic folklore in behalf of the author's idiosyncratic vision. Negative parallelism ("Those forests . . . are not
forests; they are the hair," etc.) is a time-honored device of the
Russian folk song or ballad. A typical example drawn from a
bylina is: "It was not a bright falcon that flew out there. It was
not a black raven that fluttered out there. There rode an evil
Tartar."[23] Yet this time the strategy of denying an element of a
landscape ("forests") in order to project an eerie anthropo-
morphic motif ("wood demon") embodies not only the Romantic poet's urge to animate nature, but also Gogol's characteristic compulsion to displace or debunk mere sense data. Brilliant
utilization of a mirror image—reflection of the mountain peaks
in the limpid water of the Dnieper—serves to reverse the
normal hierarchies, to blur the distinction between "above"
and "below," but more importantly, to call into question the
reliability of appearances. The distrust of our ordinary percep-
tions, the gnawing sense that things are not what they appear to
be, was to become before long an essential Gogolian theme.
Only four years separate the first volume of *Evenings* from the

22. *Collected Tales and Plays,* p. 138.
23. Quoted in Jurij M. Sokolov, *Russian Folklore,* tr. Catherine R. Smith
(New York, Macmillan, 1950), p. 207.

anxious warning in Gogol's first Petersburg tale, "The Nevsky Prospekt": "Oh, do not trust that Nevsky Prospekt!"[24]

Both the wonder and the terror, the deviltry and the romance, are conspicuously absent from the last story of the Dikanka cycle, "Ivan Fedorovich Shponka and His Aunt," a wantonly truncated tale of a tame and inane Ukrainian squire, bullied by his overpowering aunt into marrying a neighbor's daughter. This elaborately flimsy narrative has several claims on the Gogolian's attention. In his pathetic reluctance to marry and his mounting helplessness vis-a-vis the busybody aunt's matrimonial schemes, Ivan Fedorovich clearly foreshadows the chief protagonist of Gogol's later comedy, "Marriage." Podkolesin, who throughout the play reluctantly follows the matchmaker's lead only to escape matrimony at the last moment by jumping out the window.[25] In a different vein, few Freudians, or for that matter, few modern-minded laymen, will resist the temptation of reading intricate sexual symbolism into Shponka's burlesque anxiety dream which translates the squire's fear of marriage into a wild proliferation of wives who keep emerging from under his hat, from his pockets, indeed from almost every wrinkle in his clothes. At the peak of this hectic sequence, Ivan Fedorovich is being pulled by a rope up a belfry which, very much to his surprise, turns out to be his formidable aunt. To make things even more disturbing, it is his wife who does the pulling, "because [he is] a bell."[26]

There is too the studiedly nonchalant manner of narration which has reminded more than one scholar of Laurence Sterne's tampering with the conventions of prose fiction in *Tristram Shandy*. The last sentence of "Ivan Fedorovich Shponka and His Aunt"—"Meanwhile, a new scheme, of which you shall hear more in the following chapter, matured in his aunt's brain"—is deliberately misleading. We never hear

24. See below, Chapter 4, p. 80.
25. See below, Chapter 6, p. 100.
26. *Collected Tales and Plays*, pp. 196-97.

about this scheme, for the following chapter is missing. It seems—so we are told in the preamble by the garrulous editor-beekeeper—that his "old woman" lined the baking tin with a half of the pages upon which the Shponka story was written down. . .

This whimsical alibi points up, in retrospect, the precariousness and flimsiness of the plot. It is as if the tale had suddenly petered out, defeated by its own triviality. For it is triviality that is at the core of Shponka's ludicrously small universe. It is unreedemable insignificance that is both the source and the target of whatever comic effects the tale manages to achieve. Gone, along with the operatic glamor of the "singing and dancing Ukraine," is the exuberance and the "fun" of the spirited village pranksters. For the first time, we are treated to what was to become an essential Gogolian genre—the comedy of inanity, the enactment of pathetic stupidity through verbal incoherence and incongruity.

In his ludicrous inarticulateness, Ivan Fedorovich prefigures the tongue-tied anti-hero of "The Overcoat," Akakij Akakievich.[27] In a fateful encounter with a neighbor's daughter, Shponka after fifteen minutes of painful silence, takes a desperate conversational plunge by remarking: "There are a great many flies in the summer, Madam!" His notion of a "long and difficult sentence" is: "I had occasion to observe what distant lands there are in the world." The hapless squire's proclivity for irrelevance is illustrated by the following passage from his letter to his aunt: "As to your commission in regard to the wheat seed and Ukrainian grain, I cannot carry it out; there is none in all the Mogilev province. As for pigs, they are mostly fed on brewer's grain as well as a little beer when it has grown flat." Since the aunt's commission had nothing to do with pigs, there is no more logic in this sequence than in the aunt's dictum, which, to be fair, does occur in Shponka's dream: "Yes, you must sleep on one leg now, for you are a married man."[28]

27. See below, Chapter 8, p. 144 et al.
28. *Collected Tales and Plays,* pp. 195, 190, 178, and 197.

A shabbily comic outsider in the operatic world of *Evenings,* "Ivan Fedorovich Shponka and His Aunt" lends substance to Setchkarev's observation that boundaries between Gogol's various stages or periods are often fluid.[29] Both in its verbal texture and in its essential tenor, this truncated tale points beyond his first narrative cycle toward what is known as his middle period. If the parochial timidity of Shponka anticipates the placidly stagnant existence of "The Old-Fashioned Landowners," his inane non sequiturs are a modest preview of the brilliant use of incongruity in that comic masterpiece, "The Tale of How Ivan Ivanovich Quarreled with Ivan Nikoforovich."

29. *Gogol: His Life and Works,* p. 113.

4

From Dithyramb to Irony

These remarkable tales were to appear two years after the publication of the second Dikanka series in *Mirgorod*, a volume of stories bearing the name of a Ukrainian county town. On the eve of this new spurt of creativity, Gogol had a brief and ill-fated encounter with another vocation, university teaching.

Gogol's pedagogical episode—his one year stand as a lecturer in world history at the University of St. Petersburg—is bizarre, and in some respects rather difficult to assess. It is generally recognized that his bout with Academia was a fiasco. Yet, the Gogol scholars have had trouble agreeing as to the scope and nature of his failure. Once again, some recent investigations (Vengerov, Gippius, Cizevsky)[1] tend to call into question the view, which in the nineteenth-century was generally taken for granted, that Gogol was an unmitigated disaster as an academic historian.

First, the incontestable facts. Toward the end of 1833, a

1. Cizevsky is especially emphatic in refusing to reduce Gogol's short-lived academic career to his excessive craving for status and in challenging the notion of Gogol's being totally unprepared for the job: "Es gibt hunderte von Blättern mit Auszügen Gogol's aus der historischen Literatur and Quellensammlungen, die Gogol für seine Vorlesungen anlegte. Man spricht mit Ironie über seinen Plan, eine Geschichte der Ukraine "in mehreren Bänden" zu schreiben, vergisst aber, dass Gogol mindestens eine der umfangreichen Ukrainischen Chroniken des 17 bis 18 Jahrhunderts kannte und ausser dem noch die sogenannte "Geschichte der Russen" . . . Hätte Gogol diese Werken auch nur unkritisch verarbeitet, so hätte ohne Schwierigkeiten ein Werk in mehreren Bänden enstehen könnte" (*Russische Literaturgeschichte des 19 Jahrhunderts, 1,* 102).

young Ukrainian ethnographer, Maksimovich, who had just been offered the Chair of Russian literature at the newly founded University of Kiev, alerted Gogol to the possibility of his securing a professorship. Gogol responded to his friend's suggestion with alacrity. His nostalgia for the sunny Ukraine, his resentment toward the chilly, fog-bound bureaucratic capital, had been reactivated. "To Kiev! To Kiev!" becomes for a while the leitmotif of his correspondence. In anticipation of the coveted position, he savors the fringe benefits—the balmy climate and the rich food of his native land. He envisions, with his characteristic extravagance, a Ukrainian cultural renaissance, as a reward of dedicated efforts on the part of two native sons, himself and Maksimovich. "As soon as we get to Kiev," he writes on January 7th, 1834, "to hell with laziness! Let us turn our city, beloved by God, into a new Athens."[2]

The premature euphoria spills into the would-be educator's field of study, history. In one of his letters, Gogol speaks of a plan to dash off "a history of the Ukraine in six small or four large volumes."[3] Writing to the Moscow historian and editor, Mikhail Pogodin, who was to play an important role in his life, he outlines an approach to history which, not surprisingly, sets more store by inspiration and enthusiasm than by systematic research, and by folk poetry than by dry chronicles: "My history of the Ukraine is exceedingly wild (*beshenaja*) . . . Some say that my style is too gaudy, that it is vivid and flamboyant in a way which is inappropriate for history. Why should history be boring? What are the arid chronicles with which I now contend," he tells Maksimovich, compared to the singing, living chronicles?"[4] It may be worth noting that the only publication which emerged from Gogol's frenzied "messing" with the history of the Ukraine was a eulogy of the

2. *Polnoe Sobranie Sochinenij* (Complete Works), *10*, 291.
3. Ibid., p. 297.
4. Ibid., pp. 294, 284.

"singing, living chronicles," an essay on Ukrainian folk songs
in *Arabesques*.[5]

Some biographers have noted rather acidly that this
romantic enthusiasm went hand in hand with thoroughly pragmatic efforts. In seeking the Kiev Chair, Gogol left no stone
unturned. He was using his connections to the hilt. He kept
badgering his influential friends, Pushkin and Zhukovskij, and
was not above peppering his letters to Maksimovich with
brazenly self-serving tips such as this: "When you write to B.,
why not hint about coaxing Gogol into the University? You
don't know anyone so steeped in history and so much in
command of the language of instruction; some more praise of
this kind could be injected casually."[6] Understandably, some of
Gogol's contemporaries were taken aback by his nerve. A
minor litterateur and a prospective censor, Nikitenko, commented with some asperity: "A young man who has made a
name for himself in literature, but has no academic rank, has
not proven in any way his fitness for the Chair . . . this can
happen only in Russia where pull is everything."[7]

When the time came, the Kiev Chair was offered to someone
else. Gogol was too bitter to consider a consolation prize—a
visiting professorship at the University of Kiev. He angrily
turned it down only to accept a while later a lectureship in
world history at the University of St. Petersburg. His academic
career was short-lived. His opening lecture, later published in
Arabesques as an essay "On The Middle Ages,"[8] was an effective if flamboyant performance—a dithyramb rather than an
analysis. The broad rhetorical sweep of this introduction was
quite in line with his stated belief that "the professor's style
should be compelling, fiery," that "each lecture should be an

5. "O malorossijsikikh pesnjakh" (On Ukrainian Songs), *Polnoe Sobranie
Sochinenij, 8,* (1952), 90-97.
    6. *Polnoe Sobranie Sochinenij, 10* (1952), 310.
    7. As quoted in Veresaev,*Gogol v zhizni,* p. 138.
    8. "O srednikh vekakh" (On the Middle Ages), *Polnoe Sobranie Sochinenij,
8,* 14-25.

integrated whole, so as to appear to the listener as a harmonious poem."[9] The pitfalls of such an inspirational approach to lecturing, coupled with poor working habits, soon became apparent. As the initial excitement wore off, Gogol's teaching started deteriorating rapidly. His attendance became irregular, his lecturing style degenerated into a monotonous mumbling. It seemed that only once did he manage to recapture some of his early charisma. When warned that Pushkin and Zhukovskij were expected to visit his class, he managed to deliver a somewhat fanciful but eloquent harangue on a nineth-century Arab caliph, Al-Mamun,[10] only to relapse into a lethargy from which he apparently never recovered.

His most famous student, Ivan Turgenev, left a vivid, if perhaps a somewhat slanted account of Professor Gogol's pathetic decline: "We were all convinced that Mr. Gogol-Janovskij, our Professor . . . had nothing in common with the writer, Gogol, who was well known to us as the author of *Evenings on a Farm near Dkanka*. . . . During the final examination in his subject, he sat there with a kerchief tied around his head, allegedly because he was suffering from a tooth-ache, and an expression of utter despondency on his face, and didn't open his mouth. As if it were today, I see his lean, long-nosed figure before me, with the two ends of a black silk handkerchief sticking up high above his head, looking like his ears. Undoubtedly he saw very well the whole comedy and the awkwardness of his position. In the same year, he handed in his resignation."[11] The last sentence is a bit misleading. Gogol's "resignation" was not entirely voluntary. He must have felt that his position at the University was becoming increasingly untenable and provoked a cancellation of his appointment by an unauthorized extension of a leave of absence. Did he actually realize the "comedy and the awkwardness of his posi-

9. Ibid., pp. 28, 30.

10. See "Arabesques," *Polnoe Sobranie Sochinenij, 8,* 76-81.

11. Ivan S. Turgenev, "Literaturnye i zhitejskie ospominanija" (Literary and Other Reminiscences), *Sochinenija* (Moscow and Leningrad, Nauka, 1967), *14,* 75-76.

tion"? His letters to friends blame his pedagogical failure on the inadequacy and the unresponsiveness of his audience: "Do you know what it means to find no response? I lecture in utter solitude. . . . No one listens to me. . . . If only one . . . among the students understood me! . . . They are colorless . . . like St. Petersburg."[12] Though his often-quoted postmortem letter to Pogodin included the admission that its author had gotten "into the wrong business," the dominant theme is still one of having been misunderstood by an insensitive, colorless crowd. "Unrecognized, I mounted the rostrum, and unrecognized, I shall depart from it."[13]

There is scarcely any doubt but that Gogol was utterly miscast in the role of a professor of history. Yet, some uncharitable biographers notwithstanding, he was a failure rather than a fraud. Turgenev's verdict, "He understood nothing of history," should be taken with a grain of salt. True, in his already-quoted *apologia pro vita sua,* Gogol himself was to insist: "I never was attracted to the past."[14] But this dictum is no more reliable than many other retrospective assertions also found in "An Author's Confession." It is one thing to make the obvious point that Gogol cared nothing for the rigors of historical scholarship, that he saw history as a gaudy pageant dominated by dramatic personalities rather than a continuous process shaped by larger, impersonal forces; in other words, that he had trouble distinguishing between history and myth-making. It is quite another thing to deny that for a number of years he was under the spell of Romantic historicism. This fascination is attested by several chapters from a luridly melodramatic historical novel begun in Nezhin but, mercifully, never completed, as well as the burly Cossack romance, "Taras Bulba," which was emerging in 1834, and the recently published notebooks—solid evidence of a fairly extensive if erratic reading in major works of western Romantic

12. *Polnoe Sobranie Sochinenij, 10,* 344.
13. Ibid., p. 378.
14. Ibid., *8,* 449.

historiography.[15] In the light of these materials, Gogol's notion
of compiling a voluminous history of the Middle Ages remains
unrealistic, but seems a trifle less preposterous, let alone fraud-
ulent, than it had appeared to most of his nineteenth-century
biographers.

What was at work here, I believe, was neither utter ignorance nor utter frivolity, but a remarkably wobbly sense of
reality. Gogol's breezy reference to dashing off a four-volume
history of the Ukraine was not simply Khlestakov-like
braggadocio. It was also testimony to a colossal lapse in judgment. In venturing, not without genuine zest, into the "wrong
business," he misjudged his audience, his own resources—
which clearly did not include the ability for sustained scholarly effort—and the nature of his task. He mistook a brain
storm for an epiphany, an intellectual romance for a vocation,
and thus placed himself in a position both awkward and
comical—the kind of position in which he was to find himself
every time he mounted the rostrum in order to teach or preach
directly. What is so striking about Gogol's academic fiasco is
not so much the increasingly predictable failure of communication as the baffling coexistence of usually incompatible qualities, the contrast between nonchalance and enthusiasm,
between cunning and naïveté, and finally, between the bang of
the grand opening and the whimper of the final examination as
recalled by Turgenev. A hapless examiner trying to get off the
hook by pretending a toothache—"his lean, long-nosed
figure . . . with the two ends of a black silk handkerchief sticking up high above his head"—what a Gogolian, or, if I may use
our key term, what a grotesque image!

In a more positive vein, Gogol's academic fadeout was not
merely a matter of intellectual laziness, or of an increasing
erosion of interest in medieval history. The same year, 1834,

15. See especially his essay on "Schlözer, Müller and Herder" (1832), *Polnoe
Sobranie Sochinenij, 8,* 85-89.

turned out to be a remarkably productive one for Gogol the writer. A brief infatuation with history gave way to a vigorous and variegated literary activity. The early part of 1835 saw the appearance of two volumes—*Arabesques,* a miscellany which, along with several essays, contained three important Petersburg tales, "Nevsky Prospekt," "A Madman's Diary," and "The Portrait," and *Mirgorod,* which featured four narratives.

The latter work is often called "transitional." The adjective is applicable in several ways. Both the manner and the texture of "The Old-Fashioned Landowners," with its proliferation of *realia,* with the piling up of prosy physical and social detail, are a far cry from the operatic glamour and the lyrical lilt of *Evenings,* and a significant step toward the later Gogol. But the most easily definable shift here is one of locale.

In contradistinction to the Petersburg-dominated *Arabesques, Mirgorod* is set in the Ukraine. Yet most of the time it is not the Ukraine of the Cossack legend or the folk opera, but the seedy actuality of the stagnant early nineteenth-century backwater. The only significant exception is the longest narrative in *Mirgorod,* "Taras Bulba," in which Cossack balladry joins hands with the more sensational variant of French Romantic fiction—the "frenetic" prose of Jules Janin and Eugène Sue—and the expansive imagery of *The Iliad* to produce one of the most flamboyant pieces of historical fiction in the language.

Setchkarev contends that, on the whole, Gogol failed to integrate these disparate strains and that the result is partly abortive and largely uncharacteristic.[16] I would be inclined to query this latter assertion. At least in one respect, "Taras Bulba" is unmistakably Gogolian. Hyperbole, clearly Gogol's favorite figure of speech,[17] dominates not only the exuberantly inflated rhetoric of the novel, but also its narrative structure. In fact, the entire plot of "Taras Bulba," the story of a sturdy

16. *Gogol: His Life and Works,* p. 147.
17. The point will be elucidated at some length in Chapter 7.

Cossack chieftain and his intrepid band of "Christian warriors" hacking away at the infidels, could be called an extended hyperbole. Many incidents are hyperboles projected into narration, a figure of speech become event. (In a typical battle, Taras demolishes scores of enemies in one blow.) This is especially true of the final scenes which feature the "passion" of Ostap Bulba and the apotheosis of Taras Bulba. Ostap, Taras' elder son and his second in command, is captured by the Poles. A large Polish crowd gathers in a Warsaw square to savour the torture and execution of the Cossack warrior. Taras infiltrates the crowd in disguise to witness his son's ordeal and test his endurance. Ostap bears "the tortures and agonies like a hero," but in a moment of unbearable pain, he cannot help but cry out: "Father, where are you? Do you hear all this?" When, amid the absolute stillness of the square, Taras Bulba booms away: "I hear!," "a million people" shudder.[18] The standard English translation, "all the thousands of people," unnecessarily reduces Gogol's figure to plausible dimensions. The demographic hyperbole should not have been tampered with, since it is of a piece with the wild improbability of the entire sequence, surpassed in extravagance only by Taras' own execution: chained to the tree trunk and about to be burned alive Taras keeps shouting orders to the survivors of his unit who are crossing the river to freedom.[19]

It is testimony to the moral obtuseness of the Russian schoolmarms, Tsarist and Soviet alike, that this Cossack "Western" could have been taken seriously, and that its bigger-than-life protagonist could have been held up as an example to Russian youth—a paragon of civic virtue and a source of patriotic edification.[20]

Edmund Wilson, in his remarkably perceptive essay, "The

18. *The Collected Tales and Plays of Nikolai Gogol*, p. 332.
19. Ibid., pp. 337-38.
20. This preposterous notion was suggested mainly by the second, enlarged version of "Taras Bulba" (1842), where the rhetoric of distinctly Cossack jingoism is supplanted by that of Russian nationalism (see below, Chapter 7, n. 40).

Demon in the Overgrown Garden,"[21] is not far off the mark when he construes Taras as a moral monster rather than a hero, a freak not altogether dissimilar from the preposterous or sinister creatures that populate Gogol's later masterpieces. Many modern readers, I suspect, will go along with Wilson in denying their admiration or awe to a blustering bully who does not hesitate to provoke a war in order to provide his two strapping sons with a limbering-up exercise, and who, without blinking an eye, shoots his younger son, Andrij. The primitive brutality of Taras' code is revealed not so much by the act itself—Andrij, smitten by a Polish beauty, betrayed the cause— as by its rationale: "I begot you and now I shall kill you!,"[22] declares Taras before pulling the trigger. It is as simple as that.

This is not to say that Gogol intended Taras as another moral monster. The ethos which permeates "Taras Bulba" is a far cry from that of the twentieth-century liberal intellectual. The essential point, it seems to me, is that Gogol's historical romance lends itself to serious moral judgment as readily as a Superman comic strip. Its appeal is frankly and unabashedly escapist. While the sweep and sonority of its rhetoric raises "Taras Bulba" well above the level of the run-of-the-mill *roman d'aventure*, the spell which this brilliant melodrama casts on its ideal audience, the teenager, lies in its glorious implausibility, its extravagant defiance of the contingent, the immediate, the quotidian.

It is the unspectacular present that confronts us in the story which opens the *Mirgorod* cycle, "The Old-Fashioned Landowners." Indeed, it is difficult to imagine a starker contrast than the one between the rowdy daring of Taras Bulba's minions and the tame, placid, utterly uneventful existence of the kindly aged couple, pleasantly stagnating amidst the bounties of mellow Ukrainian nature. A latter-day Philemon and Baucis, Afanasij Ivanovich and Pulkherija Ivanovna Tovstogub

---

21. *The Nation, 175* (New York, 1952), 520-24.
22. *Collected Tales and Plays*, p. 314. I have tampered some with the Garnett-Kent translation.

literally live off the fat of the land—"the blessed earth [which] produced everything in such abundance."[23] Yet, at the early stage of the narrative, the myth is given a slightly ironic twist as our attention is called to the gradual deterioration of the ancestral estate, the waste of resources due to the dishonesty of servants and the complacent indolence of the masters who "took very little interest in farming the land." "However many presents the servants carried to their friends in other villages" . . . "however much was stolen by visitors, phlegmatic coachmen and flunkies. . ."[24] Though at the end of the sequence, the reader is assured that "this terrible robbery made no perceptible impression on their [the owners'] prosperity," the theme of waste and mismanagement insidiously registers and subtly undermines the legend. In the Philemon and Baucis myth, the prosperity bestowed upon the old folk as a reward for their virtue is an absolute, timeless quality. In Gogol's story, it appears at least in part as an illusion of the complacent couple, or, as an economist would put it, a wasting asset. There seems to be an intimation here that the old-fashioned landowners are living in a fool's paradise. We are forewarned: the story might be an idyll with a difference.

Not unlike some tales in *Evenings,* "The Old-Fashioned Landowners" is a first-person narrative. Yet, the voice telling it is not one of the folksy old-timer, but of a younger man who, though not to be confused with the author, is at least in one respect a Gogol-like figure. He has left behind his native Ukraine to face the challenges and the pitfalls of the big city, and returns home periodically to immerse himself in the peaceful, unruffled quality of "that extraordinarily secluded life in which not one desire flits beyond the palisades surrounding the little courtyard."[25]

As the narrative unfolds, one is increasingly struck by the constricted scope and the unabashedly passive, or, if one will,

23. Ibid., p. 214.
24. Ibid., p. 212.
25. Ibid., p. 207.

"oral" quality of the couples' way of life. The minuscule universe of Afanasij Ivanovich and Pulkherija Ivanovna revolves around food which provides the main source of gratification, the chief topic of conversation, and last but not least, the principal mode of showing affection. Pulkherija Ivanovna demonstrates her solicitude toward her husband most conclusively, catering to his palate by supplying him lovingly with "poppyseed pies and salted mushrooms."

Suddenly, the sluggish rhythm of an existence punctuated only by elaborately prepared and reverently savored meals is disturbed by what could appear on the surface an insignificant episode. Pulkherija Ivanovna's little grey cat runs away and joins, for a while, a savage and unruly breed which roamed a "wild and neglected forest" adjoining the Tovstogub estate. She reappears as suddenly as she vanished, looking thin and battered. "The grey little fugitive" greedily consumes the food lavished on her by Pulkherija Ivanovna, only to disappear for good: the "ungrateful creature had evidently grown so much accustomed to the ways of wild cats, or had adopted the romantic principle that poverty with love is better than life in a palace."[26]

It is a commentary on the nature of the story and the quality of the life featured in it that so trivial an incident could acquire a status of a turning point or a central event. To Pulkherija Ivanovna, the whole thing appears as a bad omen: " 'It was my death coming for me!' she said to herself, and nothing could distract her mind."[27] A few days later, she quietly dies, but not before making sure that her bereaved husband would not be deprived of his favorite dishes. After a lapse of five years, the narrator pays another call on the Tovstogub estate. He finds the old man listless, apathetic, disconsolate. Characteristically, he bursts into tears at the very mention of a dish in which the dear departed excelled. The visitor is left to marvel at the "long, bitter grief," and to muse at the force of emotional habit

26. Ibid., p. 221.
27. Ibid.

which seems more enduring than "all the whirl of our desires and turbulent[28] passions."

He [Afanasij Ivanovich] didn't live long after that. One day, Afanasij Ivanovich ventured to take a little walk in the garden. . . . He suddenly heard someone behind him pronounce in a fairly distinct voice: "Afanasij Ivanovich . . . He turned around, and there was absolutely nobody there. He pondered for a minute; his face seemed to brighten, and he brought out at last: 'It's Pulkherija Ivanovna calling me!'

Like his dead wife, Afanasij Ivanovich submits to the inevitable with "the readiness of an obedient child." To paraphrase Dylan Thomas, he goes gently, indeed meekly, into that good night. "He flickered out as the candle does when there is nothing left to sustain its feeble flame. 'Lay me beside Pulkherija Ivanovna,' was all he said before his end."[29]

The slightness, indeed the virtual absence of a plot in "The Old-Fashioned Landowners," is singularly appropriate in a story devoted to creatures of habit. So is the predominance of description over narration proper. The static quality of life depicted here provides ample justification or excuse for that lavish display of household detail, cluttering up the stage with domestic bric-a-brac—"chests and boxes, big and little," "little bags and sacks of flower seed, vegetable seed and melon seed hanging on the wall"—that was to become a trademark of the later Gogol, and probably the main reason for the largely erroneous view that Gogol was a realist.[30] In "The Old-Fashioned Landowners," Gogol appeared for the first time as a master of *Kleinmalerei,* or dense, viscous social landscape painting.

28. Ibid., p. 226. I have substituted "turbulent" for "boiling."
29. Ibid., p. 227.
30. For an extended discussion of this controversial notion see below, Chapter 7.

Yet when all is said and done, the most remarkable, and the most elusive element in the story is its tone. The critics have differed widely in trying to assess it. In one of the first serious critical reactions to Gogol's fiction, Vissarion Belinskij credits the story with some empathy for the protagonist, yet sees it primarily as a truthful portrayal of an ignominiously subhuman and trivial way of life.[31] Conversely, Mirsky, in his usually perceptive *A History of Russian Literature,* speaks of Gogol's "sentimentalizing the gluttony, the parochialism and selfishness" (p. 152) of Afanasij Ivanovich and Pulkherija Ivanovna.

Both assertions, especially the latter, strike me as lopsided, and thus misleading. The tenor of "The Old-Fashioned Landowners" cannot be reduced either to debunking or to idealization. The satire, such as it is, is tempered here by affection, "idealization" subverted by an uneasy sense of human waste, of stunted growth, of pathetic human limitation. To put it differently, the genre of "The Olf-Fashioned Landowners" is neither a pure idyll nor a straight satire. I would prefer to speak here, if I may be permitted an oxymoron, of a satiric idyll or a seedy pastoral. Gogol's, or the narrator's, underlying ambivalence is clearly reflected in the opening passage of the story: "I sometimes like to *descend* for a moment into that extraordinarily secluded life."[32] "Unconsciously, one renounces for a brief spell at least, all ambitious dreams, and imperceptibly passes with all one's heart into this *lowly bucolic existence*"[33] (my italics).

"Lowly bucolic"—this combination of adjectives epitomizes the predicament of a narrator torn between nostalgia and condescension. The peace and innocence of the kindly couple

31. "O russkoj povesti i povestjakh g. Gogolja ('Arabeski' i 'Mirgorod')," *N. V. Gogol v russkoj kritike i vospominanijakh sovremennikov* (Moscow and Leningrad, Detgiz, 1951), pp. 50-52.

32. *Collected Tales and Plays,* p. 207.

33. Ibid., p. 208. I have tampered with two words in the passages just quoted. "Descend" corresponds more closely to the original "sojti" than the neutral "enter" of the Garnett-Kent version. By the same token, "nizmennyj" is "lowly" rather than "humble."

beckon the traveler as a refuge and relief from the "restless promptings of the evil spirit"—a characteristically parochial notion which the narrator and the author seem to find congenial. Yet, the pathetically constricted nature of this haven does not allow one to view it as a truly viable alternative. Infantile regression makes this "solution" incompatible with self-esteem.

This hovering between two opposite attitudes is equally apparent in the ending of the tale. There is something embarrassingly regressive, not to say subhuman, about Afanasij Ivanovich's "long, bitter grief." He acts more like a helpless child who has lost his nanny than like a mature adult mourning the loss of a life's companion. Like so many subsequent Gogol protagonists, Afanasij Ivanovich is a homunculus, a stunted, morally underdeveloped creature. And yet his grief is genuine and somewhat moving. In fact, Afanasij Ivanovich has a unique status in the uncannily loveless universe of the middle and late Gogol. He is capable of a deep emotional attachment which, however infantile, proves more enduring and perhaps, more genuine, as we are told rather pointedly, than the more turbulent yet fickle passions.

This curiously unromantic vindication of "habit" at the expense of "passion" may give one pause. Is Gogol seriously suggesting that emotional routine is more "real" than emotional impulse? So it seems. I am reminded of Tolstoy's relentless debunking in *War and Peace* and "Family Happiness" of the romantic concept of love in behalf of the solid, biological realities of marriage and child rearing. Yet Gogol's emphasis obviously is quite different. Tolstoy takes potshots at romantic illusions. Gogol's target seems to be lust, the erotic. As some recent investigators have persuasively argued, [34] it is certainly a matter of some significance that the only positive, nondestructive relationship between man and woman featured in *Mirgorod* should have been a union which, in view of the protago-

34. See especially Hugh McLean, "Gogol's Retreat From Love: Toward an Interpretation of 'Mirgorod,' " *American Contributions to the Fourth International Congress of Slavists* (The Hague, Mouton and Co., 1958), p. 225-44.

nists' advanced age and their "oral fixation," is so thoroughly non- or postsexual.

It is quite proper, then, to view this aspect of "The Old-Fashioned Landowners" as another manifestation of Gogol's well-advertised fear of sexuality. Yet, within the context of the story, the regressive tendency is also, or perhaps primarily, part and parcel of that yearning for the idyllic safety of the womb which represents one of the poles of the narrator's inner conflict. We are back to the unresolved, and perhaps insoluble, dilemma of "Hanz Kuechelgarten"—the shuttling between the threat of the wicked outside world and that of parochial stagnation, between the fear of exposure and the fear of one's own passivity.

Yet these are not the only fears that stalk the deceptively placid realm of Gogol's "second idyll."[35] The gnawing doubts about the moral adequacy of this truncated haven are compounded by the sense of its precariousness and vulnerability. The theme subtly suggested at the outset of the story returns to haunt us. The oasis of mindless tranquillity is invaded and undermined by the dark, demonic forces dwelling on the other side of the fence that circumscribes the world of "The Old-Fashioned Landowners." As we have seen, the Arcadian happiness is wantonly destroyed by the "call of the wild"—the exposure of one denizen of this world to the "whirl of desires and poignant passions" as symbolized, quite in line with the preposterously small scale of the proceedings, by the savage and somber forest cats. Is the safety of the "lowly bucolic" not only humanly demeaning, but illusory as well? Is there, after all, no place to hide?

An uneasy sense of something ominous and uncanny lurking beneath the surface of pastoral quietism comes to the fore in a personal digression which follows immediately upon Afanasij Ivanovich's hearing the call of his dead wife:

It has no doubt happened to you sometime or other, to hear a voice calling you by name . . . which simple people explain

35. Gippius, *Gogol,* pp. 83-86.

as a soul grieving for a human being and calling him; and after that, they say, death follows inevitably. I must admit I was always frightened by that mysterious call. I remember that in childhood I often heard it. Sometimes suddenly someone behind me distinctly uttered my name. Usually on such occasions it was a very bright and sunny day; not one leaf in the garden was stirring; the stillness was deathlike; even the grasshopper left off chirring for a moment; there was not a soul in the garden. But I confess that if the wildest and most tempestuous night had lashed me with all the fury of the elements, alone in the middle of an impenetrable forest I should not have been so terrified as by that awful stillness in the midst of a cloudless day. I usually ran out of the garden in great panic, hardly able to breathe, and was only reassured when I met some person, the sight of whom dispelled the terrible spiritual loneliness.[36]

There are several themes here which are worth noting briefly. There is the contrast between the deceptive serenity of the day and the chilling, mysterious call; the sudden, unmotivated intrusion of the dread which strikes when we least expect it, and thus unmasks the serenity as an optical illusion. There is the phrase "terrible spiritual loneliness," which embodies a crucial Gogolian motif, that of spiritual anxiety, numbness, or deadness. Finally, let us consider the not insignificant fact that even Gogol's half-mocking, half-affectionate adventure into the idyllic should have featured so prominently the motif of man's vulnerability to the dark, the unfathomable, the ineluctable. Though the key and the setting are vastly different, one may be reminded of the somber finale of Pushkin's narrative poem, "The Gypsies," where the Rousseauist-Byronic utopia of the noble savage is shrewdly scrutinized: "and all is ruled by passions fatal and there is no escaping the fates." Yet in Gogol's story the tragedy is reduced to the level of a grotesque farce. Fate enters here via a call heard by a tottering and

36. *Collected Tales and Plays,* pp. 226-27.

superstitious old man; the fatal passions via a lean and gaunt
forest cat "mewing in a coarse, uncultured voice." A battered
tomcat as an exponent of romantic love—here is the measure
of the grotesque smallness of the story's agon, of the extent to
which this placid narrative tampers with the natural dimensions
of human events.[37]

A more mellow and subdued affair than other *Mirgorod*
tales, "The Old-Fashioned Landowners" injects, sotto voce, two
motifs essential to the cycle. The theme of the indolence and
stagnation of Taras Bulba's progeny is writ large in "How Ivan
Ivanovich Quarrelled With Ivan Nikiforovich." The dread
which breaks through the surface of the lowly idyll explodes in
the nightmarish imagery of "Viy," a horror story that strikes
me as more effective, that is, more frightening, than "A Terrible Vengeance." If, in the earlier gothic tale, the terror was
distanced by the sonorous poetic prose and framed by the
Cossack myth, where spectacularly foul deeds alternate with
feats of knightly valor, in "Viy," the demonic obtrudes itself
without a warning on a prosy and commonplace setting, on a
way of life which some of Gogol's readers could recognize as
their own. To paraphrase Wolfgang Kayser, it is "our world
that has been transformed."[38]

The time of "Viy" is not too far removed from that of "The
Old-Fashioned Landowners." In the opening passage, we are
plunged into near-contemporary Kiev and treated to what
was to become the stock-in-trade of Gogol's middle period, a
racy social reportage encumbered by homely and occasionally unappetizing trivia. We are passing in review a rowdy
bunch of students of the Kiev Theological Seminary, hurrying
every morning to the classrooms. The narrator carefully distin-

37. Obviously, "The Old-Fashioned Landowners" lacks the blatantly grotesque quality of some other Gogolian narratives. Yet, Boris Eikhenbaum is
fundamentally right in suggesting that there is something "grotesque" about
the preposterously restricted scope of the story's moral universe. (See "Käk-
sdelana 'Shinel' Gogolja," *Skvoz' literaturu, Voprosy poètiki, 4* [Leningrad,
1924], 171-95.)

38. See above, Chapter 1, pp. 4.

guishes between various classes and age groups—the "grammarians," the "theologians," the "philosophers," by the timbres of their voices, the clothes they wear, indeed, by the contents of their pockets.[39] The three protagonists who emerge from this crowd—the "theologian" Khalava, the "philosopher" Khoma Brut, and the "rhetorician" Tiberij Gorobec—are very ordinary youths about to embark on their annual summer routine, roaming the countryside and sponging on the villagers. When the narrative proper is about to begin, its focus narrows down to one of the members of that uninspiring trio, the "philosopher," "who was very fond of lying on his back, smoking a pipe." [40] The three friends decide to spend the night at a small homestead. Khoma, who is assigned to a sheep's pen, becomes a target of a strange assault on the part of the testy old landlady. Suddenly, over his feeble protest, the "granny" leaps upon his back with the "swiftness of a cat," strikes him with a broom, and has the utterly helpless and will-less Brut carry her on his shoulders through the fields, "prancing like a horse." For a while, the paralysis of Brut's will is parallelled by the blankness of his mind. It is not until he leaves the homestead behind to face the wide expanse of the plain framed by an ominously black forest, that he says to himself, "Aha, she's a witch!"

This delayed insight, which propels the narrative out of the daytime reality of the Kiev seminarians and market women back into the nocturnal magic-ridden realm of *Evenings,* occasions a major stylistic shift. Gogol's prose, hitherto weighed down by seedy detail, takes wing, acquires lyrical vibrancy, alliterative richness, feverish radiance. The scene of Khoma Brut's nocturnal ride, without any doubt, is one of the most spellbinding sequences in all of Gogol:

39. "[T]heir [the grammarians'] pockets were full of all manner of garbage such as knucklebones, whistles made of feathers, or a half-eaten pie" (*Collected Tales and Plays,* p. 338).

40. Khoma Brut's thoroughly mundane stance lends a touch of irony to the narrator's constant references to him as a "philosopher." It seems that the only philosophical attitude that could be attributed to Khoma is the indifference with which he took the thrashing administered periodically by his mentor.

The waning crescent of the moon was shining in the sky.
The timid radiance of moonlight lay mistily over the earth,
light as a transparent veil. The forest, the meadows, the sky,
the dales, all seemed as though slumbering with open eyes
. . . such was the night when Khoma Brut, the philosopher,
set off galloping with the mysterious rider on his back. He
was aware of an *exhausting, unpleasant, and at the same
time voluptuous sensation assailing his heart* [my italics].
He bent his head and saw that the grass, which had been
almost under his feet, seemed to be growing far below him,
and above it there lay water transparent as a mountain
stream . . . He saw shining there a sun instead of the moon.
He heard the bluebells ringing as they bent their little heads;
he saw a water sprite flow out from behind the reeds, there
was the gleam of her leg and back, round and firm, all
brightness and shimmering . . . did he see it, or did he not?
Was he awake or dreaming? What was that, the wind or
music? It was ringing and ringing, and reverberating, and
coming nearer and nearer and piercing his heart with a kind
of unendurable trill.[41]

The dreamlike metamorphosis of nature—"He saw shining
there a sun instead of the moon"—may remind one of the
topsy-turvy descriptive sequence in "A Terrible Vengeance,"
studded with negative parallelisms. But what lends this passage
its unique and disturbing poignancy is the strikingly conveyed
"unpleasant and at the same time voluptuous sensation," or, as
the narrator says later, "a fiendishly voluptuous feeling," the
quiver of debilitating, masochistic eroticism. In his brilliant
book, *The Paths of Russian Theology*,[42] Georgij Florovskij
observed that Gogol had "uncanny insights into the mystery of
dark passions." The word "dark" seems doubly applicable

41. Ibid., pp. 346-47. The last sentence in this quotation is drawn from
another English rendition of "Viy" in *Mirgorod: Four Tales by N. Gogol,* (New
York, Noonday Press, 1962), p. 186.

42. *Puti russkogo bogoslovija* (Paris, YMCA Press, 1937), pp. 260-61.

here, as it suggests both the self-destructive and the illicit, the guilt-producing, the shameful. Few major writers have spoken so compellingly about the sickly delights of humiliation and surrender. Fewer still have managed to parlay this painful insight into haunting poetry.

As modern psychology has told us, masochism and sadism are two sides of the same coin. The burning sense of shame produces an urge to redeem one's manliness by inflicting humiliation rather than savoring it. For a while, the roles are reversed. Suddenly overcoming his paralysis, Khoma Brut first leaps upon the witch's back, then proceeds to beat her to death. Immediately, his victim, very much to the seminarian's dismay, turns into "a beautiful girl with luxuriant tresses, all in disorder, and eyelashes as long as arrows."[43] Terrified and baffled, Khoma runs all the way back to Kiev. It is testimony to his essential coarseness and insensitivity that he should be able to recover his equanimity "the same evening." Yet his "extraordinary adventure," which he almost manages to put out of his mind, catches up with him. The price to be exacted for his sado-masochism is a heavy one. Soon he is summoned to the estate of a wealthy Cossack colonel and requested to stand vigil for three nights over the body of his beautiful daughter who died under unspecified circumstances. Needless to say, she is none other than the witch. Fearing the confrontation, Khoma makes several attempts to escape, but each time he is brought back to face the mounting fury of the evil spirits which he seeks to keep at bay by prayer and incantation. During the third night, the unholy offensive in the village church reaches its climax. The grotesque parade of evil creatures is topped by "Viy," a huge earth spirit, a "thick set, bandy legged figure . . . covered all over with black earth. His long iron eyelids hang down to the ground."[44] It is the unspeakable horror of this apparition, or to be exact, Viy's unbearable gaze, that strikes the "philosopher" dead. In the encounter between the

---

43. *Collected Tales and Plays*, p. 348.
44. Ibid., p. 373.

Christian ritual and the demonic, the latter wins handily. Is it because evil is more resourceful and powerful than the good? Or is Khoma's defeat testimony to the inadequacy and unworthiness of this particular Defender of the Faith?

On the face of it, the finale seems to suggest the latter. As the nightmare subsides we are back in Kiev, at our starting point. Khoma's former companions—the "theologian" Khalava, who in the meantime has risen to the prestigious position of bellringer, and Tiberij Gorobec, who "by now was a philosopher, and so thought himself to be in possession of all the answers" —are pondering, in a Kiev tavern, their colleague's untimely death. The bellringer is content to offer a eulogy: "He was a fine fellow. And he came to grief for nothing!" But the "philosopher" insists on an explanation: "I know why he came to grief. It was because he was afraid; if he had not been afraid, the witch could not have done anything to him. You have only to cross yourself and spit right on her tail, and nothing will happen. I know all about it. Why, the old women who sit in our market in Kiev are all witches."[45]

This reassuring notion, along with the rest of the "philosopher's" postmortem, ought to be accepted with qualification. Granted, Khoma Brut was a thoroughly uninspiring figure. His faith may well have been shallow and ritualistic; his concerns trivial and mundane. More importantly, he did not come into the church with clean hands; he had ridden the witch and was ridden by her, and he might well have been weighed down both by the vague sense of guilt and by fear of retribution. Granted too, that his death was, in part, self-inflicted, and that he paid a high price for his sinful curiosity, his lack of self-restraint. ("Do not look! an inner voice whispered to the philosopher. He could not restrain himself and he looked.")[46]

But importance of this transgression can be easily overstated. Khoma's chief vice is not so much curiosity or excessive fear—for who would not fear Viy and his ghoulish

45. Ibid., p. 374.
46. Ibid., p. 373.

cohorts?—but complacency. And this happens to be the trouble with his companion's retrospective diagnosis as well. In fact, one could go one step further: Khoma Brut is Everyman, a bumbling, careless, insensitive *homme moyen sensuel,* who was fated to stumble into the devil's trap, to look into the abyss. Gorobec, equally trivial but less severely tried, was spared this fate. Thus he can go on denying the potency of evil, construing the demonic not as an apocalyptic threat, but as a manageable nuisance that can be subdued by the right gimmick.

The complacent denial of the reality of evil, of the nocturnal threat, is an important theme in German Romanticism, especially in E. T. A. Hoffmann. In Hoffmann's famous story, "Der Sandmann," where the poet-dreamer, Nathanael, is haunted and finally destroyed by dark forces, Clara, Nathanael's sensible and cheerful fiancée, keeps assuring him that the horrors which he says have invaded his life are "all in his mind."[47]

To be sure, Tiberij's is a different brand of obtuseness. Gogol's Philistines cannot be accused of rationalism. They are superstitious provincials who take the existence of the devil and of the witches for granted and who claim to "know all about" them. Indeed, Gorobec's casual dictum sounds almost like a parody of Gogol's—or his mother's—parochial world view. But essentially the Gorobecs are no less blind to the unmitigated horror of the netherworld than Hoffmann's serene, enlightened Apollonians who blithely deny the reality of the supernatural and the irrational. They, too, smugly play down the threat by trying to domesticate it, to make it appear manageable, to absorb it casually into the fabric of daytime routine. The statement: "Why, the old women who sit in our market in Kiev are all witches," can be easily reversed. If all Kiev market women are witches, at least some witches are mere market women who can be easily spotted and disarmed. Khoma Brut's terrible ordeal seems to have been in vain.

As a grotesque crescendo of horror, "Viy" is Gogol's last tribute to the overt demonology of *Evenings,* or more broadly,

47. *Poetische Werke* (Berlin, Aufbauverlag, 1958), *2*, 371-412.

the supernatural machinery of the fairy tale. Yet, Gogol's own claims notwithstanding, the folkloristic authenticity of this strange narrative should not be overestimated. The title of the story is provided with the following footnote: "Viy is a colossal creation of the popular imagination. It is a name among the Ukrainians for the chief of the gnomes whose eyelids droop down to the ground. The whole story is folklore."[48] This, I am afraid, is a typical Gogolian mystification. Though the plot of "Viy," especially the scenes of the nightly vigils, is somewhat indebted to the Slavic legend, students of Ukrainian folklore have never encountered the ghoulish chief of the gnomes. Both the appearance of this bizarre monster and his weird one-syllable name can be credited to Gogol alone. As for sources or antecedents, the elaborately gruesome scene of the third vigil makes one think of the pageants of Hieronymus Bosch or of E. T. A. Hoffmann at his most Bosch-like, rather than of any recognizable body of folklore.

The doors were burst from their hinges, and a countless multitude of monstrous beings flew into the Church of God. A terrible noise of wings and scratching claws filled the church . . . All the while, he [Khoma] heard evil creatures whirling about him, almost touching him with their loathsome tails and the tips of their wings . . . He had not the courage to look at them; he only saw a huge monster, the whole width of the wall, standing in the shade of its matted locks, as of a forest; through the tangle of hair two eyes glared horribly, with eyebrows slightly lifted. Above it, something was hanging in the air like an immense bubble with a thousand claws and scorpion strings stretching from the center; black earth hung in clods on them.[49]

Thus Gogol. Let us now listen to a passage from E. T. A. Hoffmann's elaborately gothic novel, *A Devil's Elixirs,* a fragment of Brother Medardus' nightmare:

48. *Collected Tales and Plays,* p. 338.
49. Ibid., p. 373.

I wanted to pray. There was a confused rustling and whispering. *People I had known before appeared madly distorted* [my italics], heads crawled about with grasshoppers, lice growing out of their ears, and leering at me obscenely. Strange birds, ravens with human heads, were beating their wings overhead. . . . The chaos became madder and madder, the figures more and more weird. Satan screeched with delight: "Now you are mine alone!"[50]

An influence or a convergence? Possibly the latter. Scholars have detected many echoes from Hoffmann in Gogol's Ukrainian and Petersburg tales.[51] His familiarity with the German Romantics is richly attested. Whether he had actually read *A Devil's Elixirs* prior to the writing of "Viy" is neither certain nor, ultimately, particularly important. What matters is that the two passages belong to the same literary and artistic tradition: morbid, demon-ridden, irresistibly attracted to the hybrid, the bizarre, the incongruous, the "madly distorted." What matters is that Gogol's pandemonium, like Hoffmann's, enacts the St. Vitus' dance of the grotesque imagination.

If "Viy" is the most striking embodiment of what Kayser would have called the fantastic-grotesque strain in Gogol, the last *Mirgorod* story, "The Tale of How Ivan Ivanovich Quarreled With Ivan Nikoforovich," epitomizes the satirical-grotesque vein. In this comical and yet saddening tale, the unrelieved dullness and triviality of "plant-like" existence is featured without any redeeming undertones, without the shamefaced nostalgia and the uneasy affection that informed "The Old-Fashioned Landowners." The protagonists of "Two Ivans" are never endearing. They are merely preposterous. The

50. (London, John Calder, 1963), pp. 245-46.
51. See Gippius, *Gogol;* Setchkarev, *Gogol: His Life and Works;* Michael Gorlin, *N. V. Gogol und E. TH. A. Hoffmann* (Leipzig, Harrassowitz, 1933); Norman Ingham, *Hoffmann in Russia, 1822-1845* (Ph.D. diss., Harvard University, 1963); Adolf Stender-Petersen, "Gogol und die deutsche Romantik," *Euphorion,* (Leipzig, 1922).

sluggishness of mere existers which the Nezhin schoolboy had decried so strenuously becomes here the target of elaborate mockery.

The quarrel between the two Ivans, which is at the core of the story's flimsy plot, enacts the triviality and pointlessness of the Mirgorod way of life. Though strikingly dissimilar in appearance and demeanor—Ivan Ivanovich is thin and "refined," Ivan Nikoforovich, fat and blunt—the two squires are good neighbors and presumably the best of friends. Yet this much-advertised friendship turns into bitter enmity over an entirely trivial disagreement. Lounging around on his porch, Ivan Ivanovich sights Ivan Nikoforovich's gun which his neighbor's "old woman" airs on the clothesline along with his old uniform. This odd spectacle activates Ivan Ivanovich's lingering sense of inferiority, or, if one will, his status anxiety—he has never been in the army. He chooses to call on his neighbor, whom he finds, predictably, in a prone position, and offers a sow and two sacks of oats for a weapon which is clearly useless to either of them. Ivan Nikoforovich finds the proposition indecent and demeaning—"a gun is a gentlemanly thing!" —loses his temper and calls Ivan Ivanovich a gander. This rather moderate insult leads to a complete breaking off of diplomatic relations between the neighbors, and subsequently, to an escalation of hostilities which include Ivan Ivanovich's stealthy nocturnal attack on Ivan Nikoforovich's goose house, and the comically long-winded and ponderous complaints which the protagonists file simultaneously against each other with the Mirgorod district court. In the meantime, the long, drawn-out quarrel has become the main conversation piece in a town which has little to talk about, and increasingly, the sole concern of the two litigants who slowly and bitterly go to seed as they wait, interminably it seems, for a verdict. (The wheels of small-town Ukrainian justice grind very slowly indeed.) Their aimless existence has finally acquired a focus and goal—to show up and destroy the opponent.

Although the exposure of provincial stagnation is unambiguous this time, it can scarcely be called straightforward. Once again, Gogol had recourse to his characteristic mode of stylization—the device of hiding behind a narrator whose verbal mannerisms clearly betray a cultural status different from and inferior to the author's. The speaker who tells most of the story sounds now like a naïve Rudy Panko-like villager to whom Mirgorod is something of a metropolis, now like a local gossip who has internalized the false values of his community, and thus can view the brittle friendship between the two Ivans as a communal asset, their quarrel as a disaster, and the inane priggishness of Ivan Ivanovich as proof of refinement and delicacy of feeling. But to say this is to indicate a new twist which the strategy of impersonation has acquired here. Rudy Panko's or Foma Grigorievich's gabbing was jolly, "ethnic," folksy, but not deliberately inane. The narrator of "Two Ivans" is not merely a provincial; he is, emphatically, a fool. In fact, "Two Ivans" could be called a tale of two idiots told by an idiot. The quality of the moral universe described here is epitomized by the point of view. The comic incongruities and inanities which were at the core of the verbal grotesque in "Ivan Fedorovich Shponka," now spill into the very texture of the narrative. The story opens on a note of moronic rapture:

> Ivan Ivanovich has a superb coat! Superb! And what astrakhan! Phew, damn it all, what astrakhan! . . . There is no finding word for it. Velvet! Silver! Fire! Merciful Lord! . . . Why don't I have a coat like that! He had it made before Agafya Fedoseevna went to Kiev. You know Agafya Fedoseevna, who bit off the tax assessor's ear?[52]

The striking thing about this passage is not just its chatty irrelevance, the small-town intimacy of reference, but above all, the ironic discrepancy between the narrator's ecstasy and its target—a mere coat. We are witnessing here the emergence of

52. *Collected Tales and Plays*, p. 375.

one of the middle and later Gogol's salient strategies—the downgrading, the dehumanization of his protagonists by reducing them to their clothes, their acouterments, their status accessories. Yet the joke here, as elsewhere, is on the teller as well as on the tale. A eulogy which starts as a paean to a man's garments debunks both the eulogizer and the eulogized as it exposes the tawdry scale of values which dominates and motivates both.

The claims of the loquacious fool are constantly undercut by his own irrepressible jabbering. Ivan Ivanovich's fondness for melons is adduced as conclusive proof of the proposition that he is an excellent man. By the same token, his kindness is illustrated by his less than admirable habit of engaging a crippled beggar in a long conversation and then graciously sending him on his way without offering him a single kopek.

This proclivity for non sequiturs is especially apparent in the comparative description of the Ivans which dominates the first chapter. It is a jumble of antitheses, some of which, at closer range, turn out to be pseudo-oppositions. Gogol's language is so apt to acquire a momentum of its own that the reader, carried away by the sheer exuberance of his onrushing prose, can easily overlook much of the incoherence, indeed the absurdity of a sequence which starts from actual contrasts— "Ivan Ivanovich is thin and tall; Ivan Nikoforovich is a little shorter, but makes up for it in breadth," etc.—only to elicit the following: "Ivan Ivanovich is rather of a meek character. Ivan Nikoforovich, *on the other hand* [my italics], wears trousers with such ample folds that if they were blown out, you could put the whole courtyard with the barns and the outhouses into them."[53] The extravagant hyperbole in which this sentence culminates can easily overshadow the fact that "on the other hand" is a piece of arrant nonsense.

Toward the end of the story, the tone shifts abruptly. The ludicrous reverence for the Mirgorod shibboleths, including the

53. Ibid., pp. 378, 379.

"splendid" puddle in the middle of the city square, the preposterous readiness to take the protagonists and their silly quarrel seriously, gives away to a clear-eyed recognition of the shabbiness and triviality of it all. The mask is off. Out goes the garrulous provincial fool. In comes a relatively sensitive outsider whose moral perspective deserves some credence. He is, roughly speaking, the narrator of "The Old-Fashioned Landowners," bereft of his sentimental nostalgia:

"Five years ago I was passing through the town of Mirgorod." The "gloomy, damp weather, mud and fog" are depressing. So are the two protagonists on whom the narrator pays a call. They have grown old, haggard. Each is reduced to ludicrous fixation, kept alive only by the "positive information" that tomorrow, or next week, the case will be settled in his favor. The weather, the seedy town, the two absurd old men, blend into a dreary, all too subhuman spectacle:

> The rain poured in streams onto the Jew who sat on a box covered with a sack. The damp pierced me through and through. The gloomy gate with the sentry box, in which a veteran was cleaning his gray equipment, slowly passed by. Again, the same fields, in places black and furrowed, and in places, covered with green, the drenched cows and crows, the monotonous rain, the tearful sky without one gleam of light in it—it is a dreary world, gentlemen![54]

The finale is characteristic in more ways than one. The mounting distaste, the deep-seated sense of "*la tristesse de tout cela*", to use Verlaine's phrase, was to become a leitmotif of Gogol's later work. No less typical is the sudden shift from foolishness to seriousness. Earlier, I dealt with the breakthrough, in one of Gogol's first tales, "The Sorochintsy Fair," of the author's underlying melancholy in the midst of the noisy gaiety of the occasion. But perhaps still more significant is the

54. Ibid., p. 420.

very abruptness of the shift in the point of view, in the moral perspective of the tale. This act of puncturing the mask and thus giving the show away was to recur in his St. Petersburg stories, "A Madman's Diary" and "The Overcoat."

5

The City as Madhouse

The note of the futility of so many human pursuits that concludes *Mirgorod* is sounded time and again in the nearly concurrent St. Petersburg tales. If, in "Two Ivans," the spatial metaphor for Gogol's emerging world view is provided by the unrelieved tedium of the Ukrainian backwater, in "Nevsky Prospekt," and "A Madman's Diary" the dreariness of it all is epitomized by the metropolitan vanity fair. Once again, the setting changes significantly as the focus shifts from the periphery of the Russian Empire to its center, from a stagnant manor or country town to the teeming bureaucratic capital. To put it in terms of Gogol's personal development, *Mirgorod* enacts both the revulsion from and the residual attraction to that cozy inertia which, as a Nezhin schoolboy, he feared and denounced. By the same token, *Arabesques* (1835) offers a somewhat delayed and significantly modified literary echo of an encounter which took place several years earlier between the fevered imagination of a provincial of genius and a stunning but heartless metropolis.

Yet this latter emphasis was not merely a residue of Gogol's actual experience. As Donald Fanger reminds us in his wide-ranging study, *Dostoevsky and Romantic Realism,*[1] by the 1830s the city had become a significant literary theme, indeed an important literary myth. A collective personality with a discernible "soul" or an evokable atmosphere, a baffling labyrinth, an intricate social organism replete with opportunities

1. (Cambridge, Mass., Harvard University Press, 1965).

and pitfalls, a maze of contradictions, at once imposing and sinister, tawdry and glittering, the city both fascinated and repelled such masters of the nineteenth-century European novel as Balzac and Dickens. Likewise, in *Arabesques,* St. Petersburg appears, to use Fanger's apt phrase, as a "usable microcosm of mankind."[2] This is especially true of "Nevsky Prospekt," the tale which sets the tone of the entire cycle.

The first movement of what was to culminate in a lurid story of self-deception and disenchantment, is what, in contemporary French parlance, was labeled a "physiological sketch," and what we might call today detail-studded urban reportage. Before the melodramatic agon gets off the ground, the reader is invited to review the various strata of St. Petersburg humanity, carefully differentiated from the standpoint of rank, status, appearance, and bearing, that are seen walking, running, riding, or strolling down the capital's main thoroughfare during a typical morning and late afternoon. Gogol's recently discovered powers of minute social observation are very much in evidence here. So is his proclivity, exuberantly displayed in the parallel between Ivan Ivanovich and Ivan Nikoforovich, for depersonalizing man by reducing him to his garments or other externals indicative of his social status:

Here you meet unique whiskers, drooping with extraordinary and amazing elegance below the necktie, velvety, satiny whiskers as black as sable or as coal, but alas! invariably the property of members of the Department of Foreign Affairs. Here you meet marvelous moustaches that no pen, no brush would do justice to . . . moustaches to which their possessors display the most touching devotion, and which are the envy of passers-by . . . Thousands of varieties of hats, dresses and kerchiefs, flimsy and bright colored, for which their owners feel sometimes an adoration that lasts two whole days, that dazzle everyone on Nevsky Prospekt . . . Here you meet

2. Ibid., p. 24.

waists of a slim delicacy beyond dreams of elegance . . . In this blessed period between two and three o'clock in the afternoon when everyone seems to be walking on Nevsky Prospekt, there is a display of all the finest things the genius of man has produced. One displays a smart overcoat with the best beaver on it; the second, a lovely Greek nose; the third, superb whiskers; the fourth, a pair of pretty eyes and a marvelous hat; the fifth, a signet ring on a jaunty forefinger; the sixth, a foot in a bewitching shoe.[3]

The proliferation of dehumanizing synecdoches ("you will meet unique whiskers, marvelous moustaches") and the extravagant catalogs of disparate items precariously held together by the unity of the predicate unveil a typical day on Nevsky Prospekt as a competitive display of status symbols, a strenuous, other-directed parade of pseudoimpressive appearances.

Soon the mock reportage turns out to be a static prelude to a poignant and, at times, flamboyant narrative. Characteristically, the story proper does not begin until "dusk descends upon the houses and the streets." Is it because, as Nietzsche would have it, the night is "more deeply conceived" than the day? (*Tief is die Nacht, tief ist die Nacht, und tiefer als der Tag gedacht.*) The night, or evening, on Nevsky Prospekt is not a moment of truth; it is, rather, a time of fateful delusion, a "mysterious time when the street lamps throw a marvelously alluring light on everything,"[4] and it thus encourages the dreamer's, or the common adventurer's, longing for romance. The two young protagonists—Piskarëv and Pirogov—share this quest. Otherwise, they are as different as they could be. Pirogov simply wants to have some fun. Piskarëv craves an epiphany, an ultimate bliss.

Both fail dismally, though each in his own way. Pirogov's setback is trivial and manageable, largely a matter of bad timing. This smug young man-about-town has overestimated

3. *The Collected Tales and Plays of Nikolai Gogol,* pp. 424, 425.
4. Ibid., p. 426.

the accessibility of a pert blonde whom he chooses to pursue into her flat, only to run into her robust German ironmonger husband who bears the incongruously poetic name of Schiller. The romance is nipped in the bud. The irate husband, assisted ably by his equally vigorous and slightly intoxicated friend, Hoffmann, administers to the interloper a sound thrashing. To an aspiring young officer, being roughed up by a couple of German artisans is unpleasant and humiliating, but scarcely a shattering experience. Pirogov bounces back in no time at all. The next evening he is seen dancing away at "an agreeable party" of his regiment. You can't get a good vulgarian down.

This anecdote serves as a backdrop for the main sub-plot—the lurid story of the high-strung, idealistic artist-dreamer, Piskarëv. His error proves much more costly. A starry-eyed idealist, forever in quest of heavenly Beauty, he is tricked by the deceptive glitter of the Nevsky Avenue lamps into mistaking an attractive streetwalker for a divine apparition, an exalted creature—in a word, for a typical Gogolian beauty, dazzling and inaccessible. Smitten by the "dazzling whiteness of her exquisite brow," he follows in her footsteps, only to find himself in a brothel. He flees in horror, and promptly plunges into a gaudy dream sequence in which his sullied love object appears now and then as a fallen angel in search of redemption. As dreaming becomes his only haven from unbearable actuality, he seeks "to induce the process by means of opium," not unlike the protagonist of DeQuincey's influential *Confessions of an English Opium Eater*. The parallel is deftly drawn in *The Evolution of Russian Naturalism* by Viktor Vinogradov, who also detects echoes from French romantic pulp fiction in "Nevsky Prospekt."[5] According to Vinogradov, the motifs of a beautiful prostitute and of an idealistic artist crushed by metropolitan squalor are reminis-

5. *Evoljucija russkogo naturalizma: Gogol i Dostoevskij* (Leningrad, Academia, 1929), pp. 89-126.

cent of the now justly forgotten exponents of so-called *littéra-
ture frénetique*, Jules Janin and Eugène Sue. Some passages in
"Nevsky Prospekt" have indeed a high-pitched, frenetic quality: "by some horrible whim of a fiendish spirit eager to
destroy . . . she had been hurled with laughter into this abyss."
"The opium inflamed his thoughts more than ever, and if there
ever was a man passionately, terribly and ruinously in love, to
the utmost pitch of madness, he was that luckless man."[6] In a
pathetic attempt to make the dream come true, Piskarëv
confronts reality once more. He returns to the brothel and
urges the fallen beauty to make an honest woman of herself by
marrying the struggling but loving artist. His offer is met by
mockery and scorn. In despair, the "luckless victim of a fatal
passion" cuts his throat with a razor. The contrast between the
tragic end of Piskarëv and the happy ending of the Pirogov
story speaks for itself. The smug, the vulgar, the callous are
here to stay. The pure of heart are crushed by the unbearable
discrepancy between their dreams and "revolting" actuality.

Vsevolod Setchkarev has called attention to the parallels
between Piskarë and Anselmus in Hoffmann's tale "The
Golden Pot."[7] The point is well taken. Both the contrast
between the dreamer and the Philistine and the motif of the
dream as the only escape from grubby reality are essential
Hoffmannesque themes. Other Russian scholars, especially the
Soviet Gogolians,[8] have made much of the undeniable differences between the two plots. It has been argued that because it
dramatized the futility of the dream and the impossibility of
escape, "Nevsky Prospekt" was a polemic against Hoffmann,
and more broadly, a turning point in Gogol's career, an abandonment of Romanticism and a significant step toward Real-

6. *Collected Tales and Plays,* pp. 432, 439.
7. *Gogol: His Life and Works,* p. 132.
8. See especially Grigorij Gukovskij, *Realizm Gogolja* (Moscow and Leningrad, 1959). This, one of the best Soviet studies of Gogol, is marred by the
simplistic official notion of Gogol's literary career as an inexorable evolution
from Romanticism to Realism.

ism. (The latter assertion is predicated, of course, upon a debatable proposition which will be considered below, that the late Gogol was a Realist.)

This notion, it seems to me, is at best a half-truth. It is fair to say that "Nevsky Prospekt" is more pessimistic, or simply more gloomy, than Hoffmann's tale. In the latter, Anselmus manages to leave behind the humdrum world of tawdry witches and secret counselors for the never-never land of Atlantis. In "Nevsky Prospekt," the "reality principle" obtrudes itself upon the dream and shatters it to pieces. Yet, to speak of Gogol's turning his back on Romanticism and moving toward Realism seems a bit misleading. For one thing, in Gogol, as in Hoffmann, the dream, however fragile, remains the only thing of value: "Oh how revolting was reality. What was it, compared to the dream!"[9] For another, the view of reality which underlies "Nevsky Prospekt" is scarcely that of a Realist. For if "The Golden Pot" culminates in a Romantic daydream, "Nevsky Prospekt" builds toward a Romantic, or perhaps a grotesque, nightmare. The view of life as wanton, arbitrary, and unpredictable is explicitly articulated by the narrator toward the end of the story. "How strangely, how unaccountably Fate plays with us! . . . Everything goes contrary to what we expect."[10]

Characteristically, the treacherous quality of Fate is epitomized by "Nevsky Prospekt." We are back where we started, but now that the pitfalls of metropolitan glamor have been so blatantly dramatized, the tone has shifted appreciably. It has become frankly ominous, nocturnal, distraught. The narrator's moral panic explodes in a series of frenzied warnings, a breathless crescendo of hyperboles.

Oh, do not trust Nevsky Prospekt. Everything's a cheat. Everything's a dream. Everything's not what it seems! Keep your distance. For God's sake, keep your distance on the

9. *Collected Tales and Plays,* p. 436.
10. Ibid., p. 451.

streets there! It is a happy escape if you get off with nothing
worse than some of its stinking oil on your foppish clothes.
But even apart from the street lamps, everything breathes
deception. It deceives at all hours, Nevsky Prospekt does,
but most of all when night falls in masses of shadow on
it . . . when all the town is transformed into noise and glitter,
when myriads of carriages roll off the bridges, [11] postilions
shout and jump up on their horses, and when *the devil
himself lights the street lamps to show everything in false
colors* (my italics).[12]

"The devil himself . . ." We have traveled a long way from
the deceptively mundane opening, the pseudosober recital of
social *realia*. Are we back in the demon-ridden universe of the
Kunstmärchen? Yes and no. The folkloristic *Evenings* are
gone forever, along with the good fairies and the silver glow of
the Ukrainian night. The marvelous is now but an optical
illusion, or worse still, the devil's snare. Yet in this contemporary urban setting, amid the "realistic" bric-a-brac, our old
acquaintance, the devil, is still very much with us; in fact, it is
he who is still in control. The subtitle of Hoffmann's "The
Golden Pot" may well apply to "Nevsky Prospekt." Gogol's
story, too, could be called "ein Märchen aus unserer Zeit," an
ominously cautionary tale for the befuddled denizens of a
seedily metropolitan universe where it is too late for miracles,
but, unfortunately, not too late for black magic.

The finale of "Nevsky Prospekt" reenacts the underlying
theme of "Viy," and of "The Old-Fashioned Landowners":
There is no place to hide. The Evil One is as resourceful as he
is ubiquitous. The trouble with him, as Gogol was to tell
himself and his contemporaries time and again, is that he gets
at man not only through taking advantage of his lowly

11. I permitted myself to tamper at this point with the Garnett-Kent translation, since once again it made the text more plausible than it was designed to be.
In the original, the carriages roll *off* the bridges, rather than *over* the bridges, an
image which clearly suggests tumbling into an abyss.

12. *Collected Tales and Plays*, p. 452

impulses, his base passions, but also, and more insidiously, by distorting, twisting, and capitalizing upon his loftier aspirations such as the yearning for beauty which brought down the tragically deluded dreamer, Piskarëv.[13]

The theme of the city as half-inferno, half-madhouse, was to be heard again. The absurdity of life, which in *Mirgorod* was mainly a matter of grotesque smallness of local pursuits, becomes in *Arabesques* a hopeless muddle, a cumulative effect of an orgy of "senseless rumors" circulating within the teeming yet thoroughly atomized human labyrinth of the metropolis. "It seemed to him [Piskarëv] as though some demon had crumbled the whole world into bits and mixed all these bits indiscriminately together."[14] This phrase, drawn from the artist's dream, could serve as a motto for "The Nose," a story published a year later in the short-lived journal, *The Contemporary* (Sovremennik), edited by Alexander Pushkin.

The plot of this burlesque extravaganza is as simple as it is bizarre. Kovalëv, a smug and somewhat phony young man, a "collegiate assessor" who, stretching the point a bit, liked to refer to himself as a "major," wakes up one morning only to discover, to his considerable embarrassment, that there is "only a flat patch on his face where the nose used to be." (This "unusually strange event" is first presented in an oblique fashion. As the story opens, Kovalëv's nose pops up in a loaf of bread on the breakfast table of the "major's" barber. Thus we meet Kovalëv's nose before we are introduced to the man

13. This notion lies at the core of what is perhaps the least successful tale in *Arabesques,* "The Portrait." While the story proper centers around the malignant influence exerted upon a struggling painter by a portrait of an evil moneylender, we learn from the extended flashback that the fatal artifact was a study for a religious pageant intended to celebrate the triumph of light over darkness. The devout painter's admirable design was ironically foiled. The graphically portrayed fiend upstaged the more pallid "positive" figures. The ill-fated fragment acquired a life of its own, becoming an agent of moral corruption throughout the world, and thus perpetuating the malevolent spell of the dead villain. We might file this lurid plot for further reference: the story of evil stealing the potentially edifying show might well be the paradigm of Gogol's own plight.

14. *Collected Tales and Plays,* p. 433.

himself.) The bereaved young man promptly swings into action. Characteristically, he is taken aback rather than stunned. The disappearance of so prominent an organ strikes this self-important and self-engrossed young man primarily as a blow to his ego, as an embarrassing social handicap for a man of his status and marital aspirations. "An old woman," he explains patiently to the fugitive nose, "selling peeled oranges on the Voskresenskij Bridge may sit there without a nose, but having prospects of obtaining an important position."[15] He tries to advertise his loss in a paper, lodges a complaint with the police, and writes an irate letter to a lady acquaintance whom he accuses of using black magic in order to trick him into marrying her daughter, but all this to no avail. To add insult to injury, Kovalëv's nose, which has acquired an independent existence, cold-bloodedly snubs its owner and manages to outrank him. At some point the fugitive is seen strutting up and down Nevsky Avenue in the uniform of a "Councilor of State." The scene in which Kovalëv confronts his recalcitrant nose plays up to the hilt the typically grotesque reversal of the normal relationship between the part and the whole, with the former both impersonating and overshadowing the latter: "It seems strange to me, sir," remonstrates Kovalëv. "You ought to know your proper place. And all at once I find you in a church, of all places . . . The nose looked at the major and its eyebrows [!] slightly quivered. 'You are mistaken, sir. I am an independent individual.' "[16] Finally, after all the futile demarches and comically routine complaints fizzle out, the nose reappears on its owner's face as suddenly as it vanished thus restoring to the bewildered young-man-on-the-make his battered self-esteem. The meaningless social round can now be resumed.

Critics who insist on making some psychological sense out of "The Nose" inevitably wind up invoking castration anxiety. This interpretation may well have some validity; the story does seem to have phallic undertones. So do the frequent, indeed

15. Ibid., p. 480.
16. Ibid., p. 481.

obsessive, references to noses in Gogol's other works. In "Nevsky Prospekt," the drunken German ironmonger urges his friend, Hoffmann, to cut Pirogov's nose. In "The Tale of How Ivan Ivanovich Quarreled with Ivan Nikoforovich," there is much talk about how women take men by their noses, in connection with the relationship between Ivan Nikoforovich and his domineering aunt. The motif of separate noses living on the moon appears in the ravings of the insane clerk in "A Madman's Diary." Gogol's nose-mindedness often spilled into his personal correspondence. In a letter to his former pupil, in which he eulogized the beauty and fragrance of Rome, Gogol expressed a wish to be transformed into one big nose.[17] Much of this may be of legitimate interest to a Freudian, but I have a distinct feeling that castration anxiety is not the central theme of "The Nose." Seen against the background of Gogol's emerging view of man, "The Nose" seems rather, as Herbert Bowman put it, a "grotesque laugh at the absurd importance of appearances in a world of appearances."[18] In the universe of "The Nose," status looms larger than sex. Whether this hierarchy is a commentary on the social milieu depicted or debunked by Gogol, or on his psychic make-up may well be a moot point, but the fact itself is hardly debatable. Thus, Kovalëv's seems an acute case of status anxiety rather than castration anxiety, though perhaps both are involved. Preposterously enough, to Kovalëv the nose is not so much an important part of his body which can be symbolically substituted for a male organ as another status symbol to be shown off on the Nevsky Prospekt vanity fair. True, Kovalëv thinks of his nose as an important attribute of his manhood, and a matter germane to his marital aspirations. However, to this single-minded careerist, a right kind of marriage is in itself primarily a stepping-stone toward an "important position." To use modern terminology, on Nevsky Prospekt status is highly libidinized; in fact, it seems to be the chief focus of a libidinal involvement. In this preposterously other-directed context, where all that matters is "a good front," a nose is, in a sense, a crucial part of such a front, as the most conspicuous, exposed and protruding part of one's anatomy, as the most public or "official" facet of one's personality. This somewhat inane point is made explicitly in a mock panegyric to the nose which appeared in a Russian journal in 1831, two years before Gogol's story was written: "A nose is a sign of honor on one's face . . . A nose is an embodied honor affixed to a man."[19]

The false hierarchy of values which prevails in the metropolitan marketplace is only one of the broader implications of the plot. Another larger reality which seems to be dramatized here in an extravagantly farcical fashion is the pathetic brittleness of the average human personality. The detachability of Kovalëv's nose may be, among other things, a grotesquely metaphorical vehicle for the view of ordinary man as a *sui generis* animated automaton,"[20] an aggregate of parts rather than an organic whole, a homunculus lacking, to paraphrase W. B. Yeats, a center that holds.

While recognizing the relevance of what some scholars have dubbed Gogol's "moral anthropology,"[21] we ought to be wary of taking an unduly portentous view of "The Nose." Whatever the story's symbolic implications, "The Nose" is primarily a nonsense narrative, a piece of burlesque whimsy, and not least, an irreverent play with contemporary literary modes and conventions. In his valuable book on Gogol and the Russian "natural" school,[22] Vinogradov calls attention to the proliferation, in the Russian literary journals of the 1820s and 1830s, of fantastic adventure stories, often placed in gaudily exotic settings, where the motif of a cut-off or vanishing nose often

19. Quoted in Vinogradov, p. 15.
20. Pëtr Bicilli, "Problema cheloveka u Gogolja," *Godishnik na Sofijskii Universitet* (Yearbook of the University of Sofia) (1948).
21. Ibid., see also Cizevsky, "The Unknown Gogol," *Slavonic and East European Review, 30* (June 1952), 476-93; "Neizvestnyj Gogol," *Novyj Zhurnal, 22* (1951), 126-58.
22. *Evolucija russkogo naturalizma,* pp. 27-34.

appeared. This bizarre literary fad, which seems to have had its chief literary source in Laurence Sterne's *Tristram Shandy,* may well have been aggravated by the presence, in the Russian language, of nose-oriented colloquialisms, one of which gave rise to a pun said to have appeared in an 1836 Russian miscellany: "However unpleasant it is to be with the nose (s nosom), it is somewhat more bearable (snosno) than to be entirely without one."[23] As all literal translations of puns, this one makes no sense at all unless we consider that, in Russian, "to remain with the nose" means, roughly, to be left holding the bag, or to be in trouble, and that the adjective "snosno," which is Russian for "bearable," is derived from "nos." Incidentally, Pushkin is known to have perpetrated, in a risqué epigram addressed to a fellow socialite, the following bon mot: "And thus you surely will be 'with the nose' when you find yourself without one." It is clear from the context that Pushkin was referring not to the rather implausible contingency of losing one's nose, but to its shrinkage due to venereal disease. It occurs to me, though, that the plot of "The Nose" could be described as a literal enactment or "realization" of Pushkin's witticism.

The merit of Vinogradov's study lies not only in placing "The Nose" within a discernible literary tradition, but also, and perhaps more importantly, in bringing out the element of literary parody in Gogol's tale, which disengages the fantastic motif of a cut-off nose from its exotic paraphernalia, only to place it within a familiar, easily recognizable framework. The device of using the St. Petersburg barber's breakfast table— on which, we will recall, Kovalëv's nose makes its first appearance—as a launching pad for exercise in fantastic nosology, is a characteristically deglamorizing device, somewhat akin to providing the two-fisted German artisans in "Nevsky Prospekt" with the names Schiller and Hoffmann.

The tension between the prosiness of the setting and the wildly romantic or exotic provenience of the central motif is

23. Ibid., p. 24.

but one facet of the contrapuntal tension which underlies the
story, the contrast between the "realistic" mode of presentation
and the utterly incredible central event. The proliferation of
homely trivia and the matter-of-fact narrative tone tend to
domesticate the absurd, to absorb it almost imperceptibly into
the texture of everyday life. At the same time, the narrator's
relative "lack of astonishment"—to use Camus's apt description of a Kafka narrative—in the face of the strangest incidents, subtly undermines one's trust in the reality of the sensible, the dependability of predictability of the world around us.
Characteristically, the narrator is trying to have it both ways.
On the one hand, the strangeness of Kovalëv's predicament is
strenuously insisted upon. The opening sentence of the story
announces an "extraordinarily strange incident that took place
in Petersburg on the 25th of March," and the finale picks up
the word and the theme: "So this is the strange event that
occurred in the northern Capital of our spacious empire!"[24]
Ultimately, the occurrence is found possible, if not altogether
plausible. As the curtain goes down, the narrator mutters
sheepishly:

> Only now, on thinking it all over, we perceive that there is
> a great deal that is improbable in it. Apart from the fact that
> it is certainly strange for a nose supernaturally to leave its
> place and to appear in various places in the guise of a Civil
> Councilor—how was it that Kovalyov did not grasp that he
> could not advertise about his nose in a newspaper
> office? . . . And yet when you think it over, there really is
> something in it. Despite what anyone may say, such things
> do happen in the world—seldom, to be sure, but they do
> happen![25]

While the parodistic flavor of the above is apparent, it is less
easy to decide who and what has been mocked here. Is the joke

24. *Collected Tales and Plays,* pp. 474, 497.
25. Ibid., p. 497.

on the dull Philistine, the congenitally befogged St. Petersburg
dweller who cannot distinguish between the plausible and the
implausible, between a wild rumor and an ascertainable fact?
Or is this piece of inanity a Philistine travesty of Gogol's own
existential befuddlement, of his grotesque view of reality as a
madhouse, a hopeless muddle? Be that as it may, Gogol's, or
his narrator's, chatter implicitly calls into question the underlying assumption of realistic fiction that social reality "makes
sense," that human behavior yields a discernible pattern, a
stable structure of causation. This intent is made explicit in
"philosophical" asides. "All kinds of nonsense happen in this
world. *Sometimes there is no plausibility whatsoever*"[26] (my
italics). I am reminded of a discursive story by Franz Kafka, a
writer whose world view bears some similarity to Gogol's, "The
Investigations of a Dog." Kafka's introspective, scholarly
researcher, who happens to be a dog, reports his findings thus:
"I investigated the most senseless rumors, following them as far
as they could take me, and the most senseless seemed, to me, in
this senseless world, more probable than the sensible."[27]

"This senseless world"—the words are Kafka's but they
could easily be Gogol's. For here lies a clue to that astonishing
"lack of astonishment" which Gogol's narrator exhibits. The
tendency to treat the intrusion of the irrational as "part of the
game" is predicated upon the view that the game itself lacks
any definable rules, that every-day living is absurdly chaotic—a
web of incongruities, a series of interlocking anxiety dreams.

I am using the word "dream" advisedly. Neither the pseudo-
realistic solidity of pedestrian detail—the barber's wife was a
"rather portly lady who was very fond of drinking
coffee"—nor the pat disclaimers as Kovalëv tests the reality of

26. *N. V. Gogol, Sochinenija* (Moscow, Izdatelstvo khudozhestvennoj literatury, 1952), *3*, 87. This time the translation is my own. "Sometimes there is not
the slightest semblance of truth to it" is not a proper English equivalent, I
believe, of the narrator's inane mumbling "inogda vovse net nikakogo
pravdopodobija."

27. *Selected Short Stories of Franz Kafka* (New York, Modern Library,
1952), p. 224.

the event by pinching himself—"No, apparently he was not asleep"—should blind us to the essentially dream-like logic of the plot. For it is only in a dream that compactness and vividness of imagery can be visualized as existing side by side with, or perhaps be achieved at the cost of, logical and ontological incompatibility. It is precisely in a dream that a thing can be both a part and a whole. And it is only in a dream situation that such an incongruity can be viewed with so slight a sense of shock.

Interestingly enough, an earlier (1831) variant of "The Nose" used "dream" as the subtitle and contained the following sentence: "Incidentally, all that was described here appeared to the 'major' in his dream." Another variant explicitly toyed with this possibility. "This event was so fantastically improbable that one could call it a dream vision, if it had not actually happened."[28] In the final version, the dream escape clause is discarded. As soon as Kovalëv assures himself that he is not asleep, the absurdity of the plot is totally unmitigated, or rather, unmotivated; it is not susceptible to any realistic or rational explanation. In fact, the story in its final form discourages nonrealistic explanations as well. Kovalëv's preposterous readiness to blame his woes on the evil schemer, Mrs. Podtochina, the mother of a marriageable girl, may be said to epitomize the futility of all attempts to explain the inexplicable, to find a tangible clue to the absurd things that sometimes happen in this "senseless world."

Though the use of the dream as a framework for the story and motivation for its strange proceedings has been rejected, dream or sleep figures rather prominently both as a dimension within which the events might have been occurring, and as a direct antecedent of the agon: "Collegiate Assessor Kovalëv awoke early that morning . . . He wanted to look at a pimple which had appeared on his nose the previous evening, but to his great astonishment, there was a completely flat space where his nose should have been."[29] One is tempted to speak here of a false awakening, of an uneasy anxiety dream extended into waking hours.

Aleksej Remizov, perhaps the most Gogolian among twentieth-century Russian writers, recalls in his fascinating book, *The Fire of Things*,[30] the multi-layered nightmare of the painter, Chartkov, in that gloomily Romantic Petersburg tale, "The Portrait."[31] Chartkov is haunted by the terrible eyes staring at him from a newly acquired portrait of a demonic moneylender. Time and again, in the course of a harrowing night, the figure of the evil old man seems to emerge from the canvas. The hapless artist keeps waking up "only to find himself in the midst of another nightmare."[32] When he finally emerges, exhausted and bleary-eyed, into the bleak and foggy Petersburg day, he is confronted with a reality which differs but little from his uneasy dreams. Remizov shrewdly comments: "The world is a witches' sabbath: whether asleep or awake, man is forever under an evil spell, and there is nothing to wake up into" (p. 76).

If, in "The Nose," Gogol characteristically foregoes the opportunity to legitimize his plot and offers, as the only explanation, the fundamentally grotesque notion that the world is a madhouse, in "A Madman's Diary" the increasingly strange proceedings (a lively exchange of letters between two pups, for example) are allegedly motivated by the gradual disintegration of the story's central consciousness, the mounting insanity of the diarist, Poprishchin. This time, madness is not an inherent quality of the fictional universe, but part of the view point; not a matter of absurdity, but rather of individual schizophrenia. In fact, "A Madman's Diary" is one of the first pathological sketches in Russian literature, and more broadly, one of the early portrayals of schizophrenia in European fiction.

29. *Collected Tales and Plays,* p. 477.
30. *Ogon' veshchej, sny i predson'e* (Paris, Opleshnik, 1954).
31. See above, n. 13.
32. *Collected Tales and Plays,* pp. 520-22.

This is not to say that Gogol was alone among his contemporaries in addressing himself to the subject. (Both Nikolaj Polevoj and Vladimir Odoevskij shared his interest in madness.[33]) The Romantic age was becoming increasingly fascinated by the phenomenon of madness. In their recoil from "smug" rationalism, from "Philistine" sobriety, the Romantics tended at times to credit the madman with a finer sensitivity and a deeper insight than was vouchsafed to ordinary men, to treat *Wahnsinn* as a gateway to revelation.

Once again, E. T. A. Hoffmann seems to have authored the probable design for the story. The initial title of what was to become "A Madman's Diary"—"The Diary of a Mad Musician"—seems to point to Hoffmann's novel about a gifted but mad *Kapellmeister,* Kreisler.[34] Yet, as is so often the case, the source of the theme is less interesting and less significant than its transformation, which is, once again, a matter of giving it a prosaic twist. Poprishchin, whose very name is lowly and ludicrous,—it makes one think of "pimple" (*pryshch*)—is not a mad artist, but a mad petty clerk. There is nothing holy about Poprishchin's *Wahnsinn,* the mental deterioration of an unprepossessing, pathetic, petty official, incongruously infatuated with the boss's daughter, a little cog in the bureaucratic machine, a mere cipher for whom madness, more specifically schizophrenic delusion of grandeur, becomes an escape from crushing anonymity.

The first sentence of "A Madman's Diary" bears considerable similarity to the opening phrase of "The Nose:" "Today an extraordinary event occurred."[35] The event which the diarist

33. On Odoevskij's concern with insanity, see Pavel Sakulin's scholarly study *Iz istorii russkogo idealizma: knjaz' V. F. Odoevskij—Myslitel'—Pisatel'* (Moscow, M. M. and S. Sabashnikov, 1913); and A. Rammelmeyer's introduction to a recent reprint of Odoevskij's major work, *Russkie Nochi* (Munich, Wilhelm Fink Verlag, 1967).

34. It has been noted, too, that the talking and writing pups in "A Madman's Diary" may be a throwback to that remarkably articulate and sophisticated cat, the protagonist of Hoffmann's short novel, *Kater Murr.*

35. *Collected Tales and Plays,* p. 453.

finds startling, even though "of late [he has] begun seeing and hearing things such as no one has ever seen or heard before," turns out to be a spirited conversation between two pups, Madgie and Fido, overheard by the diarist. Since, in the early phase of the story, Poprishchin's view of reality is not yet entirely distorted, he is, at first, taken aback: "I was very much surprised to hear her (Madgie) speaking like a human being."[36] Yet, after a while, his astonishment subsides.

After a while, when I thought it all over, I was no longer surprised. A number of similar instances have, indeed, occurred. They say that in England, a fish popped up and uttered two words in such a strange language that the learned men have been for three years trying to interpret them and have not succeeded yet . . . But I must admit I was much more surprised when Madgie said: "I did write to you, Fido. Polkan probably didn't bring you the letter." Damn it all, I never in all my life heard of a dog being able to write. No one but a nobleman by birth can write correctly.[37]

Though in the context, the quality of this comment is scarcely a tribute to the diarist's sanity, it is not significantly different, in all fairness, from the comic inanity of the concluding section of "The Nose." In the opinion of the narrator of that story, the most implausible thing about it was the bad judgment shown by Kovalëv in advertising the loss of his nose in the paper.

Poprishchin's eavesdropping on the suave society pups is not merely the first in the series of "extraordinary events" which constitute the plot of "The Madman's Diary." It is also the beginning of the end of his mute and hopeless courtship of Sophie, the inaccessible daughter of Poprishchin's ambitious boss. Since Madgie is Sophie's pet, the correspondence previously alluded to becomes of abiding interest to the hapless

36. Ibid., p. 455.
37. Ibid.

clerk because of the light it is likely to shed on his standing vis-a-vis the devastatingly remote love object. Five weeks after the initial encounter with Madgie and Fido, Poprishchin takes bold strategic action by plunging into a garbage can from which he fishes out Madgie's letters. As he deciphers painstakingly her "doggy handwriting," the hopelessness of his predicament becomes inexorably clear.

It is an interesting commentary on the nature of Gogol's literary strategy that this bit of Hoffmannesque whimsy should serve as a pivotal point in the story, that all the seemingly relevant factors of the situation—the bureaucratic ambitions of Sophie's self-important director-father, her frantic "infatuation" with the dashing young officer, and her amused disdain for her father's preposterous-looking menial, Poprishchin—should have been reported by a dog! The status of this evidence is admittedly precarious. But it would be a simplification to suggest that the diarist's mounting derangement fully accounts for this new intrusion of the highly improbable. To first overhear a conversation between two pups, and then to imagine in detail their correspondence, would seem to require a greater potential for sustained hallucination than Poprishchin can be safely credited with at this early stage of the narrative. I have a feeling that his incipient madness is not so much the actual source of the fantastic nature of the proceedings as it is a handy excuse for it.

Be that as it may, there is some logic in the fact that this painful discovery should have served as the turning point in the narrative. It is bad enough to be faced with conclusive proof that to one's love object one is merely a ridiculous nobody. It is doubly humiliating to be found out and condescended to by a mere pup. Poprishchin's inward reaction is as vehement as it is impotent. The moment of truth stirs a helpless rage at the invariably successful generals and court chamberlains who grab "everything that's best in the world," and an acute resentment of the utter nothingness to which a clerk's lowly status consigns him. In a deranged mind, whose grip on reality

weakens daily, this rebellion against one's predicament, one's
degrading identity, leads to the questioning of its reality. Thus
the indignant query: "Why should it have happened to me?
Why am I a mere titular councilor?" promptly shades off into
an ontological doubt: "Perhaps I am not a titular councilor at
all?"[38] Identity becomes fluid, negotiable.

The next phase is a sudden preoccupation with international
politics, more specifically Spain, clearly a form of acute mental
escapism:

> Strange things are going on in Spain. . . . They write that
> the throne is vacant . . . It seems to me that it is extremely
> peculiar. A kingdom cannot exist without a king . . . I
> cannot get the affairs of Spain out of my head. These events
> have so overwhelmed and shaken me that I haven't been
> able to do anything all day.[39]

The humiliated petty clerk who craves esteem uses his schizophrenia to escape the unbearable truth. From this, it is but a
step to a delusion of grandeur, a new identity as glamorous and
exotic as the previous one was shabby and commonplace:
"There is a king of Spain. He has been discovered. I am that
king!" Quite appropriately the diarist announces his discovery
in an entry in which his galloping deterioration is marked by a
dislocation of a sense of time (A.D. 2000, April 43) and
incoherent raving complete with unhinged sexual fantasies. "I
believe it all arose from believing that the brain is in the head.
It's not so at all; it comes with the wind from the direction of
the Caspian Sea."[40] The antifemale demonology of this entry,
spurred in part by the stinging rebuff, seems almost a pathological travesty of Gogol's own fear of sexuality: "Woman is in
love with the devil . . . Scientific men write nonsense saying
that she is this or that. She cares for nothing but the devil, she

38. Ibid., p. 465.
39. Ibid., p. 466.
40. Ibid.

does, and she will marry him, she will marry him."[41] Otherwise, incoherence and irrelevance reign supreme:

> All this is ambition, and the ambition is because of a little
> pimple under the tongue, and in it, a little worm, no bigger
> than a pinhead. And it's all the doing of a barber who lives
> on Gorokhovaya Street. I don't remember his name, but I
> know for a fact that, in collusion with a midwife, he is trying
> to spread Mohammedanism all over the world, and that is
> why, I am told, the majority of people in France profess the
> Mohammedan faith.[42]

From then on, events roll inexorably toward institutional-
ization. Yet, characteristically, the portents are ignored or
misinterpreted. Gogol manages to wrench effective if cruel
comedy out of Poprishchin's galloping mental deterioration by
manipulating the incongruity between the actual event and the
diarist's consistently mistaken perception of it. The reader
cannot help but laugh uneasily at the various strategies
whereby the diarist's closed delusional system explains reality
away. When Poprishchin announces to his servant or to his
co-workers his newly found identity, that of the King of Spain
in exile, he interprets their stunned silence as a sign of awe and
reverence. When a few roughnecks come to his flat to cart him
away to an insane asylum, he construes this unannounced visit
as an entreaty from his loyal subjects to reoccupy the throne
which he was forced to relinquish. He is somewhat taken aback
by their rudeness—one of the "grandees" hits him with a
stick—but he is quite prepared to blame it on the tenacity of
the Spanish traditions.

In the last entry, dismal reality breaks through. The self-
styled King of Spain is forced to face the humiliating and
brutalizing squalor of an insane asylum. What ensues is a
strident cry of sheer anguish, of unbearable self-pity, embodied

41. Ibid., p. 468.
42. Ibid.

in a lyrical rhetoric which anticipates, in part, the soaring finale of Part One of "Dead Souls."[43] This is how it sounds in the best available English translation, that of Vladimir Nabokov:

No, I have not the strength to bear this any longer. God, the things they are doing to me! They pour cold water upon my head! They do not heed me, nor see me, nor listen to me. What have I done to them? What do they want of poor me? . . . My strength is gone, I cannot endure all this torture. My head is aflame and everything spins before my eyes. Save me, someone! Take me away! Give me three steeds, steeds as fast as the whirling wind! Seat yourself, driver; ring out, little harness bell; wing your way up, steeds, and rush me out of this world. On and on, so that nothing is seen of it—nothing. Yonder the sky wheels its clouds; a tiny star glitters afar; a forest sweeps by with its dark trees and the moon comes in its wake; a silver-grey mist swims below; a musical string twangs in the mist; there is sea on one hand; there is Italy on the other; and now Russian peasant huts can be discerned. Is that my home, looking blue in the distance? Is that my poor mother sitting there at her window? Mother dear, save your poor son! Shed a tear upon his aching head. See how they torture him. Clasp the poor orphan to your heart! There is no place for him in the whole wide world! He is a hunted creature. Mother dear, take pity on your sick little child . . . And, by the way, gentlemen, do you know that the Bey of Algiers has a round lump growing right under his nose?[44]

Once again the spell is abruptly, wantonly broken, and the reader left in bewilderment. The shift is a double one. A strident crescendo of pity—or should one say self-pity?—peters out into burlesque irrelevance. At the same time, the recognition of reality yields once more to schizophrenic incoherence. The

43. See below, Chapter 7. pp. 128-29.
44. *Nikolai Gogol,* facing p. 1.

finale is truly Gogolian and more thoroughly grotesque than the ending of "Two Ivans."

May I revert to one of the significant generalizations of Kayser I cited at the outset? In discussing the nightmare art of Hieronymus Bosch, he pointed to the mounting emotional disorientation due to the fact that the "viewer is in no way instructed how to react to or interpret the picture."[45] In dealing with "A Madman's Diary," the Kayser formula may require a slight emendation. If, in confronting Bosch's triptych, the viewer fails to receive any meaningful emotive instructions, in Gogol's pathological burlesque we get conflicting clues. Toward the end of the story, the reader is jolted by two successive shifts of emotional perspective. For pages, he is treated to a thoroughly unemotional, or if one will, inhuman exploitation of insanity as a source of morbidly comic effects by means of a deft impersonation of mental disarray. Finally, the recognition of the unbearable human cost of this brilliantly contrived show breaks through, so as to allow, indeed impel, the reader at long last to register the hitherto frustrated human response—to pity, to relate, to vibrate in unison. Yet Gogol would not allow his audience to indulge its humanity for too long. As the crescendo of anguish reaches an almost hysterical pitch, the last-minute empathy is subverted by a sudden lapse into bathos. It is as if Gogol's art could not sustain empathy or involvement, as if these emotions became literally unbearable to him as they escalated into hysteria, and thus had to be resolved back into verbal clowning, to be undercut by the burlesque. Whatever the underlying mechanism, the emotional perspective of the story is indeed grotesque in the Kayserian sense. The long-frustrated emotional gratification is nipped in the bud. The rug is pulled from under us. "We have stepped into a void."

45. See above, p. 3.

6

The Importance of Being a Comedy Writer

In *Mirgorod* and *Arabesques,* Gogol found an apt vehicle for his brilliantly idiosyncratic vision, a type of short narrative both akin to the Kunstmärchen and significantly different from it, a mode in which the demonic is domesticated, evil internalized, the irrational absorbed into everyday reality, where there is still room for the unfrocked devil but none for good fairies.

As he became more and more adept at narrative fiction, however, Gogol yearned increasingly for another medium. In Nezhin, and for a while in St. Petersburg, Gogol's affinity for the theater, inherited in part from his amateur playwright father, was a matter of aspiring to an acting career. Now it becomes an ardent desire to make an impact as a comedy writer. Many years later, he was to construe his turn toward comedy as an important landmark in his career, a moment at which the carefree gaiety and pointless exuberance of his earlier tales began to give way to a purposeful satire that would harness his comic gifts so as to produce a salutary, chastening effect upon society.[1] It is entirely possible that in this retrospective confession, Gogol was overstating the didactic thrust of his new project. Yet, it is a fact amply attested to by correspon-

1. In "An Author's Confession," Gogol avers that his "early works moved some to carefree laughter and made others wonder how an intelligent man could ever dream up such trifles." "Pushkin persuaded me to take a more serious view of the matter," he writes later. "I realized that in my works I had laughed pointlessly . . . If one has to laugh, one may as well . . . laugh at what is really worthy of general derision" (*Polnoe Sobranie Sochinenij* [Complete Works], *8* [1952], 439, 440).

dence and eyewitness testimony that his involvement with comedy coincided with an increasing emphasis on the writer's social responsibility, indeed with a growing sense of mission. As a schoolboy, Gogol had spoken vaguely about serving the State and doing good. Now, for the first time, he explicitly associates the idea of service with his literary activity.

As early as the summer of 1832, during his first trip to Moscow, Gogol imparted to the writer and publicist Sergej Aksakov, who was to become one of his most loyal friends, some "original" notions about Russian comedy.[2] Though Aksakov does not specify what these notions were, the context seems to suggest a view of drama which Gogol was to spell out in a freewheeling essay, "St. Petersburg Notes: 1836," where he called the theater "a pulpit from which a large crowd is taught a live lesson."[3] In February 1833, he confided in another newly acquired Moscow friend, the historian and editor Mikhail Pogodin, that he was "hung up on a comedy."[4] In the same letter he averred: "I don't know why I so crave contemporary fame." He was speaking, I assume, of a direct, unmediated impact upon an audience that only the theater could afford.

The comedy on which Gogol was "hung up" in 1833 was "The Order of Vladimir of The Third Class." This play, which was to contain, in Gogol's own words, much "malice, laughter and salt,"[5] was never completed. From the extant fragments and from Gogol's references to his design, one can infer that he intended a hard-hitting satire built around a shabby bureaucrat's obsessive craving for a promotion and an "order." As the result of a scheme hatched by an equally unsavory opponent, the chief protagonist's dream of glory fails to materialize: the frustrated careerist goes mad.

Let me note in passing that the two themes of the aborted

2. *Istorija moego znakomstva s Gogolem*, p. 12.
3. *Polnoe Sobranie Sochinenij, 8,* 186.
4. Ibid., *10 (1952), 202.*
5. Ibid.

comedy—those of a bureaucrat's overweening ambition and of a flight into insanity—found their way into "A Madman's Diary." However, in that story the motifs diverge. It is the diarist's boss who, as we glean from the pups' informative correspondence, worries about the "ribbon" which he eventually receives. Madness hits here not the aspiring dignitary, whose status needs are duly met, but the anonymous, lowly clerk.

Somewhere along the way Gogol abandoned "The Order of Vladimir of the Third Class." Presumably he chose to avoid trouble with the censor, likely to take umbrage at the pointed references to the mores of Russian officialdom. Much of the "truth and malice"—without which, he argued in his letters, no worthwhile comedy was possible—later was to spill into his comic masterpiece, *The Inspector General.*

In the meantime, the budding playwright switched to what may have seemed a safer tack, a comedy of indecision bordering upon paralysis which he called "Marriage: A Quite Incredible Incident."[6] This lively farce which abounds in echoes from French Classical comedy, especially Molière's, features a reluctant suitor somewhat reminiscent of Ivan Fëdorovich Shponka. Mercilessly manipulated by his busybody friend, but panic-stricken at the thought of women and marriage, Podkolesin resolves his inner conflict by a burlesque last-minute leap from the window on the eve of betrothal. The reception of "Marriage" was cool. The audiences were baffled and uneasy. They felt cheated out of a conventional happy ending and, perhaps more importantly, out of a genuine love interest which seemed incumbent upon a comedy ostensibly concerned with courtship and marriage.

A hilarious but rather slight affair, "Marriage" could neither satisfy Gogol's yen for "contemporary fame," nor offer an adequate outlet for the pointed social observation which had failed to jell into "The Order of Vladimir of the Third Class." Having discarded the latter design, Gogol seemed to be at a loss for a "truly Russian anecdote." Before embarking upon an

6. *The Collected Tales and Plays of Nikolai Gogol,* pp. 677-724.

important literary endeavor, he often needed an outside stimulus, an idea for the plot, preferably one drawn from some rather freakish actual happening. Allegedly, Alexander Pushkin stepped into the breach by telling his younger confrere about getting stuck once in a dingy Nizhnij Novgorod hotel and being mistaken by local notables for a St. Petersburg dignitary. Whether Pushkin actually urged this theme on Gogol, or whether, as some versions have it, the "sly Ukrainian" promptly availed himself of it, to Pushkin's noticeable chagrin, is a moot point. What is incontrovertible is that the comic potentialities of the anecdote were not lost on Gogol. Several months later, *The Inspector General,* by far the greatest comedy in the Russian language and one of the finest ever written, was completed.

In *The Inspector General,* Gogol's dazzling verbal inventiveness and his brilliant use of the comic incident give the time-honored motif of mistaken identity, a staple food of Western comedy ever since Plautus, a new lease on life. The plot can be stated in relatively few sentences which, needless to say, do not come close to suggesting the effectiveness of the play, one of Gogol's most accomplished performances. The worried officials of the town of N. gather at the mayor's house in order to discuss the imminent arrival from St. Petersburg of an Inspector General. The notables clearly have a great deal to be worried about: they are as venal as they are incompetent. The city hospital, the school, the post office are in a state of disrepair. The mayor, the greatest criminal and extortionist of them all, is about to order the police to clean up the mess. Two local busybodies, whose comically twin names of Bobchinskij and Dobchinskij epitomize their symbiotic relationship, burst into the scene to announce that the dreaded dignitary has already arrived and lives incognito in the local hotel. To Bobchinskij and Dobchinskij, the proof of his identity is unmistakable: it seems that the young man has presence and allure, and that, even though he has been staying at the hotel for some time, he has staunchly refused either to pay his bill or to leave.

This logic strikes the audience as compelling. The mayor and his henchmen promptly repair to the hotel to pay their respects to the alleged dignitary who is actually an insignificant young man from the capital, utterly penniless after an unlucky bout with gambling and about to be evicted. The arrival of the frightened officials mercifully takes Khlestakov off the hook. Stunned by his good fortune, he graciously accepts both a substantial "loan" from the mayor and his servile hospitality. He is wined and dined, fawned upon by the mayor's family and the local officialdom, blatantly bribed both by the bureaucrats who fear exposure and the local populace who seek to insure a sympathetic hearing of their complaints. He flirts outrageously and absentmindedly with both the mayor's wife and with his daughter. He barely manages to skip town before he is exposed. Prompted by his stolid and reality-oriented servant, Ostap, who plays a Sancho Panza to his tawdry Don Quixote, he departs in a huff, leaving the mayor and his family in a state of dazed euphoria. But their bliss is rudely interrupted by the postmaster who makes a practice of feeding his intellectual curiosity by sampling both the incoming and the outgoing mail. He has just perused the highly irreverent account of Khlestakov's unex-pected triumphs, which, on the eve of his hasty departure, the impostor had dispatched to his St. Petersburg chum, clearly as shiftless and frivolous a creature as himself. The cat is out of the bag. The mayor, shattered and humiliated, heaps abuse upon himself, a seasoned old charlatan taken in by a mere trifler, and in a famous monologue, steps beyond the play to anticipate and deplore its imminent impact: "There will come some scribbler, some inkslinger, who will put you in a come-dy . . . he won't spare your rank and your calling, and everyone will grin and clap!" Shaking his fist at the imaginary audience, the mayor bellows in a much cited phrase: "What are you laughing at? You are laughing at yourselves!"[7] As this frenzy of breast-beating subsides, everybody turns on the pair of gossips, Bobchinskij and Dobchinskij. The two "pot-bellied shrimps"

7. Ibid., p. 673.

are rescued from lynching by a shattering announcement made by an entering policeman: "The official who has arrived from St. Petersburg with instructions from the Government summons you to his presence. He is staying at the inn. (These words fall like a thunderbolt upon all. . . . The whole group, changing their attitude, remains petrified. . . . For almost a minute and a half, the petrified group retains its position.) Curtain."[8]

I submit that this minute and a half is, in a significant sense, a moment of truth. The lightning which strikes dumb the cast of *The Inspector General* illuminates, in retrospect, the real nature and drift of the proceedings. The shattering announcement unmasks the agon as sham, as merely a spurious prelude to the real thing. (Or is the "official who has arrived from St. Petersburg" another impostor?) More importantly, perhaps, the mute scene which ensues resolves the abrasive satire into what it was, essentially, to begin with—a grotesque pantomine, a madcap ballet. For the world of *The Inspector General* is populated by homunculi rather than by full-blown human beings, by puppets whose precariously contrived mode of existence is pointed up by their blatantly comic names, e.g. Bobchinskij and Dobchinskÿ, Ljapkin-Tjapkin, etc. Borne on the wave of the author's verbal exuberance; they are by-products or figments of his freewheeling nomenclatural whimsy. As any reader of Sheridan will readily recognize, meaningful expressive names are part of the time-honored tradition. Yet the names in *The Inspector General* are not only appropriately characterizing labels, but also richly suggestive sound gestures. This is certainly true of that of the play's chief protagonist. Nabokov shrewdly notes; "Khlestakov's very name is a stroke of genius ["Khlestat" means either "to whip" or "to guzzle"] for it conveys to the Russian reader an effect of lightness and rashness, a prattling tongue, the swish of a slim walking cane . . . the braggadocio of a nincompoop, the dashing ways of a lady-killer."[9] I may add that the "lightness and rashness"

8. Ibid., 674-75.
9. *Nikolai Gogol*, p. 55.

of which Nabokov speaks is masterfully pointed up by Khlestakov's priceless self-definition: "There is an extraordinary lightness about my thoughts."[10] This naïvely boastful phrase is a
marvelous evocation of the mindlessness, frivolity, and utter
lack of substance which is at the core of the Khlestakov
syndrome.

It was another stroke of genius on Gogol's part to have made
Khlestakov so flimsy and shadowy a creature, to have turned
the traditional figure of an impostor into the epitome of
vacuity, to have built a comedy of mistaken identity around
someone who does not choose the role of mountebank, but
drifts into it. Some of the critics and stage directors notwithstanding, Khlestakov is a phony rather than a fraud, an almost
unwitting beneficiary of a totally unearned windfall rather than
a schemer who sizes up the situation as a promising one and
cold-bloodedly sets out to take advantage of it. In contradistinction to his foil and antipode, that stolid provincial bully, the
mayor, Khlestakov does not manipulate events, but is manipulated, in a sense created, by them. He is not smart enough to be
a schemer: it takes him nearly two acts to understand the
situation in which he finds himself. Not until after the remarkable scene of bribing in Act IV, in which the whole string of
frightened officials clumsily ply him with loans ranging from
65 to 300 rubles, does it dawn on him that "they take [me] for
someone of importance in the government."[11] A marginal
boulevardier, a poor man's Casanova, a grabbag of ill-digested
clichés and literary misquotations—"as Karamzin says, 'Only
the laws condemn it' " "we'll flee to some happy dale beneath
the shade of brooks"—he is a walking parody of worldliness.
Even in his finest and funniest hour, one of the truly great
moments in Russian comedy, when in the wake of a lavish meal

10. The more idiomatic but pat rendition of "legkost' v mysljakh
neobychajnaja" found in Collected Tales and Plays, "I have a wonderfully ready
wit," misses the self-revelatory implication of emptiness and thinness of Khlestakov's "thoughts." Once again the Garnett-Kent translation has erred by grafting too much sense and coherence on Gogol's brilliant impersonation of inanity.
11. Collected Tales and Plays, p. 649.

at the mayor's, "the braggadocio of the nincompoop" success-
fully projects the image of an influential man-about-town, and
literary adviser of Pushkin's, escalating into that of a field
marshal, Khlestakov seems not so much a manipulator as a
captive of his awed audience. For it is the unearned, misdi-
rected adulation which emanates from these craven fools,
along with his own mounting intoxication, that sucks the babbling guest of honor into an orgy of daydreaming, and flamboyant enactment of ludicrous fantasies of omnipotence. Khlestakov is a nobody, literally a nobody, propelled into the limelight
by the inanity and panic, or to put it differently, by the bad
faith of the local bureaucrats.

In one of his more perceptive observations, Vissarion Belinskij went even further in questioning Khlestakov's very existence when he described him as a "figment of the Mayor's
frightened imagination, the phantom shadow of his conscience."[12] Gogol himself, in a direction to actors jotted down
in 1842, called attention to Khlestakov's lack of substance:
"Khlestakov is a phantasmagorical figure who, like an embodied fraud, vanishes into thin air with his troika."[13]

The notion of Khlestakov as a phantom, as an objectified
state of mind, was to recur in a much stodgier vein in a delayed
postscript to the play called "A Dénouement of *The Inspector
General*" (1846).[14] In this ponderous interpretation, the town
of N. symbolizes the soul of man, the corrupt officials represent
the base passions gnawing at it, while the Inspector serves as an
embodiment of man's awakened "conscience" or sense of guilt.
This reading, offered at a later and significantly different stage
of Gogol's moral evolution, provoked much skepticism and
derision among Gogolians. It is indeed tempting to dismiss it as
a dubious ratiocination, an example of what Nabokov deems
Gogol's deplorable habit of "thoroughly planning his works
after he had written and published them."[15] Yet we might do

12. See *V. G. Belinskij o Gogole* (Moscow, Ogiz, 1949), p. 140.
13. *Polnoe Sobranie Sochinenij, 4*, 118.
14. Ibid., pp. 121-33.
15. *Nikolai Gogol, p.* 57.

well to heed the warning of Cizevsky, probably the most distinguished living Gogolian,[16] and not prematurely laugh out of court Gogol's belated exegesis. For one thing, in some Russian religious tracts which Gogol read assiduously, the city does appear as a metaphor for the soul of man. For another, if—as will be argued at greater length below—the import of Gogol's satire is ethical and metaphysical rather than topical and institutional, the emphasis on traditional Christian symbolism might not be altogether misleading. The residual difficulty with "The Dénouement of *The Inspector General*" may lie not so much in misrepresenting the play's ideological implications, but in mistakenly describing its genre and trying to construe a wildly exuberant comic pageant as a morality play.

The story of the reception of *The Inspector General* and of Gogol's subsequent reaction is almost as interesting as the play itself. The initial impact was explosive. While the audiences' responses were mixed, hardly anyone remained indifferent. The bulk of the theater going public, especially the officials and the sycophants of the bureaucratic establishment, were displeased, indeed often scandalized, by the "vulgarity" and "coarseness" of the play, and by its slanderous, not to say subversive tenor.[17] Writing to a friend, the sympathetic and sophisticated conservative Vjazemskij, ironically summed up the angry mutterings of the notables thus: "How is it possible not to present on the stage a single, decent, honorable man as if there weren't any left in Russia. These functionaries," Vjazemskij commented pointedly, "want to be more monarchist than the King."[18]

The "king" in this case was the Tsar, Nicholas I, who behaved on this particular occasion with a totally uncharacteristic broadmindedness. "Had the Emperor not offered his protection and assistance," wrote Gogol to his mother on June 5,

---

16. Tschizewskij, *Russische Literaturgeschichte des 19 Jahrhunderts, 1,* 105.
17. See Debreczeny's *Nikolay Gogol and His Contemporary Critics,* pp. 17-29.
18. Letter to A. I. Turgenev as quoted in Veresaev, *Gogol v zhizni,* p. 162.

1836, "probably the play would not have been performed or published."[19] Moreover, Nicholas deigned to attend the premiere and is known to have laughed several times. (The spectacle of a tsar who fully earned the appellation "gendarme of Europe" savoring the humiliation of a provincial bully lent special relevance to the mayor's prophetic outburst: "what are you laughing at? You are laughing at yourselves!") He was even rumored to have said good-humoredly: "Everybody got his come-uppance, and I most of all"—a bit of self-criticism which I find rather implausible.

In spite of the sovereign's "assistance and protection," Gogol felt roundly and universally condemned. On April 29, 1836, he wrote to his fellow Ukrainian, the famous Moscow artist Shchepkin: "Respectable and aging officials shout that for me nothing is sacred . . . Policemen are against me; merchants are against me; litterateurs are against me." Increasingly, he insists that the comedy writer's lot is not a happy one.

> Now I see what it means to be a comedy writer . . . I am not bothered by the fact that all estates are now definitely against me, but it is sad to see that your contemporaries whom you love with all your heart are unfairly incited against you . . . Let the crooks fume. But some of the people whom I did not think were crooks fumed, too . . . I am appalled by the obtuse irritability which pervades all classes of our society. . . . To call a crook a crook is to undermine the foundations of our State.[20]

There is no question that Gogol was overgeneralizing about the negative responses. The police were indeed against him, and so were many of the merchants. But the litterateurs were split down the middle. While his traditional detractors (Senkovskij and Bulharyn, for example) tried to dismiss *The Inspector General* as trite and vulgar, some of the most serious

19. *Polnoe Sobranie Sochinenij, 11* (1952), 47.
20. Ibid., p. 38.

and independent critics of the day, including, to be sure, that
vocal spokesman of the budding intelligentsia, Belinskij hailed
the play as a remarkable and profoundly truthful work of art.[21]
Moreover, as Gogol himself noted with understandable satisfaction, the fulminations of the aging officials did not detract
from the popularity of the play; in fact, they might have added
to it. "They abuse the play, but everyone wants to see it—four
performances in a row have sold out."[22] All in all, the situation
was one which would have been scarcely disappointing to a less
paranoid author. "Another man," Nabokov rightly says,
"would have reveled in the atmosphere of praise and scan-
dal."[23] The play was making an impact; it was the talk of the
town, the focus of a lively and loud controversy. Yet Gogol was
visibly upset, overwrought, in fact traumatized. He responded
to this turmoil in his characteristic fashion. He chose to "dissi-
pate his spleen" by going abroad. This time the self-
administered cure was to be a lasting one. When on June 6,
1836, he boarded a Germany-bound boat, he was to become a
virtual expatriate for over a decade. With the exception of two
brief trips to Russia, he was to spend the subsequent twelve
years in Europe, shuttling restlessly between Italy and France,
Germany and Austria.

His case for temporary expatriation was too elaborate to be
fully convincing. Not only did he claim to need travel in order
to calm his shattered nerves; he needed moreover, and more
importantly, a perspective on his society which only physical
distance would provide. On May 10, 1836, he wrote to Pogodin: "I am going abroad to shake off the anguish which my
countrymen inflict upon me. A contemporary writer, a writer
of comedy . . . had better get away from his native land. The
prophet can have no fame at home."[24] On May 15, he told the
same correspondent: "I am going in order to shake off my

21. See Debreczeny, pp. 17-29.
22. *Polnoe Sobranie Sochinenij, 11,* 38.
23. *Nikolai Gogol,* p. 57.
24. *Polnoe Sobranie Sochinenij, 11,* 41.

spleen, to ponder deeply my duties as a writer and my future works. I shall return to you, I trust, refreshed and renewed."[25]

The time-honored cliché, "No one is a prophet in his own home," which is invoked here as a generalization after the fact was a typically Gogolian way of dealing with a crisis. Yet it is not altogether clear why the public response to *The Inspector General* occasioned such a crisis, why it proved quite so upsetting. Gogol's first flight was a relatively simple affair: "Hanz Kuechelgarten" was a resounding failure. Conversely, *The Inspector General* made Gogol one of the best-known and most talked-about writers of his time. What, then, went so terribly wrong?

I suspect that the "cacophony of praise and blame" (Nabokov) was doubly disturbing to Gogol. Though he had genuine scorn for the small-time "crooks" who recognized themselves in the comedy's protagonists and screamed in outrage, it is at least arguable that he had no intention of exposing the system and was truly worried over the displeasure of some influential dignitaries. By the same token, he may have been more embarrassed than gratified by the unsolicited support which he was getting from the liberal camp. I shall revert to the question of Gogol's implicit politics at a later stage of this narrative. Suffice it to say at this point that neither in his writings nor in his copious correspondence is there any indication that he was at any time a principled opponent of the tsarist regime.

This clearly is only part of the story. In addition to an acute embarrassment, which verges on paranoid panic, about being blamed and praised by the wrong people, one detects in Gogol's reaction a letdown, a sense of anticlimax. It is as if in his heart of hearts he had hoped that his spirited exposure of corrupt men who wormed their way into the system might shock his audiences into a moral catharsis, a spiritual regeneration. This, in turn, would suggest that his initial expectations had been extravagant, indeed utopian—a hypothesis which is not incompatible either with the solemn view of the play-

25. Ibid., p. 46.

wright's mission that incongruously brought into being a dazzlingly wacky comedy, nor with its author's notoriously wobbly
sense of reality.

Neither the embarrassment nor the disappointment, however, can fully account for the note of dejection, of real nausea,
which crept into Gogol's correspondence in the wake of the
first performances of his greatest comedy. "*The Inspector General* is on a stage," he writes to a fellow writer "and I feel so
strange, so troubled."[26] It is entirely possible that he was taken
aback by what must have been a slapdash, cheaply farcical
style of acting. Yet he seems to have been unhinged by the play
itself, as well as by its production. Dmitrij Merezhkovskij may
not have been far off the mark when he attributed Gogol's
visible hangover after his comic binge to a helpless disgust with
the unrelieved moral tawdriness of the world he so brilliantly
mimicked.[27]

A polemical postscript to *The Inspector General,* a dramatic
fragment entitled "After the Play," features disgruntled spectators who offer the objection that the play was an exercise in
negativist debunking. The Philistine complaint is challenged in
the author's soliloquy:

> It's too bad that nobody noticed one honest person who
> does appear in my play. In fact, there is an honest, noble
> person who never leaves the stage. His name is 'Laugh-
> ter.' . . . Not that laughter which is generated by temporary
> irritability, by a bitter, morbid frame of mind, nor that
> frivolous laughter which serves only for idle entertainment,
> but laughter which emerges from the man's better nature.
> . . . without whose penetrating power the pettiness and emp-
> tiness of life would not have appeared so frightening.[28]

26. See Veresaev, p. 161.

27. *Gogol-Tvorchestvo, zhizn' i religija* (St. Petersburg and Moscow, M. O.
Volf, 1911).

28. "Teatralnyj raz'ezd posle predstavlenija novoj komedii." *Polnoe
Sobranie Sochinenij,* 5 (1949), 169.

We are back to the basic ideology of Gogol the playwright. Yet, the writer's overt aesthetics and his visceral reactions need not to coincide. Even as Gogol the satirist was celebrating the right kind of laughter as a cleansing, chastising, and ultimately liberating force, to the lonely, anguished man who wrote the comedy and urged this vindication, the frightening "pettiness and emptiness of life" must have been much more real than the moral uplift to be ultimately gleaned from the act of debunking. Thus it stands to reason that when, in 1836, Gogol once again took to the road, he was running not only from a society that had presumably let him down, but also from the moral fumes of the unredeemed and unredeemable universe he had conjured up in *The Inspector General*.

7

The Payoff

Shortly before his fateful departure, Gogol embarked on a new work which was to become the crowning achievement of his career. With Part One of *Dead Souls,* he returned to narrative fiction. Yet this time his aim was nothing less than a full-length novel.

Once again, if one is to believe "An Author's Confession,"[1] it was Pushkin who gave Gogol his subject by calling the younger man's attention to a bizarre newspaper item. Allegedly, an enterprising swindler had gone around buying up dead serfs to use them as a mortgage for a brewery he intended to purchase. A novel built around an itinerant rascal such as this, Pushkin is said to have urged, would provide ample scope for Gogol's satirical gifts. It would offer him "a complete freedom to travel all through Russia with his hero and to introduce a multitude of most disparate characters."[2]

Gogol plunged into his new project with zest and enthusiasm, His hopes soared. Soon after the launching, he was deeply convinced that he was engaged in the most significant effort of his entire career. A sense of mission which antedated *The Inspector General* and which was exacerbated by the public reaction to the play—the image of oneself as a spiritual leader and guide—became a leitmotif of Gogol's numerous references to his emerging novel. "It is time to go to work . . . If

1. *Polnoe Sobranie Sochinenij* (Complete Works), *8* (1952), 439-40.
2. Ibid., p. 440.

God will help me complete my poem[3] . . . it will be my first decent work. All of Russia will be revealed in it."[4] Inevitably many people will resent this revelation." Many estates and all and sundry gentlemen will rail against me, but what can I do? It is my fate to be at war with my countrymen!" A man dedicated to the truth must be prepared for scorn and abuse—he will do well to heed posterity rather than his contemporaries. Gogol's tone in 1836-37 was often one of cryptic prophecy, of anticipatory euphoria: "Tremendously great is my creation; it shall not be completed for some time . . . Someone invisible is writing before [through?] me with a mighty rod."[5]

The first four chapters of the "poem" were completed prior to Gogol's second flight and read to Pushkin, eliciting his much-quoted groan: "Oh Lord, how sad is our Russia!" The remainder of the first volume was written fitfully in Europe within the four restless and nomadic years during which onsets of physical illness and depression alternated with periods of relative serenity and almost frenzied productivity. The last such sequence, according to an engaging eyewitness, Pavel Annenkov,[6] was the summer of 1841. By the fall of that year Part One of *Dead Souls* was complete. Rather reluctantly Gogol journeyed home to argue or plead with the censors. The difficulties were manifold: at first the Moscow censorship committee was adamant, not the least because of the novel's oxymoronic title which, said the chairman, was an attack on the Christian doctrine of the immortality of the soul. To be sure, this theological objection was grotesquely and characteristically misplaced. Within the context of the novel "soul" means "serf," a legal rather than a theological notion. It is not entirely clear whether the chief censor was preposterously literal-

---

3. Interestingly enough, Gogol called his first full-length novel a "poem." The possible implications of this subtitle will be discussed further.

4. *Polnoe Sobranie Sochinenij, 11* (1952), 77.

5. Ibid., p. 75.

6. "N. V. Gogol v Rime letom, 1841 g.," *Gogol v vospominanijakh sovremennikov* (1952), pp. 230-39.

minded, or simply disingenuous; politically, serfdom was certainly a more touchy issue than the immortality of the soul.
Had it not been for the efforts in Gogol's behalf on the part of
his influential and ever-helpful friends (Zhukovskij, Pletnëv,
Pogodin) it is doubtful whether Part One of *Dead Souls* would
have been allowed to see the light of day in May of 1842.

Puškin's alleged expectations were borne out. The permis-
sive, loose-jointed structure of the quasipicaresque novel built
around a shifty and, of necessity, mobile huckster, did allow for
a wider range of character and situation than Gogol had been
able to deploy in a small-town comedy or in a claustrophobic
Mirgorod tale. As the novel's focus shifted from manor to
manor, and from deal to deal, along with Chichikov's fast-
moving carriage, the grotesque vignettes of the "Two Ivans" and
The Inspector General grew into a freakish panorama of
provincial gentry, flanked by a supporting cast of small-town
notables, eccentric gossips and feather-brained society ladies.
The social landscape painting of "The Old-Fashioned Landowners" and the piling-up of status-oriented physical detail
that characterized "Nevsky Prospekt" catapulted here into a
descriptive frenzy, an oppressive proliferation of details that
clutter up the stage and in so doing point up the stifling, soulless
physicality of the novel's moral universe. In the same way, the
high-flown rhetoric of nature passages in the early stories found
its payoff in the rolling eloquence, the richly orchestrated
sonority of the famous finale and of other lyrical digressions in
Dead Souls. Whether or not it is Gogol's most accomplished
work—the claims of *The Inspector General* and "The Overcoat" cannot be easily dismissed—it is without any doubt his
most ambitious, his most broadly conceived effort. Thus it
could become for both Gogol's contemporaries and for modern
critics a crucial test of the nature of his art and the texture of
his vision.

The immediate response, while falling considerably short of
a moral catharsis, was vigorous and not infrequently laudatory.
Predictably, there was no unanimity. The inveterately hostile

reviewers (Osip Senkovskij, Nikolaj Grech, Nikolaj Polevoj) were as scurrilous as ever. *Library for Reading,* an influential magazine edited by Senkovskij, deplored the novel's unabashed treatment of the lowly and seedy and inveighed against the "indecency" of its language. *Dead Souls* was bracketed together with the vulgar potboilers of the third-rate French writer Paul de Kock. In a St. Petersburg quarterly, *The Russian Messenger,* Polevoj took Gogol to task for slandering life and Russia by reducing both to "dirt, dung, debauchery and vice." Yet the bulk of the serious critics, be they of conservative slavophile or liberal westernizing persuasion, hailed *Dead Souls* as a major literary event. In a wide-ranging and thoughtful essay, the conservative literary historian Stepan Shevyrëv ranked Gogol with the best representatives of European literature. Konstantin Aksakov, the ardently romantic Slavophile essayist, went Shevyrëv one better. In an article brimful of "Schillerian" enthusiasm, he placed Gogol in exclusive company with the "greatest two," Homer and Shakespeare. The parallel with Homer may have been suggested in part by Gogol's extended similes[7] and helped by the novel's subtitle "poem." The main intent of the analogy, however, was a fullthroated celebration of the novel's epic grandeur: "Only in works by Homer and Shakespeare can we come across such a fullness of creation as in those of Gogol. Only Homer, Shakespeare and Gogol possess the great identical secret of art."[8]

More influential in the long run was the verdict of Vissarion Belinskij, who by 1841 had clearly emerged as the recognized spokesman of the forward-looking, western-oriented Russian intelligentsia. Belinskij, who had written appreciatively about *Mirgorod* and *Arabesques,* and in his 1835 essays had dubbed Gogol "a poet of reality" and praised the originality and the "inexhaustible humor" of *The Inspector General,* now hailed *Dead Souls* as a "refreshing lightning amid the tedious and oppressive drought." Belinskij had little use for Aksakov's

7. See below, pp. 126–27.
8. See Debreczeny, *Nikolaij Gogol and His Contemporary Critics,* p. 40.

extravagant and allegedly misleading parallels. To him, *Dead Souls* was a "purely Russian national work emerging from the depth of Russian life, ruthlessly tearing the veil off reality."[9] To put it in somewhat more modern and less circumspect language, it was a masterpiece of social realism as well as a forthright indictment of the serf-owning, bureaucratic Russia of Nicholas I.

This view, which acquired wide currency during the second half of the nineteenth century, and which today is binding on the official Soviet critic, has been challenged with increasing vigor in the last seventy-five years or so. First, an imaginative turn-of-the-century Russian writer, Vasilij Rozanov, and such leading Russian Symbolists as Andrej Belyj, and Valerij Brjusov, punctured the notion of Gogol's realism by portraying him vividly and eloquently as a master of the grotesque hyperbole.[10] Nabokov follows suit: "The view taken by Russian readers and critics who saw in *Dead Souls* a matter-of-fact description of existing conditions seems . . . utterly and ludicrously wrong."[11]

Nabokov's vigorous objection receives assistance from a rather strategic quarter. In an 1843 postmortem on *Dead Souls*, Gogol himself stated flatly that Pushkin's much publicized comment on the first four chapters of the novel was largely beside the point. Presumably, when Pushkin exclaimed "Oh Lord, how sad is our Russia!," Gogol was "astounded": "Pushkin, who knew Russia so well, did not realize that all this was caricature and my own invention." In a later passage, Gogol suggests that this "invention" echoed his own nightmares: "I did not invent these nightmares. They were weighing upon my soul."[12]

9. Belinskij, *Estetika i Literaturnaja Kritika* (Moscow, Gosizdat, 1959), *1*, 607.

10. Rozanov, "Neskolko slov o Gogole," *Legenda o velikom inkvizitore* (3d ed. St. Petersburg, M. V. Pirozhkov, 1906); Belyj, "Gogol," and Brjusov, "Ispepelënnyj," *Vesy* (Moscow, 1909), no. 4.

11. *Nikolai Gogol*, p. 73

12. *Polnoe Sobranie Sochinenij, 8*, 294-97.

Does this obiter dictum close the matter and effectively dispose of Gogol's "realism"? Not necessarily. The author's post-factum interpretation of his work can neither be ignored nor taken at its face value, especially if the author's name is Nikolaj Gogol. The issue joined between Belinskij and Nabokov remains to haunt the modern student of Gogol. Or should I rather say "the issues"? For it is at least arguable that we deal here with two distinct, if interrelated queries: Is it meaningful or helpful to call the late Gogol a "realist" in any legitimate sense of this word, and what was the main thrust of Gogol's satire? Was his cleansing laughter aimed mainly at the social institutions of the early nineteenth-century Russia, as Belinskij had implied, or at man's ineradicable folly?

First a word about "realism." Few terms of literary criticism have been used less critically. In everyday parlance, and even more so in the high-powered jargon of publishers' blurbs and of popular book reviewers, the adjective "realistic" tends to become a rough equivalent of the naïve gasp, "how true!," of "straightforward," "hard-hitting," or simply "real," in a word, an epithet which reveals more about the reader's attitude than about the nature of the book under discussion.

Some of this is undoubtedly an echo of midnineteenth-century literary polemics, when the word "realism" was used as a battlecry and a banner of the rising movement in literature and in the arts. In challenging their rivals, the spokesmen of the Realistic school argued with partisan heat that the works they championed represented an accurate and forthright account of reality such as their convention-ridden forerunners had never managed or dared to offer.

Yet the phrase "correspondence with reality" is both ambiguous and misleading, since "reality" is a highly complex notion and since no work of literature worthy of the name can dispense with invention or artifice. As René Wellek and Austin Warren reminded us, "realism and naturalism, whether in the drama or the novel, are literary . . . movements, conventions, styles . . . The distinction is not between reality and illusion, but between differing conceptions of reality, different modes of illusion."[13] Consequently, no discussion of realism as a literary trend can be profitable if it does not address itself to the "realistic" mode of illusion.

In Roman Jakobson's provocative but little-known article "On Realism in Art," in which he explored in an iconoclastic vein the divergent meanings of the term "realism," he suggested an essential criterion in identifying the realistic style. It is a tendency toward minute, "metonymic" description, toward a lavish use of external detail, above and beyond the call of the story itself. This crucial thesis is illustrated by an anecdote: "A boy was given the following problem: a bird flew out of its cage. When did it reach the woods if it was flying at such and such speed and the distance from the cage to the woods was such and such? The boy inquired: what color was the cage?" "That boy," adds Jakobson, "was a typical realist."[14]

Jakobson's point is well taken. In realistic fiction—in Balzac and Dickens, in Goncharov and Howells—the stage is always cluttered with *realia*. Not only the characters' appearance and mannerisms, but their physical and social environment as well are described at length. While much of this detail can be deemed "irrelevant" to the narrative, it is absolutely essential to the realistic novelist's avowed intention of approximating the texture of social reality, of life as actually lived by ordinary, workaday people. The proliferation of everyday detail indicative of social status or rank helps locate the events and characters described in an easily identifiable social milieu. The density of *Kleinmalerei* seems to lend the realistic work of art a tridimensional, lifelike quality.

It goes without saying that this cumulative effect cannot be achieved by close attention to the setting alone. Other elements of the art of fiction must come into play. The authenticity of

13. *Theory of Literature* (New York, Harcourt, Brace and World, 1949), p. 220.

14. "O khudozhestvennom realizme," reprinted in *Michigan Slavic Materials* (Ann Arbor, University of Michigan Press, 1952), no. 2, pp. 30-46.

descriptive texture must be bolstered by the credibility of the plot structure. If a work of fiction is to create and sustain an illusion of reality, the story, however artfully contrived it may be, must not diverge too sharply from a world picture grounded in science and sanctioned by common sense. The incidents and situations portrayed must be such as to be accepted as plausible by the bulk of the reading public.

It is precisely such a congruence between texture and structure that is conspicuously absent from Gogol's middle and late works. What we confront here, it seems to me, is not so much a sustained illusion of reality as an intermittent illusion of realism induced by the accumulation of homely trivia, and by that lack of squeamishness in the choice of language and subject which was part of Realism's challenge to the early nineteenth-century literary and social taboos. Yet when matter as well as manner are properly attended to, it becomes clear that this "realistic" detail serves here not as the subsoil of an autonomous yet reality-like world, but as a factor of contrapuntal tension between the ultra-realistic mode of presentation and a narrative framework which brazenly disclaims credibility.

This is clearly the case with "The Nose," a story whose effect, as already indicated, rests on a grotesque discrepancy between the matter-of-fact narrative tone and an utterly incredible central event. "The Nose," which calls into question the basic realistic criterion of "plausibility,"[15] admittedly is an extreme case. In such "post-Romantic" works of Gogol's as "Two Ivans," *The Inspector General,* and *Dead Souls,* credibility is not altogether eliminated, but it is strained to the breaking point. As Dmitry Cizevsky persuasively argued,[16] Gogol's most "realistic" plots are remarkably farfetched. The tedium and inanity of the Ukrainian backwater epitomized by the preposterous quarrel between the Ivans was all too real. But it was *not* customary for brown pigs to break into county court

15. See above, Chapter 5, p. 88.
16. See above, Chapter 5, n. 21.

buildings and steal complaints lodged against their owners. By
the same token, the stupidity and venality of provincial officialdom satirized in Gogol's greatest comedy were altogether
plausible themes. Yet it does not necessarily follow that silly
chatterboxes such as Bobchinskij and Dobchinskij were likely
to jump to the conclusion that a young man who did not pay his
hotel bill and refused to move out could be no one else but the
Inspector General. Even if one pays parochial obtuseness its
full due, one may have trouble imagining a tightwad old
landlady such as Korobochka in *Dead Souls* haggling in all
seriousness about the market prices of dead serfs. Nor was it
usual for small-town gossips to proclaim a shoddy character
whose whereabouts was shrouded in mystery no less a figure
than Napoleon who had just escaped from his internment on
the isle of St. Helena. (This bizarre notion of Chichikov's real
identity makes rapid headway among the befuddled inhabitants
of the town of N.) More centrally, Chichikov's bizarre financial
scheme—that of buying up serfs who have died since the last
population census at appropriately low prices—is neither plausible nor typical. It is a morbidly extravagant parody of actual
frauds committed in the Russia of Nicholas I, rather than a
reliable example. And need I insist on the ambiguity of that
title, *Dead Souls,* which means both "dead serfs" and "dead
souls"? Need I point out that Chichikov's traffic in corpses is
symbolic, as it epitomizes the soulless vulgarity, the moral
deadness of Gogol's uncanny world?

Is it not true, a champion of Gogol's "realism" may remon-
strate at this point, that the plot of *Dead Souls* was based on an
actual happening? So it seems. Yet this would argue for a *sui
generis* authenticity of the plot rather than for its typicality.
Friedrich Engels' dictum that realistic literature portrays "typical characters under typical circumstances," mercilessly abused
though it has been by Soviet literary hacks, does have some
validity. "Realism" is geared not to what somehow managed to
happen, but to what was likely to happen. Its realm is the
plausible, the recurrent, the representative, rather than the

barely conceivable, the freakish anecdote, the stranger-than-fiction actuality.

In his already-cited 1842 postscript to *The Inspector General,* "After the Play," one of the many displeased spectators, an "experienced" official, loudly berates the author: "What does he know? He doesn't know a damn thing! That is not the way bribes are taken!"[17] The "expert" clearly refers to that brilliantly hilarious sequence in Act IV where quivering officials pop into the alleged Inspector's room one by one, engaging Khlestakov in an utterly inane conversation that leads to a clumsily timid offer of a "loan," or, as Khlestakov increasingly catches on, to his own abrupt request for such "assistance." Technically, the irate bureaucrat has a point. Moreover, it is one which, mutatis mutandis, is applicable to many other Gogolian plots or incidents. With equal justice, and equal irrelevance, a literal-minded reader of *Dead Souls* could argue, "That is not the way frauds were committed." Clearly, verisimilitude was not Gogol's forte, nor was it, most of the time, his avowed goal. "I never had the desire to reflect reality as it is around us," he declared in a moment of candor.[18]

This relative lack of concern with the way things actually happen, this whimsical or cavalier attitude toward reality, permeates much of Gogol's world. In his idiosyncratic universe where the actual is incessantly intruded upon, distorted and magnified by a disheveled imagination, there are few consistent "realists." Not only exuberant liars such as Khlestakov and Nozdryov, but also, as Nabokov shrewdly notes,[19] stolid, earth-bound characters like Sobakevich, are susceptible to wacky flights of fancy. In a memorable scene in which Sobakevich is haggling with Chichikov over the prices of his dead serfs, a rather important ontological distinction becomes obliterated as Sobakevich waxes lyrical over the late Mikheev, the carriage-maker. To be sure, Sobakevich is a man who drives a

17. *Polnoe Sobranie Sochinenij,* 5 (1949), 163.
18. See a revealing letter to Pletnëv which appears in *Zapiski o zhizni N. V. Gogolja* (St. Petersburg, 1856), *2,* 149.
19. *Nikolai Gogol,* pp. 98-103.

hard bargain, and this strenuous boosting of nonexistent wares can be construed in part as a morbid travesty of his tightfisted-ness. Yet somewhere along the line his enthusiasm seems to acquire a disinterested, nearly poetic quality. "Why, of course, they are dead," he admits reluctantly when Chichikov con-fronts him with the reality. "Moreover, it may also be said, what good are the people of today that are numbered among the living? What sort of people are *they*? They're so many flies—not people." As Chichikov timidly observes that "the others" are "but a dream," Sobakevich replies with genuine indignation, "Well, no, they're no dream! You'll never find such men as Mikheev was. I'd like to know what other place you'd find such a dream in!"[20] It may not be altogether face-tious to echo Cizevsky's observation that the only reality-oriented person among Gogolian protagonists is Welfare Com-missioner A. F. Zemljanika in *The Inspector General,* who, when confronted with a somewhat surrealistic description of himself in Khlestakov's notorious letter to his friend, addresses a plaintive query to the audience: "Who has ever seen a pig in a skullcap?"[21]

The same principle of exuberant tampering with the actual through exaggeration and intensification that shapes Gogol's later plots is discernible at the level of character-drawing. A typical Gogol protagonist is an embodiment of a single trait, proclivity, or foible generalized or extended throughout the personality, pushed to the limit of utter rigidity or absurdity. Stolid Sobakevich; insipid Manilov; the seedy martyr of greed, Pljushkin; the brazen bully and braggart, Nozdrjov; the foppish nincompoop Khlestakov; and last, that faceless "acquirer," that slick peddler of non-existent goods, Chichikov—all these are types, or "humors," to use Ben Jonson's term, "psychic automatons,"[22] role-players in a masterfully contrived puppet show rather than full-fledged human beings. Frozen in their

20. *Dead Souls,* tr. B. G. Guerney (New York and Toronto, Rinehart and Co., 1948), p. 115.

21. *The Collected Tales and Plays of Nikolai Gogol,* p. 671.

22. Bicilli, "Gogol i Chekhov," *Sovremennye zapiski, 56* (Paris, 1934), 298-308.

characteristic poses, incapable of movement, development, or growth, they are vivid rather than alive; their faces Goya-like masks.

Although in some of Gogol's earlier works man's pathetic inadequacy was often conveyed by an orgy of synecdoches, by reducing a man to his whiskers or moustache, in *Dead Souls* the characters's subhumanity is often driven home through the medium of an animal simile. Sobakevich is likened to a bear, Pljushkin to a spider. In fact, "is likened" is an understatement; it would be more accurate to say that Sobakevich becomes a bear. The fluidity of the existential boundaries is not confined to Gogol's early openly Romantic works. If in his goblin tales, metamorphosis is negotiated through black magic, in *Dead Souls* it is the novel's magnificently exuberant, disheveled style that serves as an agency of transformation, however short-lived. Time and again, the similes and metaphors are "realized," projected into the plot. Figures of speech taken literally become events. "After beginning a simile," said Cizevsky, "Gogol seems to forget about it [or rather about it being a mere figure of speech] and a strange process takes place: A vendor of hot mead who was likened to a samovar, turns into a samovar; Chichikov, into a fortress and Pëtr Petrovich Petukh, into a watermelon."[23] Chichikov's likeness to a fortress appears at the time he is being threatened by Nozdrëv and his servants. Promptly "fortress" becomes the subject of a sentence: "The fortress was experiencing such fright that its heart was in its very heels."[24] A similar shift occurs in the description of Korobochka's carriage entering the town of N.: "It resembled neither a tarantass, nor a calash, nor a light covered carriage, but rather a round-cheeked, bulging watermelon placed on wheels. *The cheeks of this watermelon* [my italics]—i.e. its small doors—closed but poorly owing to the sad state of the handles and catches."[25] No wonder that in this

23. "Gogol: Artist and Thinker," *The Annals of the Ukrainian Academy of Arts and Sciences in the U.S., 4* (Summer, 1952), 272.

24. *Dead Souls,* p. 96.

25. Ibid., pp. 204-05.

topsy-turvy world Sobakevich seems to be not so much a bear-like individual as a medium-sized bear who does his best to look like a stolid landowner.

As the boundary between the human and the animal becomes fluid, so does the distinction between the animate and the inanimate. "Every object, every chair in Sobakevich's house seemed to proclaim: 'I, too, am Sobakevich!' "[26] The statement could be reversed. In line with the dehumanizing quality of Gogol's imagery, it might be equally proper to proclaim Sobakevich as the central object, the most strategic piece of furniture in his uncannily homogenous surroundings. Gogol's compulsion to extend the characteristics and mannerisms of the protagonist into the physical environment which he dominates is matched by the characteristically downgrading strategy of reducing him to an integral part of that environment.

With notions such as the downward similes and the "realization of the metaphor," our argument has almost imperceptibly veered from the problems of plot and characterization to those of style. This is not surprising. Imaginative literature, as a German critic has put it, is "the world transformed into language." This is doubly true of Gogol's "poem," where language is a demiurge of reality in the most literal sense imaginable, where—as I shall indicate in a moment—subordinate clauses give birth to peripheral characters and potential subplots. Thus it is singularly appropriate that in *Dead Souls* a characteristic urge to grotesquely distort the natural dimensions and the relative size of objects, persons, and events, which we have already seen operate in the realms of plot and characterization should assert itself so powerfully at the level of language through Gogol's favorite stylistic device, the hyperbole.

Gogol's addiction to this figure of speech has been commented upon by a host of astute and knowledgeable critics from the Russian Symbolists[27] down to Dmitry Cizevsky. Andrej

26. Ibid., p. 107.
27. See above, n. 10.

Belyj spoke of Gogol's hyperbole-ridden vision of life which "resolves earth into ether and dung and humanity into giants and dwarfs."[28] Whether dithyrambic or debunking, satirical or rhetorical, his prose is always bent on overstating the actual, on magnifying it beyond recognition. In Gogol's earlier writings, the hyperbolic mode seemed of a piece with the rhapsodic drift of so many rhetorically "swollen" sequences, be they eulogies of the Dnieper or the Ukrainian night, or celebrations of Cossack supermen. The language of Gogol's later satirical or ironic works is less rapturous but no less exuberant. To convey the notion that someone's laughter was loud, Gogol or his narrator says: "like the bellowing of two bulls as they stand facing each other."[29] Ivan Nikiforovich's trousers, we may recall, had such ample folds that, "if they were blown out, you could put the whole courtyard with the barns and the outhouses into them."[30] In *Dead Souls* the hyperbolic impulse asserts itself time and again. Pljushkin shaves so rarely that "his chin and jaws resembled a wire-bristled currycomb."[31] In the scene in which Chichikov and Manilov visit the administrative offices of the town of N., the cumulative effect of the scratching of copying clerks' pens is described thus: "the sound thereof was as if several carts loaded with brushweed were being driven through a forest piled with dead leaves a yard deep."[32] Finally, when Chichikov enters the Governor's Ball, the provincial fool who suddenly takes over the narration starts raving about the ineffable refinement attained by the attire of the ladies: "There was no end of tastefulness about their attire: the muslins, satins and tulles were of such fashionable pastel shades that one could not even give their names, to such a degree has the refinement of taste attained!"[33] This latter passage is a good example of a hyperbole which one might call "negative." The adjective fits

28. "Gogol," *Vesy* (1909), no. 4, p. 73.
29. "Viy," *Collected Tales and Plays,* p. 360.
30. See above, p. 72.
31. *Dead Souls,* p. 130.
32. Ibid., p. 162.
33. Ibid., p. 188.

both the formal structure of this mode of overstatement—the protestation of one's inability to do justice to the subject[34]—and, more importantly, its essentially ironic or parodistic function. For the import of the "negative hyperbole" is to diminish rather than to magnify; more specifically, to point up the pathetic inadequacy of the point of view, the embarrassing smallness of the observer. This was already the case in "Two Ivans" where the parochial narrator raves about things that clearly are not worth raving about and where the misplaced hyperbole, instead of lifting the subject, serves only to reveal its essential triviality.

Ironic incongruity of this kind is an essential part of the texture of *Dead Souls*. So is the larger-scale contrast between the stagnant, petrified world of the "poem" and its magnificently disheveled, irrepressible style. It is not necessary to labor this point since it was brilliantly made and amply documented by Nabokov. His essay is at its whimsical best in showing how digressive paragraphs injected into the narrative with supreme lack of concern for relevance or coherence beget such compellingly vivid "fleeting characters" as a lieutenant trying on his shiny new jackboots while Chichikov is asleep, the forgotten people of the town of N. re-emerging amid the turmoil of the Chichikov affair,[35] or Sobakevich's dead serfs brought to life twice, first by their owner's extravagant eulogy, then by Chichikov's uncharacteristically lyrical musings. Nabokov is singularly effective in describing and exhibiting Gogol's "life-generating" syntax so fully exemplified by the remarkable account of Chichikov's first impressions of the Sobakevich household where a round face glimpsed by a traveler begets a Moldavian pumpkin which, in turn, gives birth to a balalaika, only to conjure up the vivid image of a

34. In his "Gogol: Artist and Thinker," Cizevsky invokes a concept of traditional poetics, hyperoche, i.e. ascription to an object dimensions of grandeur exceeding all possibilities of description (p. 267).

35. The marginality of these "fleeting characters" of whom "no one has ever heard before" (p. 221) is pointed up, in a typically Gogolian fashion, by their outlandish names, e.g. Sysoj Pafnutievich and Makdonald Karlovich.

nimble balalaika player and the "wide bosomed" country lasses who constitute his eager audience.[36] In this dizzyingly centrifugal orgy of subordinate clauses, language is on a rampage.

Passages such as this have been called "Homeric." It is not necessary to share Konstantin Aksakov's rhapsodic estimate of *Dead Souls* in order to grant this parallel some validity. For in Homer too, most notably in *The Iliad,* a comparison often acquires a momentum of its own. After a battlefield has been likened to a sea-tossed ship, the latter realm becomes for a number of lines the sole focus of the poet's attention, displacing temporarily the scene or event which occasioned the analogy. One might go one step further. It is at least arguable that Gogol's descriptive "digressions" perform a function not altogether dissimilar from that of the extended similes in *The Iliad.* In both works, these interpolations seem to offer a respite from the stringency or the oppressiveness of the agon. In Homer, a glimpse of the life beyond seems to provide a wider prospective on the grim proceedings, a salutary reminder that, whatever happens on the crowded battlefield, life will go on. A somewhat similar mechanism may well be at work in *Dead Souls,* where the foreground is stifling rather than tragic, where the stage is filled not by the clangor of armies, but by seedy bric-a-brac, or, in Gogol's own words, by "the slimy morass of minutiae that has bogged down our lives."[37] It is as if Gogol's erratic, freewheeling imagination, unwilling or unable to stay put within the limits of the appalling world it has conjured up, kept overflowing these boundaries, teasing out shadowy appearances and thus calling into question the seriousness, indeed the reality of Chichikov's ghastly enterprise.

The centrifugal impulse in *Dead Souls* partakes of the duality built into the structure of the novel. Thus one might distinguish between two types of digressions—the lateral darts and the upward flights. The passages mentioned or alluded to thus far clearly belong in the former category. The relief offered by

36. Ibid., p. 104.
37. Ibid., p. 151.

these picturesque detours rests entirely on their bracing irrelevance, their utter fortuitousness and, to be sure, on the verbal
dynamism which calls them into existence. No spiritual uplift,
no substantive transcendence can be derived from the spectacle
of a smug lieutenant in love with his boots or of the fatuous
village dandy. These vignettes are part and parcel of the novel's
moral universe. Their protagonists dwell, however precariously
or fleetingly, on the same plane of grossness and triviality that
harbors the Korobochkas and the Sobakeviches.

This emphatically is not the case with the rhetorical or
lyrical digressions which both in their tone and their overall
thrust point far beyond the hermetic staleness of Pljushkin's
overgrown garden, toward another world, a higher reality.
Once again we are presented with a stylistic and tonal polarity,
an alternation of pathos and bathos, of low-grade comedy and
high-pitched rhetoric.

The most famous and most widely quoted example of the
latter is, of course, the troika passage:

> And art not thou, my Russia, soaring along even like a
> spirited, never-to-be-outdistanced troika? The road actually
> smokes under thee, the bridges thunder, everything falls
> back and is left behind thee! The witness of thy passing
> comes to a dead stop, dumbfounded by this God's wonder!
> Is it not a streak of lightning cast down from heaven? What
> signifies this onrush that inspires terror? And what unknown
> power is contained in these steeds whose like is not known in
> this world? Ah, these steeds, these steeds, what steeds they
> are! Are there whirlwinds perched upon your manes? Is
> there a sensitive ear, alert as the flame, in your every fibre?
> Ye have caught the familiar song coming to you from above
> and all as one, and all at the same instant, ye have strained
> your brazen chests and, almost without touching earth with
> your hoofs, ye have become all transformed into straight
> lines cleaving the air, and the troika tears along, all-inspired
> by God! . . . Whither art thou soaring away to, then, Russia?

Give me thy answer. But Russia gives none. With a wondrous ringing does the jingle bell trill; the air, rent to shreds,
thunders and turns to wind; all things on earth fly past and,
eyeing it askance all the other peoples and nations stand
aside and give it the right of way.[38]

"Beautiful as this final crescendo sounds," comments Nabokov, "from the stylistic point of view it is merely a conjuror's
patter enabling an object to disappear, the particular object
being Chichikov."[39] This structural observation is a welcome
antidote to the portentously ideological interpretations of the
thunderous finale of Part One, a lyrical paean rather than a
coherent credo. This is not to say, however, that the frenzied
flight of patriotic rhetoric was merely a musical accompaniment to Chichikov's abrupt disappearance. It was also a grandiloquent expression of Gogol's emotional nationalism, exacerbated, no doubt, by his mounting uneasiness over having
become a virtual expatriate.[40]

Yet what gave the troika passage so wide a cultural reso-
nance was the fact that Gogol's headlong eloquence happened
to articulate the growing preoccupation with the destiny and
essence of Russia which was to characterize Russian intellectual life in the 1840s. More importantly, it fell to Gogol's
imagery to embody and anticipate the themes that were to
reverberate through a near century of Russian cultural history,
the notions of Russia's "manifest destiny"—a glorious future

38. Ibid., p. 304.
39. *Nikolai Gogol,* p. 113.
40. The stridently nationalistic, not to say jingoistic, note struck in the finale
of Part One of *Dead Souls* was sounded also in the later version of "Taras Bulba"
(1840-41). If the earlier *Mirgorod* variant was a celebration of the Cossack
ethos, in the revised scheme nationalism is of the "Russian" rather than of the
Ukrainian variety. "Wait a while, the time is coming, the time is at hand when
you will know what the Orthodox Russian faith can do! Already the nations far
and near have an inkling that their ruler will rise up from Russia, and there will
be no power on earth that will not submit to him! . . . But there are no fires, no
tortures in the world, no force indeed that can break the Russian spirit!" (*Collected Tales and Plays,* p. 337).

vouchsafed by her boundless expanse—of her distinctive mission, of her turbulent, unfathomable essence.

Viewed within its context, the much-anthologized set-piece appears to give a resounding lie to the main body of Gogol's narrative. In this unexpected ending the subject of the novel is not merely transcended or displaced; it is emphatically denied. So glaring is the discontinuity between the bleak and trivial surfaces of Russian life as reflected or burlesqued by the novel and the awe-inspiring prophecy that an inordinately literal-minded reader might be provoked into a spurious query: "How will a Russia of petty crooks, grafters and half-morons ever astound the world? How will she manage to compel universal awe and admiration?"

A partial attempt at bridging the gap between the visible shabbiness and the yet-to-be-revealed greatness, is provided by another apostrophe to Russia, a guilt-ridden declaration of love for the distant, indeed temporarily forsaken motherland.

Russia, Russia, I behold thee—from my alien, beautiful far-off place do I behold thee. Everything about thee is poor, scattered, bleak; thou wilt not gladden, wilt not affright my eyes with arrogant wonders of nature, crowned by arrogant wonders of art, cities with many-windowed towering palaces that have become part of the crags they are perched on, picturesque trees and ivies that have become part of the houses, situated amid the roar and eternal spray of water-falls . . . All is exposed, desolate, and flat about thee; like specks, like dots are thy low-lying towns scattered imperceptibly over thy plains; there is nothing to entice, nothing to enchant the eye. But just what is the incomprehensible, mysterious power that draws one to thee? . . . What is there in it, in this song of thine? What is it about that song which calls one, and sobs, and clutches at one's very heart? What sounds are these that poignantly caress my soul and strive to win their way within it, and twine about my heart? Russia! What wouldst thou of me, then? What incomprehensible

bond is there between us? . . . What does that unencompass-
able expanse portend? Is it not here, within thee and of thee,
that there is to be born a boundless idea, when thou thyself
art without mete or end? . . . Ah, what a refulgent, wondrous horizon that the world knows naught of! Russia![41]

In the stark contrast it urges between the dinginess of the
writer's native land and the showy, spectacular beauty of his
captivating exile, in its anguished insistence on the "incomprehensible bond" between Russia and her far-flung bard, the
above passage is not only more revealing that the finale of Part
One, but ideologically more resonant as well. As the guilt-
ridden expatriate blames the glamorous seductress, Italy, for
his own susceptibility to her "arrogant" charms and goes out of
his way to give the abandoned motherland the benefit of every
doubt by turning its very weaknesses into potential virtues,
Gogol's imagery once again turns personal anguish into an
archetype. The notion of the bleakness and "underdevel-
opment" of rural Russia as a sign of grace, a testimony to her
moral superiority vis-à-vis the proud West, an outward sign of
Christian humility, was to become by the middle of the nineteenth century an important tenet of the Slavophile faith.
Fëdor Tjutchev, one of the finest Russian poets of the era,
whose political verse shows a distinct affinity for the Russian
brand of romantic nationalism, was to echo Gogol's sentiment:
"The proud foreigner's gaze will neither comprehend nor
discern what . . . shines through your [Russia's] humble
beauty."[42]
Once again the reverberations of Gogol's eloquence have led
us beyond its immediate framework. For within it the conflict
between Russia as actuality and Russia as dream remains un-
bridged, indeed unbridgeable. Even if physical shabbiness could
be parlayed into Christian virtue, the moral tawdriness of the
Chichikovs and the Sobakeviches—as the failure of Part Two

41. *Dead Souls,* pp. 270-71.
42. "Èti bednye selenija" (1855), *Lirika* (Moscow, Nauka, 1966), *1,* 161.

of *Dead Souls* was to show—would remain unredeemed. Nor should this surprise a close reader of Gogol. The yawning chasm between reality and vision had been a major theme ever since "Hanz Kuechelgarten." Within the Gogolian scheme of things the tangible, the given is nauseating and oppressive. Conversely, anything that is worthy of admiration belongs perforce to the realm of the mythical, the imagined or the fervently wished for. To speak, with Cizevsky, of romantic utopianism is almost to understate the matter. For all its apparent discontinuity with the present, a utopian image of the future is presumably an extrapolation, however bold and extravagant, from incipient realities, from dimly perceptible trends. Gogol's prophecy is a spectacular escape from his sense of the human predicament, a panicky flight out of this world, so that, to quote Poprishchin's desperate plea, "nothing is seen of it—nothing."[43]

The digressions, especially those of the lofty variety, are an integral part of the overall pattern of *Dead Souls,* a strategic dimension of its elusive genre. Gogol chose to label this, his only full-length novel, a "poem." He seems to have meant by it a "small-scale epic,"[44] something like Fielding's definition of the novel as a "comic epic poem in prose." Yet to at least one reader this subtitle suggests the unwieldy image of a mock-epic blown intermittently by the gales of what Vasilij Rozanov strikingly called "upward-bound and disembodied lyricism"[45] into the interstellar spaces of romantic myth-making. Thus, the tortuous movement of Gogol's "poem" reenacts on a larger scale than any of his previous works the fundamental split in his world view as it shuttles precariously between savage satire and eulogy, between close-range nausea and long-range euphoria.

43. *Nikolai Gogol,* facing p. 1.
44. In his notes for a textbook of literary theory Gogol mentions Ariosto and Cervantes as authors of "small-scale epics" which combined wide scope with a humorous or mocking tone (see *Sochinenija N. V. Gogolja* [Moscow and St. Petersburg, 1896], *6*, 414-15).
45. "Neskolko slov o Gogole," [A Few Words About Gogol], p. 177.

It is at least arguable that Gogol was hinting at some such duality in his much-quoted, and, to my mind, widely misrepresented, aside to the reader: "But for a long while yet am I destined by some wondrous power to go hand in hand with my strange heroes and to contemplate life rushing past in all its enormity, amid *laughter perceptible* to the world and through tears that are unperceived by and unknown to it!"[46] (my italics). The italicized part of the sentence, often reduced simply to "laughter through tears," has had an inglorious career in Gogol criticism. In line with the influential notion of Gogol as a champion of the underdog,[47] it was often interpreted as satire tempered by compassion or pity. Now this cliché, I submit, may have some applicability to a truly humanitarian and at times downright sentimental "humorist" such as Charles Dickens, but it is profoundly misleading with reference to Gogol. Compassion, sympathy, empathy, as distinguished from mere pity, presuppose the basic humanity of those who might evoke them and thus, some opportunity on the reader's part to identify. Yet this is precisely the opportunity which Gogol's reader is steadfastly denied. His satire demeans its targets by reducing them to psychic automatons dominated by an *idée fixe*, forever distorted by a physical or moral deformity, scarcely worthy of our tears.

Rozanov offers a significantly different interpretation of Gogol's "tears." One of the first Russian men of letters to call attention to the willfully misshapen and truncated nature of Gogol's moral universe, he argued that the writer's "unperceived tears" were not so much those of pity or compassion for the victims of his laughter but of anguish, if not guilt, over the limitations of one's own vision, over one's accursed inability to see and portray goodness: "It is the great pity for man thus portrayed, an artist's grief over the law of his creation, his cry over the remarkable picture which he cannot draw in any other way, an artist's sobbing over his own soul."[48]

46. *Dead Souls,* p. 152.
47. See below, Chapter 8, pp. 151-52.
48. "Neskolko," pp. 199, 201.

Rozanov's reading clearly has something to recommend it. I shall later have an opportunity to cite some of Gogol's confessions, bemoaning his inability to give emphasis to the positive. However, I am even more strongly drawn to Cizevsky's view that in *Dead Souls* "laughter" and "tears" have two entirely different destinations, that they are addressed respectively to two disparate realms of existence between which the novel is precariously poised. "Laughter" derides, castigates, debunks the spiritual vacuity, the unbearable triviality of this world. "Tears" are addressed to the beauty and magnificence of the never-never land, of a lyrically projected millenium. To put it differently, they are tears not of compassion shed over one's unfortunate brethren, but of transcendent rapture, of anticipatory bliss.[49] Cizevsky's observation strikes me as a plausible one; nearly every time the narrator's voice starts to quiver, the author or the persona seems to be moved to tears by his own words and daydreams rather than by any predicament of the thoroughly disreputable protagonists.

Whatever the precise destination of Gogol's tears, they remain, admittedly, the emotional undertow of the novel rather than its principal tenor. It is "laughter perceptible to the world" that dominates the scene. Perhaps it is time to inquire about the precise nature and target of this laughter and thus to revert to the problem of Gogol's later satire.

Are Belinskij's view of *Dead Souls* as primarily an exposure of the regime and Nabokov's flat denial of the novel's social relevance the only serious options open to us? I don't think so. Yet I may as well confess that I consider the latter emphasis somewhat more congenial. To a modern reader of Gogol, not encumbered by the message-mindedness of the nineteenth-century Russian critic, the sociopolitical interpretation can easily appear a piece of high-minded wishful thinking. For one thing, from what is known about Gogol's own views and

49. "Gogol's tears," says Cizevsky, "are shed for a world created beautiful by God, yet now corrupted and disfigured" ("Gogol: Artist and Thinker," *Annals of the Ukrainian Academy, 4* [1952], 276).

intentions, it is safer, though perhaps less satisfying, to see *The Inspector General* as an attack on bad officials rather than on Tsarist bureaucracy, and *Dead Souls* as an exposure of grasping squires who took unfair advantage of the loopholes in the system rather than a challenge to the system itself. More importantly and more broadly, as Cizevsky and some others have persuasively argued,[50] the basic tenor and the ultimate thrust of Gogol's satire, the core of his ideological concern such as it was, was not social but ethical and metaphysical. Not unlike the bulk of the greatest western satirists, Swift, Molière, and Pope, Gogol aimed his laughter at foibles or follies which cut across national boundaries, at dullness, grossness, and cupidity, rather than at any recognizable set of social conditions. Thus it is fair to assume that his reported astonishment at Pushkin's famous sigh, "Oh Lord, how sad is our Russia!," was not the self-protective, pious fraud many intelligentsia spokesmen assumed it to be. The great poet's alleged exclamation may have been, at least in part, beside the point. For *Dead Souls* is not primarily about decaying Russian squires and dead Russian serfs, but about the moral stupor, deadness, and tawdriness of it all. Heine's melancholy sigh: "Gott, wie gross ist dein Tiergarten!" (*"Lord, how large is your zoo!"*) would have been more apposite. To paraphrase Edgar Allan Poe, the horrors depicted or burlesqued in *Dead Souls* are not of Russia but of the soul—the soul of man, and more specifically, of Nikolaj Gogol.

Clearly what Cizevsky calls Gogol's "cosmic satire" and the introspective dimension of his laughter are inexplicably intertwined. If the protagonists of *Dead Souls* are the objectification or projection of the writer's private nightmares, the reverse is

---

50. In addition to Cizevsky, see Bicilli, "Problema cheloveka u Gogolja," *Godishnik na Sofijskij Universitet* (1948); Merezhkovskij, *Gogol: Tvorchestvo, zhizn' i religija,* V. V. Zenkovskij, *N. V. Gogol* (Paris, YMCA Press, 1961); Florovskij, *Puti russkogo bogoslovija;* Victor Erlich, "Gogol and Kafka: A note on Realism and Surrealism," *For Roman Jakobson* (The Hague, Mouton and Co., 1956).

also true. The deformities of Gogol's "zoo" are introjected; they become part of the author's self. For a writer so morbidly self-centered, so vulnerable to moral hypochondria, so plagued by the sense of his own unworthiness, the weaknesses and vices that he detected in himself were bound to appear as a major case in point, a salient symptom, a proof positive of man's corruptibility.

In Gogol's "poem," where the wealth of personal digressions offers ample scope for self-reference, laughter at the expense of the Chichikovs and the Sobakeviches periodically turns inward as it becomes soul-searching, if not breast-beating, in one's own behalf as well as that of the reader—*mon semblable, mon frère*. The query "Come now, isn't there a bit of Chichikov in me, too?"[51] echoes in a somewhat different key the mayor's memorable outburst: "What are you laughing at, you fools? you are laughing at yourselves!"[52] *De te fabula narratur* is Gogol's pervasive leitmotif.

Yet to say all this is not necessarily to contend with Nabokov that Gogol's masterpiece bears no discernible relation to the Russia of his day. If the venality and parochialism of the Russian small-town officials in *The Inspector General,* the sloth, the greed, the stupidity of the freakish squires in *Dead Souls* are not *the* point, these are graphic illustrations of the point, a telling mode of symbolization. The social institutions which were part of Gogol's immediate environment provided here the appropriate set of images, or to use T. S. Eliot's phrase, the "objective correlative" for an idiosyncratic moral vision of reality shuttling precariously between the personal and the universal, between private nightmares and cosmic demonology. Gogol had known at first hand, however briefly, the desiccating impact, the wastefulness and tedium of the St. Petersburg office routine. Moreover, as a subject of Nicholas I—timidly loyal and wary of subversive generalizations, but endowed with an uncannily keen eye for the inane and the

51. *Dead Souls*, p. 301.
52. *Collected Tales and Plays*, p. 673.

preposterous—he found in the world around him all too many striking instances of what, as a writer and a self-styled moralist, he endeavored to exemplify and castigate. To be sure, there is nothing uniquely Russian about waste, corruption, inefficiency, and double-talk. Yet it is at least arguable that some of these qualities, endemic in any vast bureaucratic and arbitrary system, tended to acquire a special dimension in Russia. In a culture where the gap between "State" and "Society" or, as a French political scientist would put it, between "*le pays légal*" and "*le pays réel*," between stated goals and actual perform- ance, is as glaring as it was in the Russia of Nicholas I, brazen manipulation of facts becomes a built-in feature of the System, shamming becomes institutionalized. After all, it was Tsarist Russia, though the Russia of Catherine the Great rather than that of Nicholas I, that is credited with having produced that archetypal instance of window dressing known as the "Potemkin villages"—hamlets frantically cleaned up on the eve of the Tsarina's visits to the region administered by her power- ful protegé, Grigorij Potemkin: (Whether or not these alleged last-minute attempts to conceal mismanagement and squalor were actually what they rumored to be—a number of histo- rians are inclined to doubt this—the story has been a persistent strand in Russian bureaucratic folklore.) Eyewitness testimony bearing on the Gogol era abounds in instances of quite ludi- crous and self-defeating bureaucratic procedures. In his remarkable memoir, *My Past and Thoughts*,[53] Alexander Herzen, a brilliant liberal writer and publicist, tells a character- istic story: It seems that having been banned from the capital for his political activities and placed under police surveillance in Novgorod, he was assigned as a clerk to the district court headquarters. Because of the illiteracy and laziness of the local officials, the subversive was increasingly entrusted with various responsible assignments including that of writing elaborate reports on his own behavior! All in all, it is difficult to escape

53. *Sobranie Sochinenij* (Moscow, 1956), 9, 79.

the conclusion that there was something intrinsically "grotesque" about the institutional patterns to which Gogol and his contemporaries were occasionally subjected.

It would be a gross simplification and a methodological fallacy to conclude that the texture of Gogol's writings is grotesque because such was the nature of the social practices which were the immediate foil for his satire. The drift of an artist's vision, especially if, like Gogol, he is a wacky poet of genius, is never simply or primarily a by-product of his social environment. It might be more meaningful to suggest that the thrust of Gogol's imagination which included special alertness to the trivial, the preposterous, and the automatic, while not conducive to a reliable or accurate portrayal of any realities, however freakish, enabled him to dramatize the grotesque, incongruous, absurd, "as if" elements of his society more compellingly, more vividly or hauntingly than a true realist ever could. In doing so, he proved conclusively, if proof indeed were needed, that "realism" has no monopoly on social or moral relevance.

What remains is to pin down the mode of relevance congruent with Gogol's art, to identify more specifically the principal target of his laughter. The point has been made before but it is worth restating: the bureaucratic, manorial imagery serves here as a dismally fitting local vehicle for Gogol's *idée fixe,* his persistent obsession with the demeaning impact of the base passions gnawing at the heart of man, the insidious prevalence of *poshlost'*.

It is high time that this absolutely indispensable Russian noun whose untranslatability is celebrated by Nabokov on seven gloating pages be injected into our discussion. For poshlost', a disreputable and slimy syndrome which, to simplify the matter, is compounded of such notions as shoddiness, vulgarity, grossness, self-satisfied mediocrity, has been with us for quite a while now—ever since "Two Ivans" and "The Nose," and most emphatically, since *The Inspector General*. It is singularly appropriate that this cluster of traits, which Pushkin

had allegedly recognized as the field of Gogol's special compe-
tence,[54] should have become the prime subject of his largest
work, and that this, the author's *bête noire*, should have been
embodied in the "scoundrel harnessed" for the unlikely role of
the "poem's" hero,[55] Pavel Ivanovich Chichikov.

Clearly, Chichikov, the driving force of the loose-jointed
agon, is here the chief focus of Gogol's erratic yet deadly
serious moral concern. The other denizens of the vividly differentiated gallery serve primarily as foils for Chichikov's sinister
and futile acquisitive frenzy, as well as a cumulative documen-
tation of the ineradicable and unredeemable moral stupor of
the world in which Chichikov operates. (In *Gogol's Craftsman-
ship*, Andrej Belyj aptly calls Chichikov's successive visits
with various landowners a "crescendo of deadness." Each new
landowner is more dead than the previous one. Pljushkin, the
last to be approached, is the deadest of them all, "the corpse's
corpse."[56]) The limelight throughout is on that canny schemer
whose existence ever since his childhood was dominated by a
craving for status, wealth, and comforts to the complete exclu-
sion of any moral scruple, any genuine human feeling.

Yet as Belyj pointed out, the most striking thing about
Chichikov is not a lack of morals but a lack of personality. A
Nozdrëv, a Pljushkin, a Sobakevich represents a grotesque
exaggeration, a reductio ad absurdum of a single character trait
or proclivity. The rotund, smoothly-shaven Chichikov is a

---

54. In his "Four Letters to Various Persons About *Dead Souls*" (*Polnoe
Sobranie Sochinenij, 8* [1952], 286-99), Gogol insists that only Pushkin was
able to sense his central emphasis. "He would always tell me that no other writer
has had the ability to portray so vividly the *poshlost'* of life, to sketch in so
forcefully the *poshlost'* of a 'poshlyj' man so that trifles which could easily escape
one should loom so large that no one would miss them" (p. 292). Pushkin's
alleged observation seems doubly apt. Not only does it pinpoint Gogol's obsession and characteristic *emploi*, but it also hints at his essential literary
strategy—that of magnifying trifles so that "no one could miss them."

55. "It's high time to give a rest to the poor man of virtue. . . . It's high time,
at last, to put an actual scoundrel in harness! And so let us harness a scoundrel"
(*Dead Souls*, p. 277).

56. *Masterstvo Gogolja*, p. 103.

bouncy vacuum, or as Robert Martin Adams puts it, "a peram-
bulating hollow"[57] propelled by a tawdry daydream, down
the "long, long" Russian road. Most readers will recall that in
the opening paragraph of the novel the hero is introduced in
entirely negative terms: "The gentleman seated in this carriage
was no Adonis, but he wasn't bad to look at, either; he was
neither too stout nor too thin; you couldn't say he was old, but
still he wasn't what you might call any too young either."[58]
(The utter spuriousness of this pseudo-description is pointed up
by the opaqueness of irrelevant detail featured on the first
pages of the novel, such as Chichikov's many-hued neckerchief
and, to be sure, the enormous breasts of a nymph represented
in an oil painting in the local inn.) On the face of it, the absence
of any distinctive traits, any rough edges urges the image which
Chichikov is only too eager to convey—one of *comme il faut*
respectability, moderation, devotion to the golden rule. Yet at a
more significant level, this array of vaporous negatives epitomizes an utter lack of human substance, in a word, a void.

Gogol's obsessive concern, *poshlost'*, stands unveiled in this,
his last major fictional statement, as nothingness. To quote
again Adams' wide-ranging exploration, "it is Nothing which
haunts the author's [Gogol's] vision, Nothing which inspires
his most agonizing vertigo."[59] It is the fear of the void, I would
add, that underlies Gogol's already-noted desperate urge to get
away from it all, so that "nothing be seen of it—nothing."[60]

Poshlost' as vacuity had already been dramatized in *The
Inspector General*. Compared to Chichikov's slimy, relentless
drive, Khlestakov's infantile exuberance seems almost appealing. What in the self-indulgent babbler was excruciatingly
funny becomes sinister, if not frightening in the calculating,
smug, self-promoting "acquirer." Nabokov's notion of Chichikov as "the ill-paid representative of the Devil, a traveling

57. *Nil: Episodes in the Literary Conquest of Void During the Nineteenth
Century* (New York, Oxford University Press, 1966), p. 56.

58. *Dead Souls,* p. 1.

59. *Nil,* p. 51.

60. See above, p. 96.

salesman from Hades"[61] is not entirely fanciful. For this unheroic hero is truly evil. Indeed, he is a chief agent of moral decay and corruption in *Dead Souls*. No ablutions, however strenuous, could ever obliterate his moral stench, which is uncomfortably externalized the smell exuded by his seedy servant Petrushka. It is an ultimate testimony to that domestication and trivialization of evil which had begun in *Mirgorod*.

As the sinister becomes commonplace, the commonplace is increasingly revealed as sinister. Once again on his uneasy journey, Gogol stumbles upon an important and influential notion: to use a recent phrase, "the banality of evil."[62] The Devil is a sneaky customer, boring from within or from below, rather than the dark yet commanding figure Milton's Satan or Byron's Lucifer calls up. Here was a new brand of literary demonology which was to encompass the unbearably repulsive Smerdjakov in *The Brothers Karamazov* and the loathsome Peredonov in Fëdor Sologub's *A Petty Demon*. The threat becomes more insidious for being internalized, more ubiquitous for becoming ordinary, but the underlying moral is still the same: There is no place to hide. The Devil, Gogol wrote to his friend, the Slavophile poet, Jazykov, in 1845, "seeks various means of sticking his nose in. If he cannot manage to do so when we are healthy, he will squeak in through the door of sickness."[63] His best opportunity, highlighted by poshlost' is man's susceptibility to "petty" passions, to low-grade temptations.

61. *Nikolai Gogol*, p. 73.

62. I am referring, of course, to the title of Hannah Arendt's controversial book, *Eichmann in Jerusalem: A Report On The Banality of Evil* (New York, Viking Press, 1964).

63. *Polnoe Sobranie Sochinenij, 12* (1952), 477.

8

The Pitfalls of Petty Passions

The notion of the Evil One's infinite resourcefulness and of man's infinite vulnerability, which was about to become Gogol's *idée fixe,* is deployed at length in a rather ponderous discursive postscript to a flashback featuring Chichikov's past misdeameanors. Having enunciated the principle that "acquisition is the root of all evil" the narrator proceeds to muse thus:

> Everything transforms itself quickly in man; before one has a chance to turn around there has already grown up within him a fearful cankerworm that has imperiously diverted all his life sap to itself. And more than once some passion—not merely some sweeping grand longing but a *mean, sneaky yen for something insignificant* [my italics] —has developed in a man born for great deeds, making him forget great and sacred obligations and see something great and sacred in insignificant gewgaws. As countless as the sands of the sea are the passions of man, and no one of them resembles another and all of them, the base and the splendidly beautiful, are in the beginning submissive to the will of man and only later on become fearful tyrants dominating him.[1]

The digression does not stop here, but goes on to suggest that the emergence of a grand passion is as unfathomable as that of a "sneaky yen" and that even "in this very Chichikov something may stir some day which will yet cast man into the dust

1. *Dead Souls,* p. 297.

before the wisdom of heaven."[2] I will discuss later this rather
unexpected vista which clearly points beyond the moral perspective of Part One. For the time being, the dangers bulk
much larger than the opportunities. The emphasis lies heavily
on the impulses unworthy of man's high vocation, as indicated
in a typically Gogolian enumeration, clearly reminiscent of the
parade of "sneaky yens" in "Nevsky Prospekt":

> Every man has some ambition of his own: the ambition of
> one may turn on wolfhounds; to another it seems that he is a
> great lover of music and amazingly sensitive to all the
> profound passages therein; a third may be a great hand at
> putting away a huge dinner; a fourth feels that he can play a
> better part in this world even though that part be but a
> fraction of the one assigned to him; a fifth fellow . . . sleeps
> and dreams of how he might promenade on a gala occasion
> with some aide-de-camp . . . a sixth may be gifted with a
> hand that feels a preternatural urge to bet big on an ace or
> deuce of diamonds, say, while the hand of a seventh simply
> itches to set things a-right wherever he may happen to be,
> to get under the skin of a station master or a stagecoach
> driver."[3]

A lowly ambition in lieu of a grand passion, a mundane
fixation rather than a meaningful emotional involvement, or to
put it differently, an overinvestment in trivia, such is the lot of
the typical Gogolian homunculus. This is also, as has been
recently argued, the principal theme of Gogol's most remarkable short narrative, begun in 1839-40 and completed almost
simultaneously with Part One of *Dead Souls,* "The Overcoat."
This view of the story, which was most fully articulated by
Cizevsky,[4] is a far cry from the traditional interpretation that

2. Ibid., p. 298.
3. Ibid., p. 22.
4. See especially his "O 'Shineli' Gogolja," *Sovremennye zapiski, 67* (Paris,
1938), 172-95.

prevailed through the nineteenth century and is now canonic in the Soviet Union. Through the good offices of Vissarion Belinskij and another immensely influential radical publicist-critic, Nikolaj Chernyshevskij,[5] "The Overcoat" came to be seen as a humanitarian plea for the little man, pushed around by the powers-that-be. It is a matter of record that the appearance of "The Overcoat" was followed by a spate of more or less mediocre sociohumanitarian tales.[6] Whether they were legitimate progeny of Gogol's masterpiece is something else again. I, for one, would be inclined to maintain that what mid-nineteenth-century Russian fiction was so eagerly and often bleakly emulating was not what Gogol had in fact created, but what had been read into his work by critics and by their followers who were more compassionate and more attuned to social issues and straightforward messages than the author of "The Overcoat" seems to have been. Once again, it appears, the reception of a literary work was shaped less by its essential tenor than by the urgency of the reader's emotional needs and ideological compulsions.

But let us return to the story itself. Its plot is far from intricate. A slow-witted, harassed copying clerk, Akakij

5. In an essay written in 1861, Chernyshevskij contrasted the refreshing tough-mindedness of the contemporary radical satirist Saltykov-Shchedrin with Gogol's alleged tenderness toward his underdog hero: "Does Gogol mention any defects of Akakij Akakievich's? No, Akakij Akakievich is always in the right. . . . His misfortunes are attributed to the heartlessness, vulgarity and coarseness of the people on whom his fate depended. . . . [Gogol must have felt that] to tell the whole truth about Akakij Akakievich would have been useless and heartless. One can say about him only those things that are likely to evoke sympathy." (Quoted in Vladimir Ermilov, *Genij Gogolja* [Moscow, Sovetskaja Rossija, 1959], p. 268.)

6. This is apparently what is at issue in the famous *bon mot* attributed to Dostoevsky: "We have all emerged from under Gogol's overcoat." It is far from certain that Dostoevsky, whose literary debut, *The Poor Folk*, was both an echo of "The Overcoat" and an implicit polemic against Gogol, ever uttered this phrase. The notion that he had done so was inferred from a passage in the influential book by Melchior de Vogüé, *Le Roman Russe* (1897), which credited with this dictum "a Russian very much involved in the literary history of the last forty years" (p. 96). Thus far, Dostoevsky scholars have not been able to locate the quote.

Akakievich Bashmachkin, ignored by his superiors, jostled about by his colleagues, acquires at the cost of considerable privations a new made-to-order overcoat. Shortly after this event, the high point of the clerk's bleak and uneventful existence, the coveted object which clearly outshines and outranks its owner is snatched from his shoulders by a husky robber. Shaken by this disaster out of his usual timidity, Akakij Akakievich bursts into the office of a self-important dignitary, dubbed by the narrator a "Person Of Consequence," and demands action, only to be sternly rebuked for not going through channels. Shattered by it all, Akakij Akakievich goes home and dies. Yet this is not the end of his ordeal. Suddenly a semicomic, semipathetic tale replete with "realistic" detail, turns into a ghost story. An Akakij Akakievich-like specter starts haunting the city. At one point he seems to confront the "Person Of Consequence" and brusquely to claim "his" overcoat—an experience which allegedly both frightens and chastens the overbearing official. I'm saying "seems," since we cannot be absolutely sure that this is what actually happens. So fluid is the boundary between reality and delusion in the murky world of this St. Petersburg tale, so dense the fog of absurd rumors which thrive on the metropolitan muddle, that the "ghostly clerk" might well be a figment of the overbearing bureaucrat's frightened imagination, a phantom emerging from the vapors of his bad conscience.

But this is merely the skeleton of the story rather than its actual essence.

"The real plot (as always with Gogol) lies in the style,"[7] in the twists and turns of the narrative tone, in the dazzling manipulation of the point of view, the intricate verbal play. As the Russian Formalist critic Boris Eikhenbaum brilliantly demonstrates in his path-breaking essay, "How Gogol's 'The Overcoat' was Made,"[8] the tale is a masterpiece of grotesque styliza-

---

7. Nabokov, *Nikolai Gogol*, p. 144.
8. "Kak sdelana 'Shinel' Gogolja," *Skvoz' literaturu, Voprosy poetiki, 4* Leningrad (1924), 171-95.

tion, a supreme example of Gogol's uncanny adeptness at the narrative technique known in Russian criticism as *skaz,* the mimicry of intonational, lexical, and phraseological mannerisms of a lowbrow narrator, thus achieving that worm's-eye-view of events which was so effectively featured in "Two Ivans." The stylizing, spoofing bent of the story is especially apparent in its first movement which enacts and parodies the pattern of a bumbling, chatty oral narration:

> In the department of . . . but I had better not mention which department, there is nothing in the world more touchy than a department, a regiment, a governmental office, and in fact any sort of official body. Nowadays every private individual considers all society insulted in his person. I have been told that very lately a complaint was lodged by a police inspector of which town I don't remember and that in this complaint he set forth clearly that the institutions of the State were in danger and that his sacred name was being taken in vain . . . and so to avoid any unpleasantness I had better call the department of which we are speaking, 'a certain department.'[9]

In the next paragraph, where we are introduced to the chief protagonist, the implications and uses of this narrative manner are further clarified: the chatty irrelevance imperceptibly shades off into incoherence and incongruity. Verbal mimicry becomes a matter of helpless stumbling into what Eikhenbaum aptly calls "articulatory gestures"—a quality, I may add, which is only dimly perceptible in the English translation. The passage which follows is not so much a description as a minutely articulated enactment, a verbal impersonation of the shabby and ludicrous appearance of "poor" Akakij Akakievich: "and so in a *certain department* there was a *certain clerk,* a clerk of whom it cannot be said that he was very remarkable; he was short, somewhat pockmarked with rather reddish hair and

9. *The Collected Tales and Plays of Nikolai Gogol,* pp. 562-63.

rather dim, bleary eyes.[10] The recurrence of "certain" and "rather" in the English version is but a faint echo of the original with its obsessive repetitions of "neskolko," of mockingly rhyming "-ish"-type adjectives ("neskolko riabov*at*, neskolko ryzhev*at*, neskolko dazhe na vid podslepov*at*"). This verbal clowning and grimacing is a good preparation for the hilariously implausible scene of the naming of the infant, capped by that strategic "sound gesture" which is the hero's "rather strange and contrived name Akakij Akakievich Bashmachkin." While the last name is clearly demeaning and thus expressive in the same way as are most names in *The Inspector General* and in Sheridan's plays—"bashmak" is Russian for shoe—the first name and patronymic, dominated by four k's, combines cacophony with ludicrously profane connotations ("kakat" in Russian baby talk means "defecate"). Characteristically, this gratuitous insult to the infant is construed by the narrator as a perfectly logical choice: "the circumstances were such that it was quite out of the question to give him any other name."[11] At the time of the christening, the hapless mother was confronted by a list of names so outlandish and grotesque-sounding (Mokkij, Khozdazat, Pavsikakhij, et al.) that naming the child after his father Akakij could indeed appear as a highly desirable option. This elaborate tomfoolery is scarcely an appropriate prelude to a heartrending tale about an indigent clerk. In fact, I would be inclined to agree with Vasilij Rozanov's[12] view of the opening sequence of "The Overcoat" as a bit of rather heartless fun which the author or the narrator is having at the hero's expense.

Nor does the immediate sequel to this "torrent of mockery"[13] enhance our regard for Akakij Akakievich. "He was always seen in the same place in the same position at the very same duty, precisely the same copying clerk, so they used to declare that he must have been born a copying clerk, uniform,

10. Ibid., p. 563.
11. Ibid.
12. See below, n. 20; p. 141-142.
13. Ibid, p. 144.

bald patch and all. No respect at all was shown him in the department."[14] A victim of soulless bureaucracy, of merciless exploitation? The matter is not as simple as that. For the most pathetic aspect of Akakij Akakievich's predicament is not his externally imposed poverty and lack of status, but his ability to derive satisfaction from meaningless and menial chores, his "zeal in service," more specifically, his delight in calligraphy. He was once given a chance to "do something more important than his ordinary copying": he was instructed to tamper with a report from another department by altering the headings and occasionally changing the first person into the third. Yet this proved too taxing for Akakii Akakievich. "He mopped his brow and said at last: No, I'd rather copy something.' "[15]

Clearly, Akakij Akakievich is a "little man" not only in terms of his "station" but also in those of his human potential and ambitions. The embarrassing smallness of his aspirations seems to be highlighted, indeed parodied, by the plot of the story, a short-lived infatuation with an overcoat.[16]

I use the word "infatuation" advisedly. Shortly after Akakij Akakievich reluctantly comes to terms with the indispensability of a new overcoat—his old threadbare garment is clearly beyond reprieve—he is visibly changed. The strenuous program of hardship upon which he embarks in order to save up the hitherto unthinkable sum of 150 roubles yields a new sense of purpose, a goal which, at long last, Akakij can call his own.

14. *Collected Tales and Plays,* 564.
15. Ibid., pp. 565-66.
16. Rozanov's view that Gogol demeans Akakij Akakievich's humanity rather than asserting it was supported by, among others, Makar Devushkin, the chief protagonist of Dostoevsky's first novel, which allegedly emerged "from under Gogol's overcoat." *Poor Folk* is a poignant story of a middle-aged indigent clerk's futile affection for a young girl whom he is unable to save from a dire fate. Devushkin is not an impressive, let alone an effective, man, but, as distinguished from Akakij Akakievich, he's in love with a girl, not a piece of garment. In one of his letters to Varvara, Devushkin takes time out to inveigh against "The Overcoat," which she had the bad judgment to send him, as a slur on the dignity of a petty clerk: "It is a malicious book, Varen'ka. The whole thing is simply implausible—it cannot happen that there should be such a civil servant." Dostoevsky, *Sobranie Sochinenij* (Moscow, Izdatelstvo khudozhestvennoj literatury, 1956), *1,* 147.

He even became quite accustomed to being hungry in the evening; on the other hand he had spiritual nourishment, for he carried ever in his thoughts the idea of the future overcoat. His whole existence had in a sense become fuller as though he had married, as though some other person were present with him, as though he were no longer alone but an agreeable companion had consented to walk the path of life hand in hand with him and that companion was none other than the new overcoat with its thick padding and its strong durable lining. He became as it were more alive, even more strong-willed like a man who had set before himself a definite goal. . . . At times there was a gleam in his eyes: indeed the most bold and audacious ideas rushed through his mind. Why not really . . . have marten on the collar?[17]

Perhaps the most striking thing about this passage, as Cizevsky has already pointed out,[18] is the incongruously erotic quality of its imagery. Phrases like "as though he had been married," and "an agreeable companion," lavished on a mere overcoat clearly suggest a displacement of the libido. The overcoat has transformed Akakij Akakievich's "poor, drab life." It has become the focus of an intense emotional involvement, in a word, a love object. (Conveniently, "shi-nel"—Russian for "overcoat"—is a feminine noun.) No wonder its loss acquires the dimension of an existential disaster, a trauma which first leads the bereaved clerk to forget himself in the dignitary's antechamber, to violate drastically the code which governed his existence and, when faced with a dressing down to peter out promptly. So firm is the hold of the "petty passion" that no respite is granted even after death. Akakij is doomed, or so it seems, to roam the streets of St. Petersburg in search of the "agreeable companion with its thick padding and its strong durable lining." After so much triviality, what transcendence?

Viewed in this light, the alleged exploits of the "ghostly

17. *Collected Tales and Plays,* pp. 574-75.
18. "O 'Shineli' Gogolja" p. 189.

clerk" appear as an additional posthumous proof of his human inadequacy rather than a belated vindication of his essential humanity, unless, to be sure, one works on the assumption that in Gogol's world to be adjudged human is to be found wanting. More broadly, the import of the entire story—if it can be said to have any paraphrasable import—would appear to be not the edifying dictum like "petty clerks are human too," but rather another existential sigh, "how embarrassingly petty are so many human pursuits, involvements, aspirations," the St. Petersburg civil servant version of Verlaine's "et la tristesse de tout cela!"

Whatever is known about the genesis of "The Overcoat" seems to sustain this interpretation. Apparently the plot was again suggested by a true anecdote. If one is to believe Gogol's engaging contemporary Pavel Annenkov,[19] sometime in 1834 Gogol listened attentively at a St. Petersburg party to a tale about an indigent clerk who loved to hunt, and who, at the cost of considerable hardship, bought himself a gun only to lose it on his first hunting trip. He was saved from an acute depression, if not suicide, by the generosity of his co-workers who made a collection and bought him a new gun. If this anecdote did indeed provide the nucleus for Gogol's greatest and most widely misinterpreted story, the transformation it underwent in the procees is far-reaching and significant. Gogol's narrative is both gloomier and more pathetic than its alleged model. The happy ending which featured the rescue of the chief protagonist, along with the heart warming theme of human solidarity, was eliminated. The hero's fixation became less "manly." More importantly, the motif of the hero's material hardship was overlaid with that of spiritual poverty. According to Rozanov,[20] the tendency to downgrade the petty clerk was even more apparent in the earlier version of "The Overcoat" which contained such condescending phrases as "essentially he [Aka-

19. "N. V. Gogol v Rime letom, 1841 G.," pp. 260-61.

20. "Kak proizoshel tip Akakija Akakievicha," *Legenda o velikom inkvizitore,* pp. 262-82. Gippius notes that the earlier variant of "The Overcoat," whose title, interestingly enough, was "A Tale About the Clerk Who Steals Overcoats," portrayed the chief protagonist as smug rather than pathetic.

kij Akakievich] was a rather good-natured sort of beast."

Is it then sheer myopia that accounts for the persistence through so many decades of the view of "The Overcoat" as a vindication of the underdog? Critics with an ax to grind have been known to clutch at straws. The fact is that Gogol, or rather his rambling, fickle, protean narrator, has provided such a clutchable straw in the form of the vastly overquoted "humanitarian passage," wedged in between the burlesque nomenclatural orgy occasioned by the naming of the infant and the tongue-in-cheek account of Akakij's dedication to calligraphy. After telling us that no respect was shown Akakij Akakievich in the department, that he was often a defenseless butt of clerkly wit, and that most of the time he behaved "as though there were no one there," the speaker perceptibly shifts gears:

It was only when the jokes became too unbearable, when they jolted his arm and prevented him from going on with his work, that he would say, "Leave me alone! Why do you insult me?" and there was something strangely poignant in the words and in the voice in which they were uttered. There was a note in it of something that aroused pity so that one young man, new to the office, who following the example of the rest had allowed himself to tease him suddenly stopped as though cut to the quick and from that time on everything was somehow changed and appeared in a different light to him. Some unseen force seemed to estrange him from his companions and long afterwards during moments of the greatest gaiety, the figure of the humble little clerk with a bald patch on his head appeared before him with his heart-rending words "Leave me alone! Why do you insult me?" and within these moving words he heard others; "I am your brother!" And the poor young man would hide his head in his hands and many times afterwards in his life he would shudder seeing how much inhumanity there is in man, how much savage brutality lies hidden under refined,

cultured politeness, and, my God! even in a man whom the
world accepts as a gentleman and a man of honor.[21]

To Boris Eikhenbaum this crescendo of emoting is
essentially a matter of grafting a sample of "declamatory style"
upon comic skaz for the sake of a contrapuntal tension. More
broadly, it is a significant instance of the alternation of two
contrasting styles—the elaborately comic narration and sentimental rhetoric—which, in the Formalist critic's view, shapes
the pattern of "The Overcoat." Yet readers questing for a
positive social message were only too eager to construe this
incongruously compassionate sequence as a clue to the story
and the phrase "I am your brother" as the burden of its
message. That in so doing they were vastly overrating the
relative weight of this set-piece and blithely ignoring the larger
context in which it appears was probably the inevitable cost of
their well-intentioned single-mindedness.

In all fairness, a critic intent on a humanitarian interpretation of "The Overcoat" can derive some further comfort from
its ghoulish ending. On the face of it, the avenging ghost
appears to inject into the proceedings the theme of poetic
justice, of a long delayed blow for the little man's injured
dignity. Indeed, a compassionate reader is bound to derive a
measure of emotional satisfaction from the clerk's belated
assertiveness and the well-deserved fright of the arrogant
"Person of Consequence." Yet the satisfaction is, or ought to
be, short-lived, for, as Nabokov properly reminded us, just
before the curtain goes down there occurs yet another abrupt
shift which has gone largely unnoticed.

After telling us that having struck his blow the "ghostly
clerk" quite ceased to appear, Gogol, or rather the chatty
narrator whose mask he wears, treats us to the following:

However, many active and vigilant persons refused to
be appeased and kept asserting that in a remote part of the

---

21. *Collected Tales and Plays*, p. 565.

city the ghostly clerk still showed himself. And indeed a
suburban policeman in Kolomna saw with his own eyes a
ghost from behind a house but being by nature something of
a weakling (so that once an ordinary full-grown young pig
which had rushed out of some private house knocked him
off his feet to the great merriment of a group of cab drivers
from whom he demanded and obtained as a penalty for this
derision ten coppers from each to buy himself snuff), he did
not dare to stop the ghost but just kept walking behind it in
the dark. The ghost suddenly turned, stopped and inquired:
"What d'you want, you?" and showed a fist of the size rarely
met with even among the living. "Nothing," answered the
sentinel and proceeded to go back at once. That ghost,
however, was a much taller one and he had a huge moustache. It was heading apparently towards Obukhov bridge
and presently disappeared completely into the darkness of
the night.[22]

The function of this oddly whimsical finale is not altogether
different from the end of "A Madman's Diary"—a spell-
breaking sentence which so wantonly undercuts the nearly
unbearable stridency of Poprishchin's plea. Once again the emotional perspective of the story is willfully, indeed frivolously,
dislodged. A torrent of irrelevant detail bursts upon what could
have been mistaken for—and is still widely assumed to be—a
heartrending tale of the insulted and the injured. "Together
with the mustachioed ghost the grotesque disappears in the
darkness, resolving itself into laughter."[23]

The sudden shift which occurs in the final passage seems to
be one of casting as well as of tone. Is the man who stole
Akakij's overcoat now stealing his posthumous thunder as the
poor clerk is about to come into his own? Surely, the apparition
at the Obukhov bridge looks more like the robber than like his
victim. As he displaces the man whom he wronged beyond
reprieve and with whom we were finally invited to identify, we

22. Quoted in Nabokov, *Nikolai Gogol,* pp. 147-48.
23. Eikhenbaum, "Kak sdelana 'Shinel' Gogolja," p. 195.

are cheated out of the opportunity to register a "normal" human response, which at long last seemed to be within our reach.

At least one articulate contemporary seems to have reacted, indeed perhaps overreacted to this emotionally subversive twist. In his unfinished essay on "F. Dostoevsky and The School of Sentimental Naturalism,"[24] Apollon Grigoriev admits to being "chilled" by "The Overcoat": "Fear, actual marrow-chilling fear grips one when one reads this icy, ruthless tale about a man created in the semblance and image of God whose only delight lay in writing letters on paper in a clear hand." Grigoriev's emphasis here is not on the ghoulish post-script but on the main body of the story, or, more specifically, on those passages which dramatize or point up the chillingly small stature of its chief protagonist. (Grigoriev anticipates here Rozanov and Cizevsky.) Yet one is permitted to wonder if some of the critic's discomfort might not have been due, in however subliminal a fashion, to the unsettling *Verfremdungseffekt* of the final passage.

Be that as it may, to this reader the ending of "The Overcoat" is the salient manisfestation, if not indeed a clinching proof, of the not-quite-human strain in Gogol's masterly tale. It would be a simplification or, if one will, a counter-simplification to reduce the tonality of Gogol's short master-piece to anything as tangible and clear-cut as "heartlessness." A stranger force, more elusive and more subtly disturbing, seems to be at work in the wanton shifts of the narrative tone, in the intricate game of teasing out the "appropriate" responses such as pity, empathy, compassion, only to undercut them all in a final guffaw. The audience, uneasily amused yet baffled, is left stranded in that emotional no-man's-land which may well be, as Kayser has suggested, the characteristic province of the gro-tesque imagination.

In his already-quoted essay, Boris Eikhenbaum calls the

24. See *N. V. Gogol, Materialy i issledovanija* (Moscow and Leningrad, Akademija Nauk SSSR, 1936), *2*, 252.

finale of "The Overcoat" a brilliant "apotheosis of the grotesque." The phrase is applicable, it seems to me, to the main
body of the narrative as well. Its last movement epitomizes
what, following Kayser, I have chosen to call the emotional
perspective of grotesque art, but the story *in toto,* Gogol's
greatest and most closely woven work of short fiction, can be
viewed as a most consistent and elaborate tribute to the literary
mode which, at the outset of this book, was assumed to be
his characteristic vehicle. Both in its intricate verbal texture
and its moral orientation, or rather disorientation, "The Overcoat" is dominated throughout by the central grotesque quality,
that of incongruity.

This principle is clearly operative in the chatty irrelevance of
the lowbrow oral improvisation which at times almost imperceptibly shades off into nonsense,[25] in the setting off of two
contrasting styles against each other, in the sudden, unmotivated shifts from the ludicrous to the poignant, from comic
"sound gestures" to emotive crescendos. The same tension
which shapes the language and the tone of "The Overcoat" is
seen at times to infiltrate and unsettle the intonational pattern,
the syntax of individual sentences and paragraphs. Thus an
extravagantly long, almost Faulknerian period full of parallel
constructions starting with "when" ("Even at those hours when
the grey Petersburg sky is completely overcast, when the clerks
are hastening to devote what is left of their time to pleasure,"
etc.) peters out anticlimatically into "in short when everyone
was eagerly seeking entertainment, Akakij Akakievich did not
indulge in any amusement."[26] The imbalance between the
cumulative bang of the antecedent subordinate clauses and the
uneventful whimper of the main clause epitomizes the strategy
already employed to good effect in *Dead Souls,* one of pitting

25. "From the very name [Bashmachkin] it is clear that it must have derived
from shoe [bashmak]. . . . Both his father and his grandfather and even his
brother-in-law and all the Bashmachkins without exception wore boots" (p.
563).
26. Ibid., p. 567.

elevated language against trivial subject matter. As Cizevsky
has conclusively shown,[27] the emphatic "even" (*dazhe*) keeps
haunting with glaring inappropriateness the most ordinary con-
texts, the most unspectacular propositions which do not call
either for awe or for surprise, e.g. "At that time when even
those in the higher grades have a pain in their brows and tears
in their eyes from the frost."[28] Cizevsky, whose remarkable
essay helpfully points beyond Eikhenbaum's brilliant awareness of verbal devices toward an inquiry into their moral
import, argues persuasively that the high incidence of these
misplaced "evens" in "The Overcoat" betrays what I would like
to call a worm's-eye view of reality, the narrator's or, by
extension, Akakij Akakievich's pathetic readiness to be
impressed or overawed by anything that carries the slightest
implication of status.

Cizevsky's observation strikes me as perceptive and possibly
central. For in "The Overcoat," as in any truly grotesque work
of literature, the dislocation of language serves to articulate
and project a freakish, distorted moral universe in which the
normal proportions are drastically reversed. As we have seen, it
is a world where the notion of putting a piece of marten on
one's fur coat can be an acme of boldness, where the most
striking thing about a man can be his hard toenail (Akakij's
tailor Petrovich), where calligraphy can be a source of delight
and an overcoat a love-object, where the dead deal blows
which the living do not dare to strike.

"He who sees the world as full of false grandeur," said the
German aesthetician Volkelt, "who observes everywhere vain
glitter and false pretensions and wants to unmask these false
values by laughter, will be inevitably drawn to grotesque distortion."[29] This, as we know by now, sounds like a relatively mild
description of the way Gogol felt about the world around him.

27. "O 'Shineli' Gogolja," pp. 173-74, 179-84.
28. *Collected Tales and Plays*, p. 568.
29. Quoted in A. Slonimskij, *Tekhnika komicheskogo u Gogolja* (Petrograd,
Academia, 1923), p. 26.

In the long run, this vision proved increasingly difficult to live with. The last years of Gogol's life were marked by a series of desperate attempts to escape or moderate his brilliantly rendered but essentially hopeless world view by granting more emphasis to the positive, by achieving, in his own words, a "reconciliation with reality." The effort was slated to end in a tragic failure.

9

In Quest of an Epiphany

In his vivid and sympathetic memoir, "N. V. Gogol in Rome, Summer 1841," Pavel Annenkov terms 1841 "the last year of his [Gogol's] fresh, vigorous and versatile youth."[1] Clearly, Gogol was then at the peak of his creative powers. His major literary effort, or what by then he saw as the first installment of his grand design, Part One of *Dead Souls* was being completed. He was putting the finishing touches on "The Overcoat" and rewriting two earlier narratives, "Taras Bulba" and "The Portrait." This is only part, though an important part, of the story. Gogol's so uncharacteristic serenity and vitality, noted by Annenkov, was due in no small measure to his love affair with Italy which, since 1837, had been the only element of stability in his increasingly unsettled, nomadic existence.

Judging by Gogol's voluminous correspondence with friends and by reliable eyewitness testimony, the period of 1837-42 was the happiest, indeed the only relatively happy, period in Gogol's anxiety-ridden life. At first, out of a vague sense of guilt about his motherland, Gogol seems to have made a conscious effort to resist the blandishments of what he called in *Dead Souls* a "far-off, beautiful" land. The strident, compensatory patriotism of the "Russia, I behold thee" apostrophe in *Dead Souls* is anticipated in an 1837 letter to Pogodin:

It's almost a year now that I live in a foreign land, look

1. "N. V. Gogol v Rime letom, 1841 g.", p. 247.

at the beautiful skies and a world rich in art . . . but not a single line will I devote to things foreign. An unbreakable chain ties me to our land . . . our humble, poor, unspectacular world, our bleak distances I prefer to the more clement skies gently shining down upon me!"[2]

Then, as if anticipating Pogodin's question, "If so, why don't you return?" Gogol falls back on his post-*Inspector General* jeremiads: "But to return to endure the haughty pride of people who puff themselves up before me? No, many thanks!"[3]

There was also, at the beginning, bad news from home. A report on Pushkin's death shocked Gogol into vocal, grandiloquent mourning: "All the joy in my life," he wrote to a mutual friend Pletnëv, "vanished with him. I undertook nothing without his advice. I did not write a single line without seeing his face before me."[4] In a letter to Pogodin he wailed;

My life, my highest bliss died with him. The bright moments of my life were moments of creation. When I created, I saw only Pushkin before me. Even my present work is his creation. I rejoiced at the thought as to how satisfied he would be, that was my highest reward. Now no reward is waiting for me. What will become of my work, what will become of my life?[5]

To suggest that Gogol here indulged his proclivity for the hyperbole is not to cast any reflection on the essential sincerity or momentary intensity of his grief. "I undertook nothing without his advice" need not be taken literally. By the same token, Gogol's insistence that his capacity for bliss was now irretrievably lost was an exaggeration which was soon to be

2. We might note in passing the striking similarity between this and the query in *Dead Souls*: "What incomprehensible bond is there between us?" (p. 270).

3. *Polnoe Sobranie Sochinenij* (Complete Works), *11* (1952), 92.

4. Ibid., p. 88.

5. Ibid., p. 91.

disproved. As "Rome and Italy took effect,"[6] the sense of bereavement mingled with bad conscience gave way to unabashed euphoria.

Gogol's letters of late 1837 and 1838 breathe a sense of liberation from an oppressive nightmare. "O Rome, Rome, Italy!" Gogol raves to his former Nezhin soulmate, Danilevskij, on February 2, 1838, "whose hand can tear me out of here? What skies, what days! In my soul there is heaven and Paradise . . . never was I so gay, so confident."[7] "One falls in love with Rome slowly, gradually," he writes in an earlier letter, "but then for your whole life."[8] "I was born here," he tells Zhukovskij.[9] His life hitherto, he insists, was a bad dream, a series of false starts:

> Russia, St. Petersburg, snow, the scoundrels, the office, the university, the theatre—that was all a dream . . . I am joyous, my soul is bright, I labor and rush my work to completion. Life! Life! Still more life! . . . Will you not look at Italy, will you not pay her the tribute that each worshiper of Beauty owes his Lady Fair![10]

The same note is sounded in April 1838 letter to his former pupil, Balabina: "Not my homeland, but the homeland of my soul did I find here."[11] Gone, at least for the moment is the theme of homelessness, the image of oneself as a hapless exile. "There is no better fate than dying in Rome: man is closer to God here by a whole mile."[12]

In a stimulating if somewhat arbitrary study, *Gogol: Work,*

6. Setchkarev, *Gogol: His Life and Works,* p. 52.

7. *Polnoe Sobranie Sochinenij, 11,* 121.

8. Ibid., p. 95.

9. Ibid., pp. 111-12.

10. Ibid., p. 141.

11. This freewheeling, cosmopolitan notion of one's primary loyalties, so blatantly incompatible with the sense of being chained to one's native land voiced only a year earlier to Pogodin, finds a close counterpart in the impassioned outburst of the love-struck Andrij Bulba: "Our country is what our soul seeks, what is most precious of all things to it. My country is you!" (p. 282).

12. *Polnoe Sobranie Sochinenij, 11,* 114.

Life, and Religion,"[13] Dmitrij Merezhkovskij, with his characteristic partiality for antinomies, discerns two strains in Gogol's
personality—the heathen and the Christian, the sensual and the
ascetic—and insists that in Gogol's love affair with Rome, his
pagan self reached its fullest expression. "The dead and magnificent Campagna," (Annenkov) the land of dead gods, was for
Gogol presumably the embodiment of flesh triumphant, of
"tangible substantiality."[14] In support of this thesis,
Merezhkovskij cites an interesting statement contained in a
letter to Gogol's Ukrainian ethnographer friend, Maksimovich,
in which he deplored what we might call today an excessive
sublimation: "We are terribly separated from our primordial
elements."[15] Other critics, less enamored of the pagan versus
Christian dichotomy, including the judicious Vasilij Gippius,
spoke—more relevantly, I believe—of Gogol's overwhelmingly
aesthetic response to Italy and saw the early phase of his love
for the Eternal City (1837-39) as the last fling of his "romantic
aestheticism" to be superseded shortly by the religio-ethical
didacticism that was to dominate the last decade of his life.[16]

While both views have some validity, a few qualifications
may be in order. It is a matter of record that Gogol responded
powerfully to the purely sensuous attractions of Italy—the
luxurious scenery, the blinding skies, the grandeur of Antiq-
uity, the dazzling richness of renaissance painting and sculp-
ture, the lushness of the Roman baroque, the intoxicating blend
of colors and smells that was Campagna—a far cry indeed from
the bleakness of the Moscow winter and the eerie mistiness of
St. Petersburg. One of the writer's most emphatic reactions to
the Italian countryside is a yelp of purely sensory, to be exact,
olfactory delight: "Would you believe me" he writes to Balabina, "that sometimes I am seized by a frienzied desire to
transform myself into one big nose . . . whose nostrils would be

13. *Gogol: Tvorchestvo, zhizn' i religija.*
14. Ibid., p. 120.
15. Ibid.
16. *Gogol;* see especially pp. 109-22.

as large as pails so that I could imbibe as much fragrance of spring as possible."[17] Not less patent was the effect of the "arrogant wonders of art" on Gogol's painterly side. Daily exposure to Raphael, Titian, and Michelangelo was a powerful boost for that rapturous cult of Beauty of which he speaks grandiloquently in his first essay, "The Woman" (1831), an extravagant eulogy of dazzlingly lovely Alcinoe, and which underlies the assertion in "The Portrait": "a great creation of art is higher than anything else on earth."[18] Gogol's visiting friends, be they the gentle Zhukovskij, the bumptious Pogodin, or the shrewd and vivacious confidante, Alexandra Smirnova, were amazed and pleased to find this generally morose and rather sluggish man transformed into a tireless sightseer, a knowledgeable and enthusiastic *cicerone* who, according to Smirnova, displayed an almost proprietary pride in Rome's churches, museums, and fountains.

I would suggest at this point that the "aestheti-cism"-"didacticism" dilemma should not be pressed too hard. For one thing, in speaking of Gogol, the term "aestheticism" ought to be used with care since romantic worship of art is not to be confused with aesthetic purism or with art-for-art's sake doctrine, clearly, a turn-of-the century phenomenon. For another, as already indicated, Gogol's attitude to art and to his own writing was never one of unselfconscious delight in what the Dutch historian, Huizinga, calls "sacred play." Indeed it is fair to say that there was no period in Gogol's life when he did not seek to justify or to legitimize art in general and his own writings in particular by invoking a transcendent moral pur-pose.[19] It is easy to agree with Nabokov that Gogol was much more compelling a stylist than he was a thinker. Yet it is one of the many incongruities in his contradiction-ridden career that he thought of himself as a rather imperfect and clumsy writer and saw the only justification of his literary endeavors in

17. *Polnoe Sobranie Sochinenij, 11,* 144.
18. *The Collected Tales and Plays of Nikolai Gogol,* p. 560.
19. A problem to be considered on p. 168.

whatever psychological insight or moral illumination they were likely to yield.[20] Even at the peak of his so-called aestheticism, he valued art as a source of spiritual uplift, or divine revelation rather than of an autonomous sensory gratification. This didactic strain, this urge to measure one's art by nonaesthetic criteria, was to become increasingly acute over the years, culminating after 1841 in a grim imperative that each work of art be justified by its tangible moral benefits, and worse still, consecrated by the purity of the writer's motives. It would be foolhardy to minimize this significant shift of emphasis and to underestimate its impact on Gogol's creativity. It would be equally erroneous, I believe, to play down its continuity with Gogol's earlier concerns. What is involved here, it seems to me, is not an essential shift from aesthetic to religio-ethical values but rather an unsettling of a precarious but temporarily viable balance between the lay and the sacred, a reconciliation of the artist with the moralist, which Gogol somehow managed to achieve at the peak of his career. For it is at least arguable that Gogol felt free to revel in the dazzling blend of nature and art, of the religious and the secular presented by Rome just because the "wonders of nature" served as a backdrop for a major center of Christendom and the "wonders of art" were so often replete with traditional Christian symbolism.

It is true that the Christian tradition embodied in Rome's churches and museums was not the one in which Gogol had been raised and to which, from his childhood, he owed formal allegiance. Yet this, to the considerable dismay of his Moscow friends, did not seem to matter to the quasiexpatriate. In fact, his often-expressed admiration for the Catholic ritual, and his contacts with persuasive and sophisticated Polish Jesuits who frequented the villa of the glamorous and brilliant Catholic

20. In a letter to Pletnëv, Gogol insists that he stumbled into a literary career "by chance" out of a desire to embody in writing "some of my observations on certain aspects of life, essential to my inner experience. . . . I still have not managed to master the primary, necessary tools of each writer—style and language. . . . Everything I have written is important only in the psychological sense" (*Zapiski o zhizni N. V. Gogolja, 2,* 148-49.

convert Princess Zinaida Volkonskaja, made some of his friends and relatives back home rather uneasy. One of them must have been Marja Ivanovna Gogol. In a letter dated December 22, 1837, Gogol assured her that there was no danger of his converting. There was no point, he argued, in becoming Catholic since the differences between Russian Orthodoxy and Catholicism were negligible.[21] The statement may strike one as odd or disingenuous. Was it a matter of Gogol's talking down to a gullible provincial, or of genuine theological naïveté? Or was it rather that Gogol's Christianity was fundamentally nondenominational, ecumenical? For whatever reason, it is quite apparent that Catholicism attracted Gogol not as a more meaningful dogma, but as a highly satisfying spectacle. In other words, the distinctive appeal of Catholicism, might well have been primarily aesthetic. But once again the fact that the framework and intent of the gorgeous pageant on which he was feasting his eyes was religious, more specifically Christian, was scarcely beside the point: "Only in Rome does one really pray; elsewhere one goes through the motions."[22]

In the little known and ostensibly unfinished story, "Rome," written in 1841 and published in 1842, the author's or, to be exact, the chief protagonist's aesthetic appreciation of the "magnificent Campagna" has a marked ideological underpinning. This predominantly descriptive fragment, weighed down, indeed stopped in its tracks, by the proliferation of massively sculpturesque imagery, features the rediscovery by a young Italian prince of the grandeur of Rome after a brief and unsatisfactory sojourn in Paris. His return provides an occasion for a eulogy of the Eternal City as a traditional way of life, a repository of enduring vaules as well as a thing of beauty, and for an invidious contrast between the meaningless hustle and bustle of the teeming Paris and the austere calm of Rome, a remarkable blend of the "powerful Middle Ages" with a genius

21. *Polnoe Sobranie Sochinenij, 11*, 118-19.
22. Ibid.

of "painter giants and with Pope's magnificent generosity,"[23] the unhurried dignity of the *populo romano,* uncorrupted by the "cold perfection" of the European Enlightenment. To the nostalgic aristocrat who seems to speak for Gogol throughout, the original sin of the obnoxious nineteenth century—so fatuously and stridently represented by Paris—is precisely the abandonment of that traditional faith which alone could hold together, and confer ultimate significance upon, the European civilization. "We carried the holy images out of the shrine and the shrine is a shrine no more; bats and evil spirits dwell in it."[24] Owing to its firm spiritual leadership, Rome had been spared the blight of secularization.

Rome clearly seemed an answer, in 1841, to one restless exile's prayer, for it could gratify simultaneously his secular and his spiritual needs, his craving for sensuous beauty and his increasingly exacting religiosity. This dual appeal of Italy is reflected in a letter to Danilevskij: "You ought to experience the artistic-monastic life in Italy."[25]

A felicitous balance between the "artistic" and the "monastic," which contributed appreciably, one assumes, to the serenity enjoyed by Gogol through much of his Roman period and to the creative affiatus of 1837-42, proved short-lived. Even in Gogol's middle period his romantic belief in the intrinsically ennobling power of great art which, as he was to say in "Rome," "lends nobility and marvelous beauty to the stirrings of the soul,"[26] was undermined by an insidious fear lest the ever-resourceful fiend use man's yearning for beauty for his own purposes.[27] In the early forties the fear escalates into a moral panic, becoming indeed an obsession. By 1842-43 Gogol is in the throes of a full-fledged "religious crisis."

23. "Rim", *Polnoe Sobranie Sochinenij, 3,* 234.
24. Ibid., p. 236.
25. *Polnoe Sobranie Sochinenij, 11,* 96.
26. "Rim," p. 236.
27. As already indicated, the plot of "The Portrait" is the most explicit and lurid exemplification of this danger (see Chapter 5, n. 13).

The nature and the onset of this travail is among the many controversial problems that beset the Gogol biographers. Predictably, Soviet scholarship has been of little help here. Not unlike that apocryphal psychoanalyst who is rumored to have said to his unappealing patient "I disapprove of your problem," the typical Soviet Gogolian reduces the syndrome to a deplorable mental aberration which allegedly set in during the last five or six years of Gogol's life, well after the completion of his major works. Gogol's "religious mania" is thus proclaimed a complete repudiation of his "progressive," ergo secular, literary achievement.[28] Biographers who have a special affinity for Gogol's spiritual quest naturally take the opposite view. The Russian theologian-philosopher, V. V. Zenkovskij,[29] who quite properly sees religious concern as a persistent theme in Gogol's life and work dates his "spiritual awakening" at 1836, that is, the very beginning of Gogol's expatriation. To Setchkarev, the turning point is the summer of 1840 in Vienna, where Gogol stopped after a brief visit in Russia on his way back to Italy.[30] I lean towards Setchkarev's timetable rather than Zenkovskij's, though the latter's view cannot be easily dismissed. A great deal hinges on what exactly is meant by "spiritual awakening." Zenkovskij is quite justified in viewing 1836 as a major landmark in Gogol's moral evolution. The escalating sense of excitement over the "wonderful creation" which was emerging within him, a nascent awe for his own yet to be revealed powers lent, as I have already suggested, a vaguely prophetic tinge to some of his utterances. The image of oneself as someone in need of a special dispensation, as a frail vessel of a higher truth to be cherished and handled with care, was very much in evidence in Gogol's letters in the late thirties. So was the concomitant impatience with the importune mundane demands made on his precious time: "I am dead to the topical," he writes pointedly to Pogodin when the latter solicits his contribution to

28. See especially Ermilov, *Genij Gogolja* and M. B. Khrapchenko, *Tvorchestvo Gogolja* (Moscow, Sovetskij pisatel, 1961).
29. *N. V. Gogol*, pp. 137 ff.
30. *Gogol: His Life and Works,* pp. 62-63.

a journal which he edits. "Like a silent monk, the poet lives in the world without being part of it, and his pure innocent soul communes only with God."[31]

Though the rhetoric of these protestations is religious, their import is not unambiguously so. The "silent monk" is a simile for a dedicated poet's monastic withdrawal—a prerequisite for creating enduring works of art. It was not until 1841-42 that religio-ethical considerations—the gnawing worry about his personal salvation becomes the pivot of Gogol's inner life.

What did happen in Vienna? The question is not easily answered. Ever since his departure from Russia Gogol's physical frailty and/or his hypochondria had been a pervasive theme in his correspondence and in eyewitness testimony. Some of his potentially finest hours in Rome were marred by insistent complaints about intestinal troubles, "my dastardly stomach," which, as one of Gogol's companions remarked, must have been taxed beyond endurance by the exile's unrestrained enthusiasm for spaghetti. Such symptoms as "nervous stomach" and "arrested digestion" must have recurred in a particularly acute and threatening form in the summer of 1840 during Gogol's ill-fated trip from Moscow to Vienna and Trieste to Rome. They may well have been complicated by what seems in retrospect an onset of depression, an aftermath, perhaps, of the frustrations and strains of a highly unsatisfactory homecoming. A rather striking account of what a psychiatrist would call an instance of altered consciousness found in an 1842 letter to Balabina may be relevant here: "My illness is expressed now in terrible fits such as I have never had before . . . I felt that turbulence which turns every state of mind into a giant, every insignificantly pleasant feeling into a joy so intense as to be unbearable and every pang into . . . a heavy, agonizing sadness."[32] In view of Gogol's proclivity for the hyperbole, this "terrible" intensification of any and all feelings seems an uncannily symbolic symptom.

31. *Polnoe Sobranie Sochinenij, 11* (1952), 77, 78.
32. Ibid., *12* (1952), 36.

Whatever the precise nature and the actual seriousness of the illness that overtook Gogol in Vienna, at some point he seems to have thought himself on the verge of death. An overpowering sense of moral urgency triggered by this prospect may well have contributed to what Setchkarev terms Gogol's "mystic-religious frame of mind."[33]

On second thought, Setchkarev's phrasing strikes me as less tenable than his chronology. The term "mystic" is somewhat misleading. As I will try to show later, Gogol's religiosity was socioutilitarian rather than mystical. What he was after was not so much an immediacy of religious experience as salvation earned through adopting a Christian code of conduct, a proven ability to do God's bidding on earth. Gogol himself was aware of his unmystical bent. Desiring to clarify a recent "misunderstanding" caused by his unsuccessful attempt at unburdening himself to his Moscow friends, he wrote, "Let me tell you that my nature is not mystical at all. Misunderstandings occurred because I started talking [about my inner experience] prematurely."[34]

A salient feature of Gogol's new stance is incessant, at times almost obsessive, introspection verging on moral hypochondria, and the concomitant shift of emphasis from his writing to the fussing and fretting over his "soul." There was some dialectical irony in this situation. The mounting urge to legitimize his art in the eyes of God and man had exacerbated the question of the artist's spiritual worthiness and impelled a program of self-improvement that would make him worthy of his calling. As a result, the writer's preoccupation with "moral housekeeping" relegated his work to the background, even while the "monastic" strain, enhanced by soul-searching, reactivated lingering doubts about the legitimacy of the creative act, the original beneficiary of the elaborate spiritual exercise.

Yet if for the artist the enterprise proved costly and self-defeating, its immediate effects upon the man were not always

33. *Gogol: His Life and Works,* p. 63.
34. *Polnoe Sobranie Sochinenij, 12,* 301.

negative, it seems. In June 1842, Gogol wrote to Zhukovskij: "Every day my soul grows more luminous . . . my journeys and withdrawals from the world have not been in vain . . . I have become much better than the man imprinted in the sacred memory of my friends."[35] This, of course, could have been a delusion. Yet the reaction of Sergej Aksakov, one of Gogol's more perceptive friends, was not altogether different. In his memoir, he claims to have noted a personality change in Gogol during his second visit to Russia in 1841-42: "He had become emaciated, pale, quiet; submissiveness to God's will was felt in every word of his; his gluttony, former mischievousness, his slyness were no more."[36]

Gogol's deliberate, quite self-conscious attempts at Christian humility on occasion verged nearly on masochistic self-abasement. One of the obsessive leitmotifs in his correspondence during the early forties is a craving for "reproaches"—for harsh, unsparing criticism, if not abuse. He encourages his friends in Russia to be relentlessly frank in telling him about his shortcomings as man and a writer, as well as in bringing to his attention the adverse opinions of others. "Reproaches are salutary," he writes to his mother, on April 6th, 1844. "I would give much for being able to hear how I am abused [at home]."[37] The often-repeated requests for the fullest possible reports on the public response to *Dead Souls*, with particular emphasis on hostile criticism, pointed to a characteristic and complex syndrome. It reflected at once the neopenitent's desire for punishment, his characteristic insistence on self-castigation as a necessary prerequisite for purity, the desire to eavesdrop on anything that was said or whispered about him, however painful and injurious, as if he were afraid of being knifed in absentia, and finally, a mounting concern over losing contact with the country which he'd left behind and to which he was not too eager to return.

35. Ibid., p. 69.
36. *Istorija moego znakomstva s Gogolem*, p. 54.
37. *Polnoe Sobranie Sochinenij, 12*, 281.

The need for self-abasement coexisted, in thoroughly Gogolian fashion, with moral presumptuousness which bordered on
delusions of grandeur. In fact, it may be argued that Gogol's
strenuously moralistic inwardness gave his congenital egotism a
new lease on life. The sense of the transcendent importance of
his spiritual travail lends an overbearing quality to many of his
letters, makes him still more demanding and manipulative
vis-à-vis his long-suffering correspondents. In behalf of the
heights that he was yet to scale, Gogol now demands from
everyone a long-term moral credit, total trust and occasionally
considerable sacrifices. Thus, he does not hesitate to ask his
three Moscow friends, Aksakov, Shevyrëv, and Pogodin, to
assume for several years, at considerable discomfort and financial risk, full responsibility for his worldly affairs since he
simply cannot be bothered with mundane details. ("I shall now
request from you a sacrifice. You must make it for me.")[38]
Thus, he sets himself high-handedly as a spiritual teacher and
guide to his correspondents, volunteers pedantic and unsolicited advice not only to his easygoing and generally admiring
Nezhin friend, Danilevskij, but also to men older and more
mature than himself. (The gentle Aksakov lost his temper
when, after being urged by Gogol to read and ponder Thomas
a Kempis' *Imitation of Christ,* he received detailed instructions
as to how he should read it so as to get the maximum spiritual
benefit from it.) "From now on my word is clad in a higher
power. Anything can disappoint or . . . betray you, but my
word alone will never betray you! . . . All I can tell you now
is—have faith in my words! I do not dare myself not to believe
in my words!"[39]

Some of this spiritual imperiousness is heard in several
digressions in Part One of *Dead Souls,* notably those which, in
both tone and substance, point beyond the moral void of the
Sobakeviches and Manilovs toward another realm and another

38. Ibid., p. 145.
39. Ibid., *11,* 343 and 347.

universe of discourse. "And still far away is that time when with a gushing force of a different origin the formidable blizzard of inspiration will rise from an austere and blazing brow and in an abashed trepidation humans will harken to the sublime thunder of a different speech."[40] So eager was Gogol's anticipation of that "different speech," in the process of composing Part One, that in his mind his nearly completed masterpiece was dwarfed by the shadowy and yet to be carried out grand design. On March 17, 1842, he places the job he has just completed in a larger perspective: "I cannot think about anything else now but this continuing work of mine. It is significant and great—and it is not to be judged by that portion of it which is now going to see the light of day. [It is] nothing more than a gateway to that palace which now rises within me"[41]

The overall design of the amply conceived "palace" cannot be reconstructed with any degree of certainty from the extant fragments of Part Two of *Dead Souls*. The outward history of the unfinished and twice destroyed sequel to Part One is both bizarre and murky. After nearly three years of more or less steady plugging away at Part Two, Gogol was thoroughly disheartened by the results of his labor. In a characteristic fit of exasperation he burned the bulk of the manuscript. After an interval of about three years, dominated in part by his ill-starred journalistic venture,[42] he resumed his work on Part Two and continued it through various ups and downs until the beginning of 1852, that is, nearly up to his death. Through much of this period he was tight-lipped about his work, reluctant to show it to others and often impatient to the point of rudeness when confronted by overly insistent inquiries about the progress of the novel and its approximate timetable. Yet he

40. Quoted in Nabokov, *Nikolai Gogol,* pp. 106-07. Nabokov's rendition of this grandiloquent passage is more effective than the one contained in B. G. Guerney's otherwise rather adept translation from which I have drawn most of my *Dead Souls* quotations.

41. *Polnoe Sobranie Sochinenij, 12,* 46.

42. See below, Chapter 10, pp. 184-99.

did give his intimates a few glimpses of the work in progress. In 1849 and 1850 he read several chapters to Alexandra Smir- nova, Sergej Aksakov, and Stepan Shevyrëv. On the whole, their reactions were favorable. It is interesting to note that Aksakov, who had become apprehensive lest Gogol's moral hypochondria undermine his creative powers, was somewhat reassured by the readings. Yet this did not prevent the second and final auto-da-fé. As I will recount at greater length in the next chapter, on the eve of his death Gogol threw into the fire a bundle of papers which contained most of the then extant version of Part Two of *Dead Souls*.

All that survived these two destructive fits was the first four chapters and fragments of the concluding portion—remnants too limited to permit more than tentative assumptions about their relative status and chronology.[43]

Amid so much uncertainty, however, two propositions can be safely ventured. Whether or not Gogol envisioned the total edifice as a *sui generis Divine Comedy* moving from the petty hell of Part One through the purgatorial zone of Part Two to the heavenly bliss of the ending, it was clearly his intention to redress the moral balance and to effect a "reconciliation with reality" by demonstrating that vice could be redeemed and *poshlost'* transcended. Secondly, measured against the negativ- istic but stunning achievement of Part One, and more relevantly still, the euphoric advance billing, the fruits of Gogol's post-1842 labors were bound to appear to him profoundly disheartening.

Speaking in absolute terms, Part Two of *Dead Souls* may not have been the total failure it seemed. Yet it does appear to have been an oddly unsatisfying compromise between the old and the new Gogol. Characteristically, the one indubitable if minor

43. Even at this late juncture, Gogol scholars still fail to agree as to whether the sections available to us represent the first (1842-45) or the second (1848-51) version. Even if one accepts the latter hypothesis—as, following Gippius' lead, I am inclined to do—there is no indication that we are dealing with a draft which Gogol was prepared to view as final.

triumph is the exuberant vignette of the gargantuan glutton Petukh, clearly a throwback to the comic-grotesque vein of Part One. By comparison, the opening section of the truncated purgatory is rather pallid. The scenes that feature the encounter between the still unredeemed Chichikov and the potentially worthwhile but lethargic young landowner, Tentetnikov, lack the Goya-or Daumier-like vividness of the earlier visits. Yet they are of considerable interest as a portent of the incipient shift from physiology to psychology,[44] from a brilliantly utilized fixation on dazzlingly graphic surface detail to modulated character studies. I may add that Tentetnikov proved a nascent literary archetype. The theme of good intentions gone to seed, of naïve idealism frustrated by recalcitrant realities and degenerating into inertia, barely sketched in by Gogol, was to blossom some fifteen years later, under the pen of Ivan Goncharov, into one of the most massive symbols of lethargy in Russian or any other literature, Ilja Il'ich Oblomov.

Both the budding psychological finesse of the Tentetnikov sequence and the comic vitality of the Petukh episode are conspiciously absent from those sections of the manuscript that deal with the positive characters—the wealthy yet virtuous squire who bears an implausible name of Kostanzhoglo, a paragon of such Puritan virtues as thrift, efficiency, and drive, as well firmness and kindness in dealing with the peasants entrusted to him, and the fabulously rich government contractor who, to Chichikov's considerable surprise, came by his millions honestly. In fact, one message clearly emerging from these encounters is the homey tenet that honesty is the best policy. In the world of Gogol's newly found positive characters, the Kostanzhoglos and the Murazovs, virtue is not exactly its own reward, but it pays off handsomely, a fact which is not lost on the dazed Chichikov. His profound belief in the operational connection between crookedness and financial success is undermined, if not altogether shattered. Though greatly impressed

44. Gippius, *Gogol,* pp. 167, 209-10.

by Kostanzhoglo's wealth and by his self-righteous homilies, Chichikov relapses into his old ways. He comes into some money and is just about to realize a long-cherished dream and purchase a spectacular frock coat—again a fixation on a garment!—when he is exposed and thrown into jail. The vehemence of his despair, moves the already mentioned Murazov, an influential and pious merchant, to intercede in Chichikov's behalf with a crusading bureaucrat, referred to in the rough draft of the last chapter as a "Prince," who is determined to stamp out corruption and has decided to make an example of Chichikov. What apparently motivates Murazov here is not just pity for the desperate wretch. He is under the impression that "something new is stirring within Chichikov,"[45] that the seasoned malefactor is about to turn a new leaf. This long-term credit is extended to Chichikov mainly on the rather tenuous assumption that he is a richly endowed man gone astray. With efficiency and enterprise raised to the status of central values, the very acquisitiveness which in Part One was proclaimed the root of all evil becomes an essentially constructive force unless it is deflected from its legitimate goal and degenerates into immoral blindness when, in Murazov's words, "one is unable to think of one's own poor soul."[46]

Since the manuscript breaks off shortly after Chichikov's release, in the midst of the Prince's vigorous and somewhat implausible sermon to the assembled local officialdom, it is not quite clear whether Murazov's hopes were meant to be borne out. Just as Murazov decides to plead for mercy on behalf of Chichikov's half-awakened new soul, the affair takes a new turn. Due to the not altogether selfless effort of some "friendly" officers of justice, Chichikov is released. This welcome news, which may well be construed as a pragmatic vindication of Chichikov's traditional *modus operandi,* seems to inhibit his incipient moral growth. Do we have to conclude that he is not

45. *Dead Souls,* tr. David Magarshack (Baltimore, Maryland, Penguin Books, 1961), p. 371. (This translation, unlike Guerney's, contains Part Two.)
46. Ibid., p. 369.

yet ready? A last reference to our hero in the truncated manuscript contains an intimation that a change of heart is in the offing: "This was not the old Chichikov. It was a sort of ruin of the old Chichikov. The inner state of his mind could be compared to a building that has been pulled down in order to erect a new one in its place, and a new one has not yet been begun, because the final plan has not yet arrived from the architect and the workers are left in the state of bewilderment."[47]

"Bewilderment," the absence of a "final plan," phrases such as these seem eminently applicable to the frame of mind of the anguished architect of the strange and suspended edifice. The frequent absence in the second section of the "poem" of that sureness of touch which marked Part One might possibly be a symptom of an acute emotional perplexity, of a confused groping towards a definite blueprint and a clear-cut moral stance. This confusion is especially apparent in the scenes dominated by the ideal landowner, Kostanzhoglo. There is some connection, I believe, between the latter's ponderous lifelessness and the blurred image of his would-be disciple and admiring guest—our old acquaintance, Pavel Ivanovich Chichikov. Surely, there is something morally incongruous about a situation in which a still-unredeemed swindler can genuinely seek to emulate someone the reader is enjoined to admire. "He [Kostanzhoglo] was the first man in the whole of Russia for whom he [Chichikov] felt a personal respect. Until then he had respected people either for their high rank or for their great wealth. He had never respected a man simply because of his intelligence."[48] This, I submit, is hardly a major change of heart, especially if, as is the case here, intelligence is manifested mainly in making money. Conversely, the new positive hero, presumably a shrewd judge of men, is disconcertingly eager to view a practiced manipulator who hangs on his words as a

47. Ibid., p. 380.
48. Ibid., p. 333.

personable and sound man of affairs. " 'Our visitor is not a
stupid man,' thought Kostanzhoglo. 'He's measured in his words
and is no scribbler.' "[49] As Andrej Belyj and Dmitrij
Merezhkovskij have noted, a strange reversal of roles seems to
have occurred here. Instead of raising Chichikov to the level of
his own ideals, Gogol seems to have been affected by the
tawdry pragmatism of his creation. (To Gogol's famous rhetorical question, "Whither art thou soaring away to then,
Russia?," Belyj offers the sardonic answer, "From Pljushkin to
Kostanzhoglo."[50])

To say this is to suggest that Gogol's positive message turned
out to be, putting it mildly, anti-climactic. The mountain has
labored and brought forth a mouse. The virtuous acquirer, the
self-satisfied paragon of managerial efficiency—is this what all
the fretting and fussing was about, what all this talk about
spiritual renaissance and yet unheard-of deeds portended? The
discrepancy between the anticipatory rhetoric and the pedestrian ethos of a Kostanzhoglo or a Murazov is so glaring as to
be, to use the key term once more, nearly grotesque.

What strikes one about Gogol's utopia in Part Two of *Dead
Souls* is not that it is conservative or retrograde, but that it is so
timidly pedestrian—the last thing an utopia can afford to be. It
is at least arguable that such qualities as efficiency, thrift, hard
work, good accounting, etc.—though highly uninspiring when
exercised within a morally unacceptable and antiquated system—are intrinsically more worthwhile than an embattled
Russian liberal was likely to allow. The fact remains that for
several years of spiritual travail to yield a Kostanzhoglo was
testimonium paupertatis—a dismal failure of moral imagination. Was it also, as is widely asserted, a failure of nerve, a
craven surrender to the powers-that-be? Russian radical critics
had no doubts on this score. Their argument ran roughly as

49. Ibid., p. 329.
50. *Masterstvo Gogolja*, p. 106.

follows: Gogol was producing major works as long as he was boldly critical of the society and of the oppressive tsarist regime. When he recoiled from his relentlessly bleak vision and embarked upon an uncritical idealization of the *status quo,* upon prettifying ugly realities, he committed himself to an untruth and thus hamstrung, and finally betrayed, his genius.

This account of Gogol's dilemma simplifies a complex problem. (So many factors were at work in Gogol's post-1842 creative stalemate that the partial failure of Part Two seems almost "overdetermined.") For one thing, the critical view I have just expounded hinges on an overly political interpretation of Gogol's literary achievement. My own contention, as already indicated, is that Gogol's exuberant debunking of the "given" was a matter of an existential nausea rather than of social protest. By the same token, his last-minute attempt to be fair to reality, at least overtly, had more to do with giving the "slandered" human community an opportunity to redeem itself than with justifying any particular social system or institutional arrangement. For another thing, while Gogol was admittedly eager to effect a "reconciliation with reality," or as he put it in his letter to Zhukovskij,[51] "Sing a hymn to heavenly Beauty," this thrust toward apotheosis seems to have coexisted precariously with efforts at a more "realistic" treatment of actuality. Many of Gogol's references to Part Two of *Dead Souls* suggested that, he saw his new endeavor primarily as one of eschewing the distorted, "trivializing," lopsided view of Russia and of mankind, and of arriving at a more balanced portrayal of a differentiated human community than he was capable of offering thus far. In a letter to Konstantin Markov, he said:

> I did not have in mind a hero of virtues. On the contrary, practically all the protagonists could be called heroes of defects. The point is, though, that the new characters are more *important* than the earlier ones, and that the

51. *Polnoe Sobranie Sochinenij, 14* (1952), 269.

author's intent is to reach more deeply into the higher meaning of life we have trivialized, to present the Russian from more than one angle.[52]

Whether one diagnoses Gogol's new project mainly as the idealization of the actual or as its more modulated portrayal, it is fair to conclude that the trouble with the sequel to Part One of *Dead Souls* lay not so much in Gogol's surrendering his creative integrity as in his saddling himself with a task that, in retrospect, appears virtually intractable—both because it was intrinsically difficult and because it was thoroughly at variance with the natural bent of Gogol's genius.

Aldous Huxley has made a spirited case for the proposition that a credible portrayal of a truly good man is one of the most difficult assignments that ever confronted a writer. Few literary artists have proven equal to the task. Dostoevsky, whose moral imagination was immeasurably richer than Gogol's, did not fully succeed in this endeavor, and certainly not for want of trying. But Gogol was singularly unsuited for the job of portraying goodness within a broadly conceived panorama of Russian society. His notion of public good, as I have already suggested, was held back by his parochial timidity, his conformist reverence for the established authority. Unable to think imaginatively beyond the status quo, he was virtually impelled to retreat into an idealization of the familiar—the thoroughly uninspiring world of an allegedly transformed manor. Thus, his utopia was bound to shrink to the size of a conservative idyll. More broadly, however, and more essentially, Gogol's attempt to feature virtue alongside vice seems to have been frustrated by the inherent lopsidedness of his moral vision. It was noted by both friend and foe that his imaginative grip was much firmer on evil than on good. The Devil was always an immediate presence to him, God an ever-receding goal of an arduous spiritual journey.

52. Ibid., p. 152.

Few imaginative writers have managed to be morally reassuring or edifying without sounding smug. Yet the dilemma
faced by the satirist of the grotesque who suddenly decides to
switch his emphasis to the positive is an especially tricky one. It
is difficult enough to render credible a moral transformation, a
basic personality change in a man, be he Hugo's Jean Valjean,
Dickens' Scrooge, or Dostoevsky's Raskolnikov. How much
more difficult it is to make us suspend disbelief in the spiritual
regeneration of a homunculus! The tragic irony of Gogol's
situation in the forties lay in that he proceeded to vindicate
mankind, which he had allegedly slandered or "trivialized," by
seeking to redeem one of its most trivial and despicable speci-
mens, Pavel Ivanovich Chichikov. Whether the new show such
as Gogol envisioned it could have been a success under any
circumstances is altogether doubtful. Saddled with the old cast,
it was clearly doomed to failure. By setting out to redeem the
obviously unredeemable, by using a suavely sinister scoundrel
as a test of Everyman's potential for moral regeneration, Gogol
hopelessly stacked the cards against his intrinsically precarious
enterprise.

Chichikov's grotesque unsuitability for the role of the chief
protagonist in an emerging morality play was only part of the
difficulty. The further perhaps more significant trouble was
that the dynamic view of human character, bound up with the
very notion of personality change, called for a kind of imagination and a literary mode that was thouroughly alien to Gogol.
More broadly, as Gippius has shrewdly pointed out, the root
cause of Gogol's creative impasse in his post-1841 period
seems literary rather than purely ethical or ideological. In
attempting to articulate a modulated and fluid view of man, a
view which allowed for change, development, and growth, in
reaching toward a differentiated picture of a society, in featuring gray along with black and white, Gogol was forcing himself
into a style and a manner that went against his grain. Gippius is
quite justified, I believe, in defining this mode as an approach
to psychological realism.

Significantly enough, it is precisely in Gogol's last and largely unsuccessful fictional endeavor that one finds for the first time a reaching toward such realistic qualities, techniques, and criteria as extended psychological analysis, which includes an inquiry into character development and motive, an analytical rather than lyrical or brilliantly impressionistic descriptive style, [53] a balanced and reliably accurate portrayal of social realities.

This latter concern is more apparent in what, as evidenced by his correspondence, Gogol was trying to do than in what he succeeded in doing. In his letters to friends back home Gogol fusses about social *realia,* about the comprehensiveness and accuracy of his treatment of Russian life, more than he ever did before. He urges his corespondents to collect data on the mores of various classes of Russian society, to supply what he calls rather inaccurately the "moral statistics" of present-day Russia. "These fleeting sketches are as essential for me," he writes to Danilevskij on December 24, 1844, "as studies are essential for a painter who works on a large canvas."[54] "[Your] letters should contain nearly a diary of thoughts, feelings, and sensations . . . ," he tells Alexandra Smirnova, "so that I will be able to hear *life itself*. Without it, I'm lost and cannot do a thing."[55] About two years later he addresses to the same intimate, now a governor's wife, an urgent plea for minute observation of the Russian provincial mores, for vignettes under such headings as

53. A remarkable example of the latter is the famous set piece in Part One of *Dead Souls*—the description of Pljushkin's garden—characterized by a singularly keen awareness of "the moving pattern of light and shade on the ground under trees or the tricks played by sunlight with leaves" (Nabokov, p. 87). The only extended descriptive passage in Part Two of *Dead Souls*—one dealing with Tentetnikov's estate (Magarshack, pp. 261-62), eschews both the rhapsodic emoting of the earlier nature passages and the postrealistic use of color and shade, noted admiringly by Andrej Belyj and Nabokov. The "new" descriptive style, though not averse to such epithets as "gigantic" and "magnificent," combines close attention to sensory detail with an apparent attempt to reproduce with some accuracy the actual layout of the scene described.

54. *Polnoe Sobranie Sochinenij, 8* (1952), 202.

55. Ibid., *12, 412*.

a "town lioness," "a misunderstood woman," etc.[56] Obsessive emphasis now is on facts, all the facts, and nothing but the facts. Raw data, as we might put it today, seems to matter more, being real and down-to-earth and clearly there, than intellectual preconceptions, general ideas, floating around among the intelligentsia. In the same letter Gogol warns his socialite friend: "Do not discuss this [my work] with my Moscow friends. They are intelligent people but they talk too much and . . . beat around the bush."[57]

To be sure, this new craving for facts was exacerbated by the predicament of the near-expatriate. In a sense, Gogol was trying to have his cake and eat it, too. For a variety of reasons he was not ready to return to Russia and subject himself once more, as he saw it, to malicious abuse and misrepresentation on the part of his countrymen. At the same time he was becoming increasingly fretful over losing direct contact with the setting of his evolving epic, and sought desperately to do the job of the novelist by proxy. Gogol's harping on the importance of being able to smell and hear life itself was not an altogether novel theme. Whether in the form of an overheard anecdote or a reported piece of social observation, he always needed to eavesdrop on actuality, not as a controlling factor or ultimate focus, but as an essential irritant for his keen, indeed hypertrophied sense of the false and the ludicrous. What was relatively new was his apparent concern not just with the slimy minutiae, but with the inner rhythms, the essential stirrings, the manifold moral forces at work within Russian society as reflected in discernible patterns of behavior. Needless to say, neither part of the job could be done by remote control. To the extent that rubbing shoulders with Russian realities was essential to the writer's emerging sense of the society's moral drift, it could not be supplanted by mediated fact gathering, by cannibalizing the research potential of already hard-pressed correspondents. By the same token, no amount of reported social observation could bridge the gap between the inherent

56. Ibid., *13* (1952), 225-26.
57. Ibid., p. 224.

exigencies of realistic fiction—comprehensiveness, differentia-
tion, tri-dimensionality—and the natural proclivity of Gogol's
grotesque vision for an extravagant distortion of the actual. It
is almost as if, during this intensely difficult stage of his career,
Gogol was driven by a literary death wish. In trying to eschew
and redeem the pattern of his earlier work, he was reaching
toward two incompatible and, at least for Gogol, equally
unpromising genres—a realistic novel of manners and a morality play. Even without his religio-didactic design, he probably
would have failed in his attempt to create what E. M. Forster
has called "round" characters within a reliably rendered social
setting. As it is, he seems to have been defeated not only by his
artistic temperament, but also by the blight of didacticism,
thoroughly inimical to incipient psychological realism. Ironically, with the partial exception of the Tentetnikov episode,
the result was a new brand of "flatness" or twodimen-
sionality—not the brilliantly illuminated starkness of a masterful cartoon, but the pallid flatness, the moral schematism
of a tedious morality play. For Gogol the moralist the shift from
Pijushkin to Kostanzhoglo was hardly an epiphany; for the
writer it was a major setback.

Hence, one assumes the gnawing sense of failure that lay
behind the 1845 auto-da-fé. But, though profoundly discour-
aged, Gogol was not prepared to abandon his effort. To give up
altogether a project which, in his own words, was to unravel at
long last the riddle of his existence, and bestow, in retrospect,
transcendent significance upon his earlier, ostensibly trivial and
frivolous, literary endeavors, would have been tantamount to a
spiritual suicide. It was somewhat easier to conclude that he
had reached a stalemate, that he had been groping in the dark,
or simply that he was not yet ready. The obsessive introspection which had characterized Gogol's frame of mind since
1841 made this a plausible inference. For several years he had
been telling his well-wishers, eager for news about Part Two
of *Dead Souls*, that he would not be rushed, for he was
engrossed in things that matter most—his spiritual reeducation,

his moral retooling—that he could not be expected to utter the new word before cleansing his soul of the impurities that had fastened upon it. Confronted with an impasse, he now proceeded to take time out of his fictional ordeal in order to devote himself fully to "moral housekeeping," the strenuous, time-consuming task of beating his own, and other people's, breasts. He needed a moratorium, but he could ill afford a withdrawal. The friends and countrymen he left behind were waiting, or so he felt, for a reassuring message, a word of guidance, an indication of the direction his work was about to take. Thus far he had failed to find an adequate fictional vehicle for the vision toward which he was straining. Perhaps what was called for was a shift to a discursive mode, an explicit statement of his emerging beliefs, a statement that would share his spiritual concerns, hitherto conveyed only to his personal friends, with a larger audience—the literate Russian public. By 1846, Gogol was in the grip of the notion of gathering some of his more significant letters to friends, properly edited and amplified, as well as some of his yet unwritten think pieces, into a small volume which "in our troubled times" might be of considerable use. Thus originated that strange and ill-starred book, *Selected Passages from Correspondence with Friends* (1847).

10

The Ordeal

As Gogol's actual correspondence in 1846-47 amply demonstrates, he seized upon the idea of an epistolary tract with an almost feverish eagerness. For a while extravagant expectations associated with the sequel to Part One of *Dead Souls* were deflected to this half-didactic, half-confessional venture. Gogol's hopes were high; his belief in the importance, the urgency of the task he set himself were all too apparent.

The first intimation of the plan is found in a letter to the Slavophile poet, Jazykov, dated April 22, 1846: "As for my letters, do not destroy them. As I reread all that I have been writing lately to various people, especially those who needed and requested from me spiritual guidance, I see that [these letters] could be turned into a helpful book."[1] Two weeks later, Gogol reiterates his plea: "Hang onto my letters, especially the recent ones . . . I have not abandoned my intention to publish selected passages from my letters; therefore I think I shall be conveying to you more and more often thoughts that should be given wider circulation."[2]

By July 30, 1846 Gogol's enthusiasm was unbridled. He wrote to Pletnëv, whose help was absolutely essential to the success of the new enterprise, "Put everything else aside and busy yourself with the publication of the book *Selected Passages from Correspondence with Friends*. This book is needed, badly needed . . . . everything will become clear and misun-

1. *Polnoe Sobranie Sochinenij* (Complete Works), *13* (1952), 53.
2. Ibid., p. 62.

derstandings will be promptly dispelled."[3] In October of the same year, Gogol told Shevyrëv: "This is my first sensible book. With God's help, it will do many of us a lot of good. What comes straight from one's soul is bound to benefit many a soul."[4] On the eve of the publication of *Selected Passages*, November 19, 1846, Gogol was serene and hopeful: "My soul looks ahead brightly. Everything will be as God has willed it; thus everything will be beautiful."[5]

Less than a year later, in the painful aftermath of the debacle, Gogol was to argue rather lamely that his "first sensible book" was a mere trial balloon, a testing ground for his major literary endeavor, that all he had wanted to do was to clarify his new ideas by verbalizing them and to gauge the readiness of the Russian public for the message yet to be embodied in Part Two of *Dead Souls* by its reaction to his tract. Presumably, he was prepared, even eager, for "rebukes." Presumably, the very shrillness and presumptuousness of his spiritual testimony were strategems designed "to stir up and provoke a number of intelligent people" into talking about things that mattered.[6] This post-factum construction strikes me as a strained attempt to rationalize the defeat away; it does not square with the available evidence. The statements just cited clearly indicate that *Selected Passages* was Gogol's first explicit bid for spiritual leadership. It is a matter of record that the bid backfired with a vengeance.

Once again Gogol's attempt to teach directly ended in dismal failure. Once again he thoroughly, indeed grotesquely, misjudged his audience. He reached for acclaim and gratitude only to be confronted with a nearly unanimous repudiation. "Everybody is against me!" was a paranoid overstatement in 1836; in 1847 it would have been almost literally true. The

3. Ibid., pp. 91-92.
4. Ibid., p. 106.
5. Ibid., p. 144.
6. Ibid., p. 251.

Westernizers and the Slavophiles, the radicals and the conservatives were as one in decrying with varying degrees of intensity
Gogol's epistolary treatise as presumptuous, sanctimonious,
and obscurantist. Gogol was not exaggerating this time when,
in a much-quoted March 6, 1847 letter to Zhukovskij, he
described the reception of *Selected Passages* as "the most
resounding slap in my face."[7] (Interestingly enough, one of the
letters in *Selected Passages,* a homily addressed to a "shortsighted friend," ends in the following sentence: "Oh how we
sometimes need a slap in our face, delivered in everybody's full
view!"[8])

The most virulent attacks came from Gogol's erstwhile radical admirers who had seen in him not only a writer of genius
but also and primarily a forthright challenger of the hateful
status quo. They were understandably shocked and dismayed
by the ultraconservative tenor of Gogol's preaching, by his
unabashed nostalgia for the old-fashioned, paternalistic ways,
his uncritical eulogy of the Russian Orthodox Church, and
more broadly, his boundless trust in Russia's traditional institutions and the beneficence of her rulers. Vissarion Belinskij gave
voice to this sense of shock in his famous "Salzbrunn letter" to
Gogol which was soon to become the fighting manifesto of
budding Russian radicalism. (When Dostoevsky was sentenced
to hard labor in Siberia, one of the charges against him was the
distribution of this explosive document.) Writing in a rage both
eloquent and blinding, Belinskij branded his former idol as a
"preacher of the knout, apostle of ignorance, defender of
obscurantism and darkest oppression," an opportunist and
sycophant who betrayed his initial ideals in order to curry favor
with the powers-that-be.[9] This brutal charge was compounded
by what, to Gogol, was perhaps a more wounding accusation,
that of invoking Christ's name in vain: "The Church was
always asked to support the knout, but what does Christ have

7. Ibid., p. 243.
8. "Vybrannye mesta iz perepiski s druz'jami," ibid., p. 348.
9. Quoted in Veresaev, *Gogol v zhizni,* p. 364.

to do with it all? He was the first to announce to mankind the gospel of liberty, equality and fraternity . . . [10] No, it is not the truth of Christ's teachings, but a morbid fear of death and damnation that pervades your book."[11] For a man of Gogol's persuasion this was a more telling blow as it was a more penetrating observation.

Characteristically, it is not the politics of *Selected Passages,* but the integrity of its stridently "Christian" message that is at issue between Gogol and many of his critics, including such thoughtful conservatives as Sergej Aksakov. The latter may well have been dismayed and embarrassed by the blatantly conformist statement of a position for which, as a Romantic traditionalist, he had some affinity. Yet his chief objection was to what he had diagnosed even before the appearance of *Selected Passages* as a mixture of spiritual arrogance with moral exhibitionism. In a letter to Gogol he decried the presumptuousness of "setting up in the full view of entire Russia a philanthropic society of your own,"[12] a pointed reference to an extraordinary document that opens the volume, in which Gogol urges his countrymen not to erect a statue of him after his death and enjoins all journals and agencies to publicize his will. In January 1847, Aksakov wrote to his son, Ivan, apparently the only member of the Aksakov family who was not repelled by *Selected Passages*: "The whole book is permeated by flattery and a terrible pride under the guise of humility."[13] The implicit charge of sycophancy and insincerity, which for a while Aksakov shared with Belinskij, was withdrawn a week later: "I am thoroughly convinced by now of the author's complete sincerity. . . . He is at the crossroads, but his book is exceedingly harmful."[14] In his last letter to Ivan bearing on the painful and, to him, clearly important subject, he reverts to the theme of Gogol's presumptuousness, accusing him, in fact, of a Christian

10. Ibid.
11. Ibid., p. 367.
12. Aksakov, *Istorija moego znakomstva s Gogolem,* 163.
13. Ibid., p. 167.
14. Ibid., pp. 167-68.

heresy. "In my opinion, it is a terrible mistake to drag God into all our affairs." The fundamental weakness of Gogol's post-1842 project is astutely diagnosed: "The notion that in order to portray holiness one has to become a saint is preposterous."[15]

Only a handful of friends, such as Alexandra Smirnova, and more or less like-minded men of letters, found *Selected Passages* worthy of praise, or at least of respect and serious consideration. Pletnëv, who, to Aksakov's dismay, was instrumental in the publication of the book, was virtually alone in striking an enthusiastic note. He hailed the book as "a great deed," and congratulated Gogol on the "wonderful world which he revealed in his new book".[16] The poet-critic, Vjazemskij and a gifted if erratic essayist, Apollon Grigoriev, went out of their way to be sympathetic and fair.[17] Interestingly enough, Pëtr Chaadaev, a highly unorthodox thinker, who, over fifteen years earlier, had scandalized official Russia by his relentless critique of Russia's past and his eloquent gloom about her future, was much more charitable than most of Gogol's closest friends. He found Vjazemskij's rather favorable review "the most honest statement about this book,"[18] and observed rather shrewdly, in a letter to Vjazemskij: "He (Gogol) is too gauche to be a Jesuit. Nevertheless, he is still the same man of genius he was before; even in his present, rather morbid, state of mind, he towers above all his detractors."[19]

Compared to his paranoid overreaction to the controversy over "The Inspector General," Gogol's response to the nearly unanimous ostracism shows a rather unexpected resilience and restraint. Or is it that the ordeal catered to his incipient moral masochism, played into his proclaimed need for public chastisement? Be that as it may, he did not break down, nor did he

15. Ibid., p. 168.

16. *N. V. Gogol, Materialy i issledovanija 1,* 175.

17. "Gogol i ego perepiska s druz'jami" (1847), *Sobranie sochinenij* (Moscow, 1915-16); for Vjazemskij's comment see P. N. Barsukov, *Zhizn' i trudy M. P. Pogodina* (St. Petersburg, 1894), *8,* 558.

18. Barsukov, p. 587.

19. Ibid., p. 579.

spend too much time in wallowing in defensive self-pity. At times when the pain was too acute to conceal or explain away, he would share his anguish with those who were still willing to listen: "Don't you know," he wailed to Shevyrëv on March 4, 1847, "that even people close to me now call me a hypocrite, a Tartuffe, a two-faced man? Do you think this is easy to take?" "It is possible to quarrel with one's avowed enemies, but let God protect us from that terrible war with one's friends!" "Believe me, my friend, it is hard to find oneself in this whirlwind of misunderstandings!"[20] But most of the time he tried to cope with the nearly unbearable situation, now through feigned naïvete verging on denial ("How did it happen that everybody in Russia got mad at me? . . . I can't understand it at all!"[21]), now through a rather transparent deviousness ("I expected it all. I just wanted to try out some ideas on the Russian public."), now through self-criticism no less genuine for being extravagantly harsh. Clearly some of the "rebukes," especially those of Aksakov, had rubbed off on the defendant: he pleaded guilty of inexcusable lack of restraint: "The devil, who poisons with self-assurance every one of us, blew up to monstrous dimensions some of the passages [in my book]. . . . As I recall how immoderate and brash were so many of my statements, I burn with shame. . . . I carried on like a regular Khlestakov."[22]

Though deeply troubled and contrite, Gogol was not prepared to repudiate the substance of his book, to disavow his basic beliefs or the integrity of his motives. Yes, he erred grievously, but his was a tactical, not a fundamental error, a matter of wrong timing (he was not yet ready, he was still a disciple, he had a great deal to learn), of wrong phrasing (he could not find the right words), of a wrong tone, and finally, a wrong genre. This latter emphasis is especially worth noting, for it was the reverse of the process which brought *Selected Passages* into being. Two years earlier a creative stalemate

20. *Polnoe Sobranie Sochinenij, 13,* 238, 347, and 348.
21. Ibid., p. 326—his first letter to Belinskij, written about June 20, 1847.
22. Ibid., p. 374, 264, and 243.

impelled the detour into explicit preaching. Now the staggering
failure of the discursive strategy sent the writer back reeling to
his natural tack, that of a creative writer. In a much-quoted
letter to Zhukovskij, Gogol avers: "It is not my business to
teach by means of sermons. My task is to speak in terms of
living images, not by reasoning."[23] Narrative fiction he recognized ruefully, was a mode more appropriate to his gifts than
explicit moralizing. One could not agree more.

Was *Selected Passages*, the cause of all this uproar and
breast-beating, as loathsome a book as so many of Gogol's
contemporaries found it? The question is not easily answered,
for the reactions I have just reported were as "unfair" as they
were understandable, and, within their historical context, to
some extent legitimate. One can hardly expect fairness from
such a long-suffering victim of Gogol's avowed presumptuousness as Sergej Aksakov, less still from an *engagé* radical
critic locked in a life-and-death battle with the oppressive
Tsarist establishment. Today, a hundred and twenty years after
the appearance of the "strangest book ever written in Russia,"
we can at least attempt a relatively balanced view of this
disturbing and largely dismal, but not altogether worthless
volume—a strange mixture of personal confessions and
entreaties, of homespun theology, moral philosophy, and literary criticism.

It is not easy to glean from the numerous attacks on the
political obscurantism of *Selected Passages* the fact that a large
portion of this miscellany is devoted to literary topics such as
the distinctive tenor of Russian poetry, the mission of the lyric
poet, or the genesis and the true significance of *Dead Souls*.
The wide-ranging epistolary essays, as well as the retrospective
interpretations of the author's own work, are admittedly quite a
conglomeration. Gogol's extravagant eulogy of Zhukovskij's
translation of *The Odyssey*, an exercise in hortatory rather than
analytical criticism, is weighed down by the author's obtrusive
and archaistic bias in favor of the grand, "patriarchal way of

23. Ibid., *14* (1952), 36.

life" allegedly immortalized by Homer, and vitiated by the
utopian assumption that the translation of a great epic, no
matter how successful, can have a discernible effect upon the
mores of Russian society. The disquisition on the "lyricism of
our poets" is also often turgid and pompous. On the other
hand, the longest piece of literary criticism in *Selected Passages*, by far the most extensive "letter" in the volume, dealing
with "the essence and distinctive character of Russian poetry,"
is at its best a brilliant performance. For all its high-pitched
rhetoric, it is much more than another inspirational talk about
Russian literature. This bird's-eye view of Russian poetry from
its beginnings up to the 1840s, replete with keen insights and
felicitous formulations,[24] helps one understand why, shortly
before his death, Pushkin, then editor of the short-lived literary
journal, *The Contemporary*, urged Gogol to undertake a history of Russian criticism.[25]

By the same token, it would not quite do to dismiss some of
the salient statements which Gogol makes here about the
nature of Russian literature or his own writings as misleading
rationalizations (as Nabokov would have it), or sanctimonious,
self-protective *obiter dicta* designed to explain away the explosive potential of his own works. When, in his already cited
survey, after paying an eloquent and modulated tribute to
Pushkin's towering achievement, Gogol argued that in the

---

24. The shift from Derzhavin's grand manner to the mincing urbanity of the
Alexandrian era, "neat, proper, polished" (*Polnoe Sobranie Sochinenij, 8*
[1952], 375), is conveyed in a vivid phrase: "The chords of Derzhavin's church
organ subsided; having left the church, our poetry suddenly found itself at a
glittering ball" (p. 375). A little later, in celebrating Pushkin's "infinite variety"
and receptivity to various cultural stimuli, Gogol anticipates Dostoevsky's
famous speech in which he hailed the master as a truly Russian poet and, therefore, a great European: "How accurate is his response, how keen his ear! We feel
the smell, the color of the land, the era, the people. He is a Spaniard in Spain,
a Greek in Greece, a free mountaineer in the Caucasus; . . . let him peer into a
peasant's hut—he is a Russian from head to toe; all aspects of our nature are
reflected in him, often summed up in one word, in one aptly chosen adjective" (p.
384).

25. *Pushkin-Kritik,* p. 408.

1840s it was too late simply to echo Pushkin, or more broadly to serve art without grasping its higher purpose, he was giving voice to what had been for years his profound conviction and his abiding need. When toward the end of his post mortem on *Dead Souls*, he averred, "I was not born in order to start a new era in literature; my job is a simpler one . . . it has to do with the *soul and with the basic business of how to live*," (my italics),[26] he was articulating once again what had been his *idée maîtresse* since 1840-41. And when in describing the imaginings that ushered in Part One of *Dead Souls*, and which, one suspects, kept undercutting his later attempts at reconciliation with reality, he wrote: "Anyone who could have seen the monsters that were emerging from my pen . . . would have shuddered,"[27] the master of the grotesque was offering what I would take to be an accurate description of the way in which he often felt about his brilliantly freakish, distorted creations.

The principal reason this spotty but not insignificant body of criticism has been so widely slighted or ignored, was, one assumes, the vehement preoccupation of so many readers with the epistles that were construed as the ideological core of Gogol's tract, e.g. "The Russian Landowner," "To The Governor's Wife," "To One Holding An Important Position," "A few Words About Our Church And Clergy." Much of this still makes dismal reading. As one wades through fulsome tributes to the Russian Orthodox clergy "which alone is in a position to solve all our problems" and "work an unheard-of miracle in full view of all Europe,"[28] the misplaced enthusiasms for the "administration of our provinces" which is proof positive that "God has built invisibly with the hands of the Sovereigns,"[29] the injunctions to the Russian landowner to be a just yet stern father to the peasants entrusted to him, along with grave and detailed instructions as to how the good squire should take to

26. Polnoe Sobranie Sochinenij, *8*, 298-99.
27. Ibid., p. 294.
28. Ibid., p. 246.
29. Ibid., p. 357.

task a recalcitrant peasant, one is equally dismayed by the clumsy pedantry of the unsolicited advice, by its moral obtuseness and unrelieved obscurantism. No wonder Belinskij flew into rage and cried sellout!

And yet this later charge, spawned by the unreasoning fury of spurned love and by the rhetoric of radical exposure,[30] appears profoundly unjust. This is not to say that Belinskij, understandably infuriated by the tenor of Gogol's homilies, engaged in deliberate character assassination. It is rather to suggest that he was impelled to impugn Gogol's integrity in part as a result of a wishful misreading of his major works, in part because of his inability to imagine that an honorable man would actually hold such "barbarous" beliefs as are dispensed in *Selected Passages*. What clearly did not occur to Belinskij is that a man of genius could be a reactionary or, to put it differently, could be an obscurantist without being an opportunist.

Actually, what seems to have happened here is a typically Gogolian "misunderstanding." To Belinskij, *Selected Passages* was a craven act of opportunism, a cowardly apologia of the hateful system which Gogol's earlier works had done so much to undermine and expose. Yet what Gogol apparently intended was a plea for amelioration or humanization of an order of things which he had always viewed as immutable. It is testimony to Gogol's thoroughly static view of society, to the already mentioned poverty of his political imagination, that in the face of the nonconformist ferment of the 1830s and 40s, he could still look upon the institutional pattern of the Russia of Nicholas I as a God-given norm. A past master at the art of debunking the lower and middle echelons of tsarist bureaucracy, he apparently never wavered in his provincial's awe for the central authority, never felt free to question its legitimacy. There is no reason to assume that Gogol wrote his tract in

30. "Betrayal" is a standard radical response to a "reactionary" statement of a previously admired personality. In an analogous situation many a reactionary might cry "treason."

order to vindicate serfdom and tsarist autocracy. Yet everything he said clearly suggests that he was taking their appropri-
ateness and staying power for granted.

Though the political implications of Gogol's preaching are
as obvious as they are objectionable, *Selected Passages from
Correspondence with Friends* is not primarily, even in its
nonliterary dimension, a piece of political apologetics or
polemics. It is, rather, an attempt at a religio-ethical treatise.
Taking the existing conditions as the given, in fact, the God-
given, Gogol pleads that they be imbued with the spirit of true
Christian faith, that within this sturdy framework everyone, be
he high or lowly, a country squire, a governor, a society
woman, or a small-town official, do his Christian duty so as to
meet the exigencies of his particular divinely ordained station
with kindness, responsibility, and integrity. What is needed in
this murky period of transition, Gogol never tired of repeating,
is a Christian code of individual conduct. The acute spiritual
crisis and prevalent confusion of values have given the forces of
selfishness and corruption a new lease on life. Along with vague
and potentially hopeful groping for a better life, signs of
spiritual malaise and of intellectual pride are abroad. "Life is
becoming increasingly arid, everything becomes smaller and
smaller. The great image of Boredom grows all the time,
assuming fantastic dimensions. Oh Lord, how empty and terrifying your world has grown!"[31]

Yet, as already indicated above, Gogol's obsessively religious inwardness is neither ascetic nor mystical. For one thing,
personal salvation, individual self-improvement so ardently
sought and so strenuously proclaimed as a major goal, is not an
end in itself here. It is, rather, a means to be useful to one's
fellow humans, a prerequisite for Christian service. By the
same token, even if in his letter "One Ought to Travel Across
Russia," Gogol declares at some point that there is no higher

31. *Polnoe Sobranie Sochinenij, 8,* 416.

vocation than the monastic one, he does not recommend to his reader withdrawal from the world, a life of spiritual contemplation, "Since it is open only to those who get the call."[32] The rest are ordained to remain in the world and do their duty there by radiating Christian influence, by giving a good example, thus showing their fellow humans a path to salvation. "Your monastery [that is a God-ordained field of Christian activity] is Russia," Gogol writes to a dignitary friend, Count Alexander P. Tolstoy.[33] Love for Russia, he argues, is a necessary prerequisite for the love of God and personal salvation. "No, you do not yet love Russia, and without loving Russia you cannot love your brethren, and without loving your brethren you will not be aflame with the love of God, and without being aflame with the love of God you shall not be saved."[34] In this scheme of things, the connection between the effectiveness of Christian service and the purity of one's soul is so organic as to turn moral perfection as Mikhail Gershenzon puts it, into a "socio-utilitarian vehicle." The same critic states the matter rather forcefully: "There is, perhaps, no other work in the Russian language that is so totally, so thoroughly permeated by the spirit of social service."[35]

Another distinguished student of Russian spirituality, George Florovskij speaks of Gogol's bent for "religious action." According to Florovskij, Gogol's contact with some brilliant Polish Jesuits at the villa of Princess Zinaida Volkonskaja made a distinct impact. These sessions, he argues, left their mark not be making a Catholic convert out of him, but by exposing him to the concept of an "Apostolate of Truth," a program of Christian action whose tenets loom large in the discursive writings of the great Polish Romantic, Adam Mick-

32. Ibid., p. 301.
33. Ibid.
34. Ibid., pp. 300-01.
35. *Istoricheskie zapiski* (Moscow, I. N. Kushmerev and Co., 1910), pp. 99, 88.

iewicz, and, still more relevantly, in the influential tract by
Lamennais, *Paroles d'un Croyant*.

Yet if Gogol emulates or parallels Lamennais in the
socioethical, extrovert thrust of his preachings, his notion of a
good society is a far cry from the reforming zeal which permeates the utopian vision of Mickiewicz or Lamennais. An ardent
if erratic fellow traveller of utopian socialism, Mickiewicz is
reported to have forced his way into the Pope's antechamber
during the barricade fighting in Paris in June 1848, and,
shaking His Holiness by his shoulders, urged that "today God is
under the shirts of the Paris workers." Can one imagine Gogol
ever shaking a metropolitan by his shoulders to drive home a
comparably subversive message?

Herein lies the inherent flaw of Gogol's brand of social
Christianity. The timid attempt, however genuine, to breathe
the true Christian spirit into such institutions as autocracy and
serfdom was both futile and unworthy. What was intended as a
brake on abuses of power, on corruption and irresponsibility in
high places, was all too likely to be interpreted as bestowing
religious sanction upon inhuman and antiquated social practices. Gogol, the religious thinker, was paying a heavy price for
his inability to translate the Christian ethos into commensurate
social terms, and for his reluctance to tamper with the existing
institutions. Clearly he was straining after the impossible as he
preached a salutary inner transformation without any significant outer change. To Christianize serfdom was as hopeless a
project as to redeem Chichikov.

In his excellent book Vasilij Gippius uses the phrase "the
third idyll" in speaking about *Selected Passages*.[36] (The first
two idylls are, of course, "Hanz Kuechelgarten" and "The
Old-Fashioned Landowners.") The label is an apposite one. In
his recoil from, or his denial of, the nauseating present, Gogol's
"frightened imagination"[37] had no choice but to retreat into the

36. *Gogol,* pp. 168-86.
37. A. O. Rosset, Smirnova's brother and a relatively sympathetic reader,

stifling coziness of a conservative pastoral where squires are firm yet fundamentally benign taskmasters, where peasants reap the benefits of a hard day's work and gladly pay heed to the spiritual guidance of zealous village priests.

To say that *Selected Passages* is a bizarre and largely misbegotten book is not to suggest that it was simply a freak, a product of a mental aberration, of a sudden onset of "religious mania." Gogol's sermons fall within a recognizable ideational and literary tradition. They have many significant links with the vast and heterogenous body of inspirational literature. Gogol scholarship has conclusively demonstrated[38] that his reading in the 1840s was ecumenical enough to encompass such high points of Western Christianity as Thomas à Kempis' *Imitation of Christ,* Bossuet's *Oeuvres Philosophiques* and Thomas Aquinas' *Summa Theologiae,* along with the homiletic works of famous Russian Orthodox preachers, e.g. Tikhon Zadonskij and Joann Zlatoust. Yet as Cizevsky and Florovskij have shown, the general thrust of *Selected Passages* is especially indebted to more recent tracts such as *On The Duties of Man* (Dei doveri degli uomini) by an early nineteenth-century Italian moralist, Silvio Pellico, who apparently spent much of his sojourn in an Austrian jail writing a treatise on the Christian duty of obeying a God-given authority, and *Patriotic Fantasies* by Justus Möser, an eighteenth-century German pietist. The insistence on personal morality and service, the conservative notion that everyone is where God willed him to be, finally, the hailing of thrift, efficiency, and resourcefulness as Christian virtues, all these salient emphases are writ large within the pietistic brand of German Protestantism. In fact, the

---

described the dominant tone of *Selected Passages* as one of "morbid, physical weakness and of a frightened imagination." (See Merezhkovskij, *Gogol: Tvorchestvo, zhizn' i religija,* p. 173.)

38. Cizevsky, "Gogol: Artist and Thinker," *Annals of the Ukrainian Academy,* 4 (1952), 261-78; "The Unknown Gogol," *Slavonic and East European ~~v~~, 30* (1952), 476-93; Florovskij, *Puti russkogo bogoslovija.*

idealization of a Kostanzhoglo is a good example of what Max Weber has called the Protestant ethic. One may add that this blithe acceptance of the status quo as a socioethical norm remained a major theme in Western European inspirational writings through much of the nineteenth century. The words of a Victorian hymn, "The rich man in his castle, the poor man at the gate, God made them high or lowly and ordered their estate," express an attitude which was widely held and frequently articulated.

If, nevertheless, Gogol's position can properly be called "archaic," it is not only because it is substantively reactionary or retrograde, but because, in the context of Russian intellectual discourse of the 1840s, it is fundamentally anachronistic. The cleavage between Gogol the moralist and the bulk of his generation was not simply a matter of a value conflict; it was also one of a time lag. The issues that plagued and harried the author of *Selected Passages* were no longer important even to his formally religious and traditionalist friends. That is why, to Aksakov, *Selected Passages* was an embarrassing and a tediously irrelevant book. As a thinker, the self-proclaimed prophet was at least partly behind his times. He was an epigone of the era of Alexander I (1800-25), an era which was characterized in Russia by a proliferation of Bible societies, the rise of pietism and eschatology, as well as a heavy emphasis on the rules of individual conduct, on how a truly Christian sovereign or dignitary ought to conduct himself. Partly under the impact of German Romantic philosophy, the 30s and 40s saw a shift toward more secular preoccupations. Theology gave way to ontology, religious didacticism to social ethics and political philosophy. By 1840, the Russian intellectuals fought over such issues as the nature of a good society, the relative merits of tradition and progress, the meaning of Russian history, the optimal relationship between Russia and the West. On the whole, Gogol's interest in these matters was none too keen. He failed to enlist in either the Slavophile or the Western c

though his views definitely overlapped with the former. His apostrophes to Russia in Part One of *Dead Souls* had gladdened the hearts of his nationalist friends such as Aksakov and Pogodin, and his eulogy of the Russian Orthodox clergy in *Selected Passages* seemed to argue the superiority of the Russian brand of Christianity. Yet on the other side of the ledger, there was Gogol's guilt-ridden but ardent love affair with Rome and the essentially ecumenical nature of his Christianity. If his Moscow friends found his frantic injunctions pedantic, his dire warnings strident and largely pointless, he in turn thought their political stance too rigid, too doctrinaire, too partisan. Did he simply get "stuck" in early nineteenth-century rhetoric and eschatology, or is it rather that the apocalyptic premonitions of that crisis-ridden era provided a congenial text for his "frightened imagination"?

One of the immediate lessons which Gogol drew from the *Selected Passages* debacle was the conviction that he had chosen a wrong genre, an inappropriate mode of expression. The discursive detour proved a dead end. To borrow a metaphor from one of Gogol's letters, he thought he would gain a reprieve from his impatient readers clamoring for the treat which was promised them, by giving them a tour of his moral kitchen and demonstrating the culinary implements needed to prepare the long-awaited meal. But all he accomplished was to antagonize and confuse the would-be diners.[39] Clearly there was no escape from the pain and frustrations of the creative process, from the arduous task of embodying a new vision in "living images." In other words, there was no substitute for Part Two of *Dead Souls*. Still, he sought to postpone the ultimate test. Allegedly, before resuming the full-scale creative effort, he had to attend to his soul. The job of spiritual housecleaning undertaken some seven or eight years before was not yet completed, he insisted strenuously. And no literary

39. *Polnoe Sobranie Sochinenij, 13,* 241-42.

activity could be morally significant or salutary without such self-clarification. "Few people were able to understand," he wrote to Pletnëv in August 1847, "that I had to leave altogether the realm of literature and to busy myself with my soul and my inner life so as to return to literature a complete man."[40]

In the fall of 1847, this meant primarily to make good on a promise Gogol had made himself quite a while earlier to go on a pilgrimage to the Holy Land. In the wake of an ordeal which strained almost beyond endurance his faith in his mission, the long-delayed voyage seemed to offer a hope of a desperately needed spiritual uplift. In January 1848, he left Naples for Palestine. His mood on the eve of the journey was more apprehensive than hopeful. He asked Smirnova to pray for him and added significantly, "I will try to pray for you as best I can, but I must confess my prayers are so arid!"[41] Even more telling is his admission to his father-confessor, Matvej Konstantinovskij: "How can one pray if God is not willing? I see so much in myself that is dead, such an abyss of selfishness, of inability to subordinate the earthly to the divine. . . . It even seems to me that I have no faith. . . . *I only want to believe!*" (my italics).[42]

"I only want to believe!"—Gogol's *cri de coeur* brings to mind one of the most poignant moments in Dostoyevsky's turbulent masterpiece *The Possessed,* a memorable encounter between the demonic Stavrogin and his erstwhile disciple, Shatov, the tortured ex-radical turned latter-day Slavophile. Shatov delivers a credo, an impassioned statement of Dostoyevsky's own belief in the God-bearing mission of the Russian people. Yet this mouthpiece for Dostoyevsky's Christian nationalism shares his creator's lingering religious doubts—a fact which Stavrogin's shrewdness ruthlessly brings to light: "But how about God?," he asks Shatov. "Do you

40. Ibid., p. 370.
41. Ibid., p. 395.
42. Ibid., *14*, 41.

believe in God?" Faced with this fundamental query, Shatov is reduced to stammering helplessly: "I . . . I . . . will believe in God."[43] For the Gogol of 1848, as well as for Shatov, faith is an ardent wish rather than an urge, an act of will rather than an immediate reality.

Quite predictably, the pilgrimage proved anticlimactic. The miracle failed to occur. At the Holy Sepulcher, Gogol felt as keenly as ever the "powerlessness of [his] prayers."[44] "How can I thaw out my soul, cold, arid, unable to rid itself of earthly, selfish, lowly thoughts?"[45] Curiously enough, the voyage to Palestine did more for Gogol's aesthetic sensibility than for his ability to pray and to open up, to feel God. His attempt to explain to Zhukovskij in a letter of February 18, 1850 why rendering the sights and the smells of the Holy Land was an impossible task, yielded one of the most vividly suggestive letters he ever wrote.[46]

Disheartened, depressed, Gogol left Paris in April 1848 and proceeded via Beirut to Odessa. The near-expatriate had returned. He was never to leave home again. Yet it seems that the homecoming was not a particularly joyous affair. Though during the course of over ten years of wandering, Gogol frequently must have been homesick, it may not be unfair to suggest that he drifted back to Russia not so much because he could not stay away any longer, but because, ultimately, the "beautiful, far-off land" let him down, too. For three relatively happy years Rome seemed the "homeland of his soul." After 1842, however, Italy's glamour somehow turned to ashes. Anxiety, real or imaginary illnesses, and above all, the mounting sense of frustration and creative stalemate, swallowed up the euphoria. Gogol's soul was homeless and adrift once again. He might as well return to his physical homeland, the setting of

43. *The Possessed,* tr. Constance Garnett (New York, Modern Library, 1936), p. 256.
44. *Polnoe Sobranie Sochinenij, 14,* 53-54.
45. Ibid., p. 49.
46. Ibid., pp. 165-70.

his magnum opus, the home of his detractors, but also of his
closest friends and confidants.

What immediately followed is not easy to describe or evalu-
ate. The widespread notion, especially prevalent in Soviet studies of Gogol, that the last four years of his life were a period of
steady deterioration, of gathering gloom, of escalating religious
mania and concomitantly creeping creative paralysis is not
entirely borne out by the evidence. It seems that the stretches of
acute depression and stagnation alternated with those of relative serenity and productiveness. As usual in Gogol's case,
eyewitness testimony is contradictory. Some observations
whether by new acquaintances or old friends, sound as if his
spiritual travail had not been altogether in vain. The Aksakovs
found Gogol, upon his final return to Russia, mellower, more
considerate and open, more genuinely interested in his friends
than he had been prior to the crisis. The Slavophile poet and
essayist Khomjakov, who saw much of Gogol in the winter of
1849-50, thought him "very gay" and assumed that he must
have been productive.[47] Yet the reaction of Gogol's family tells
quite a different story. During his visit at Vasil'evka in the
spring of 1848, Nikolaj Vasil'evich struck both his mother and
his sister as distant and gloomy. "How serious he has become!,"
noted Gogol's sister in her diary. "He never smiles. He is so
distant and cold with us!"[48]

Evidence bearing on the progress of Part Two of *Dead Souls*
is equally inconclusive. Sergej Aksakov, who admitted to
having had grave misgivings about the artistic worth of the
emerging opus, claimed to have been considerably reassured
after attending a reading of excerpts from the manuscript.[49]
Other intimates such as Alexandra Smirnova and Arnoldi seem
to have been equally encouraged. And yet Gogol's letters
written in 1849-51 abound in complaints about the creative
slump, reminiscent of his most despondent statements of the

47. Cf. Veresaev, *Gogol v zhizni,* p. 416.
48. Ibid., p. 379.
49. *Istorija moego znakomstva s Gogolem,* p. 199.

period preceding *Selected Passages*. In 1845, he had groaned to Alexandra: "I have tortured myself, forced myself to write, suffered severe pains when I saw my impotence . . . everything came out forced and inferior."[50] Four years later he confided to the same addressee: "Work moves so slowly and the inexorable, irreversible time races so rapidly that occasionally fear invades my drowsy soul.[51] However, it seems that something did get written. Shortly before his death, at the end of 1851, Gogol reported to Zhukovskij that the second part of *Dead Souls* was almost complete. Was it an overstatement or self-deception? Or was the anguished writer indeed on the verge of reaching his immediate objective? We have no right, I believe, to speak with any certainty either about the precise nature of the difficulties which beset Gogol in 1849-51 or about the extent to which they actually crippled his endeavors. It is fair to assume, however, that the pain and futility of working against his creative grain, of inhibiting his bent for the grotesquely satirical for the sake of a homiletic or "realistic" reconciliation with reality, was compounded by the renewed doubts about the moral legitimacy of the literary vocation.

There is no question but that these misgivings were powerfully activated by the man who, since 1847, had acquired an inordinately strong hold on Gogol, Father Matvej Konstantinovskij. Few Gogol scholars have managed to steer clear of either demonology or apologetics in discussing the role of this devout Rzhev priest whom Gogol described to his rather retrograde friend and confidant, Count Alexander P. Tolstoy, as the "wisest man I have ever met."[52] The view of Father Konstantinovskij as Gogol's evil genius, as a grim, religious fanatic who diverted him from the path of secular creativity, made him renounce art as the devil's handiwork, and drove him into a religious mania that finally resulted in his death, is obviously a lurid simplification. For one thing, as already

---

50. *Polnoe Sobranie Sochinenij, 12* (1952), 471.
51. Ibid., *14*, 151.
52. Ibid., p. 59.

indicated, Gogol's intense concern with saving his soul and
justifying his art antedates his encounter with Father
Konstantinovskij. For another, eyewitness testimony does not
quite bear out the image of the priest as a small-scale Russian
Savonarola. Yet Konstantin Mochulskij's attempt to clear him
of the charges of antiaesthetic bias and religious intolerance is
not altogether convincing either.[53] I am inclined to agree with
Setchkarev that Father Matvej's "outlook was very narrow and
that his sincere and honest faith bordered on blind fanaticism
and permitted no deviation from dogma."[54] It is easy to see
how this forceful rigidity, this firm, unreflecting faith in the
dogmas of the Russian Orthodox Church could have attracted
and fascinated Gogol. Nor is it difficult to fathom the dangers
of such an influence on an artist whose religiosity was, to begin
with, one of fear rather than awe, and whose uneasiness about
the literary pursuits was as pronounced as Gogol's.

In all fairness, Gogol's surrender to Father Matvej's brand of
orthodoxy was less than unconditional. In spite of his inordinate regard for the priest's opinions, he fought a strenuous and
at times a pathetic rearguard battle against the notion of
renouncing literature. In a letter written in September 1847, at
the very beginning of this special relationship, Gogol engaged
the issue directly: "I do not know whether I shall cast off the
name of a litterateur, for I don't know if this is God's will."[55]
He then proceeded to offer a characteristic apology for this
reluctance to disengage from literature and a mild polemic
against a purely ascetic view of the good life:

> As I have talent, as I have the ability to portray vividly
> man and nature . . . is it not my duty to portray good men,
> men who believe and who live by God's law? This . . . not
> fame or money, is the real motive of my literary activity. If I
> knew that there was some other realm where I could accom-

53. *Dukhovnyj put' Gogolja* (Paris, YMCA Press, 1934).
54. *Gogol: His Life and Works*, p. 89.
55. *Polnoe Sobranie Sochinenij, 13*, 390.

plish more . . . I would promptly switch to that field. If I learned that I could leave the world behind by going into a monastery, I would become a monk. But there is no place or realm in the world where we could leave the world behind.[56]

It has been alleged that the issue was joined once more during Gogol's last encounter with Father Matvej in February 1852. According to some unconfirmed reports, the priest confronted his disciple on that occasion with an urgent request to renounce Pushkin as a sinner and to abandon literature once and for all as a wicked pursuit. Once again Gogol refused to submit. Yet he was profoundly troubled, if not shattered, by what must have been a frighteningly graphic recital of the wages of sin. At some point he is said to have exclaimed: "Enough! Stop it, I can't listen any longer! It's too terrible!"[57] It is also known that during the period which intervened between Father Matvej's last visit and Gogol's death on February 22, 1852, the writer stubbornly refused to take any food.

Once again, let us beware of simplification. Although Father Matvej did enjoin Gogol to exercise restraint in eating and thus subdue his gluttony, which was admittedly one of his venial sins, the nearly suicidal fast cannot properly be laid at the door of the fire-and-brimstone-breathing preacher, less still at that of the Church authorities. By the time this fateful confrontation took place, the strain and anguish of the literary forced labor must have broken Gogol's spirit and sapped his will to live. Also, an event which occurred a few days before Father Matvej's visit seems to have been even more traumatic than the priest's admonitions. The death of Madame Khomjakov, a gentle and pious lady for whom Gogol had a very high regard, had a profound effect upon him. He saw her sudden demise as a portent, a signal that his days, too, were counted. It was then

56. Ibid., p. 391.
57. A. T. Tarasenkov, *Poslednie dni zhizni N. V. Gogolja* (St. Petersburg, 1857), p. 9.

that his fatal hunger strike began. According to Pogodin's testimony, he avoided taking food "under various pretexts."[58] One such pretext was the beginning of Lent which fell in the early part of February. But Gogol pushed his self-destructive abstinence above and beyond the call of the ritual. He stubbornly refused to abandon his fast well after Lent, despite urgent appeals of his friends and the injunction of the metropolitan who urged the emaciated writer to follow his doctor's orders.

A slow, passive suicide, a stubborn refusal to live? Sergej Aksakov's niece, M. G. Kartashevskaja, put it a little differently: "It seems to me that Gogol died only because he was convinced that he was going to die. There were no clear-cut physical symptoms."[59] This observation seems rather apt. Gogol's entire demeanor in the last two weeks of his life, especially his steadfast resistance to the doctor's unsolicited attempts to bolster his waning strength, breathes a fatalistic or perhaps superstitious resignation which is all too reminiscent of Pulkherija Ivanovna's reaction to the brief reappearance of her fugitive cat in "The Old-Fashioned Landowners": "I'm not ill, Afanasij Ivanovich. I know that I shall die."

No less strange than Gogol's way of dying was the episode which capped his literary career—the second burning of Part Two of *Dead Souls*. Pogodin relates this story as told him by Gogol's servant. In the middle of the night of February 11-12, Gogol got up from his couch, had his servant fetch him a batch of notebooks and tossed them into the fire. When the manuscripts turned to ashes, he crossed himself, kissed the boy, laid on the couch and broke into sobs.

According to the same account, Gogol's anguish over what he had done deepened as he realized that he had consigned to fire more than he had intended. "Imagine how powerful is the Fiend!" he is alleged to have said to his host, Count Tolstoy. "I wanted to burn papers which were long earmarked for destruc-

58. See Barsukov, *Zhizn' i trudy M. P. Pogodina, 8,* 532.
59. "Pis'ma o Gogole," N. V. Gogol, Materialy i issledovanija, p. 188.

tion, and burned the chapters of *Dead Souls* which I meant to leave to my friends as a keepsake."[60]

Was the second auto-da-fé a tragic mistake or was it rather a matter of deliberate decision which, for some reason, Gogol chose to explain away or deny afterward? All one can say is that the former possibility cannot be ruled out. Of course, Gogol could have been tampering with the truth even at this late stage of the game. But, as Gippius so sensibly urges, his well-documented proclivity for mystification is scarcely sufficient grounds for disbelieving anything he ever said. It stands to reason that Gogol may have intended to preserve those chapters of Part Two that had elicited warm praise from a number of his discerning friends. From what he allegedly said to Tolstoy, one could infer that at least some sections were inadvertently destroyed. On the other hand, it is said that some of the missing chapters featured a clergyman who sounded too much like a Catholic priest for Father Matvej's comfort, and that the latter urged Gogol to eliminate or drastically modify these passages. It is conceivable that Gogol was doing just this. If so—provided that he actually said to Tolstoy what Pogodin claims he did—along with the chapters slated for destruction, he may have consigned to flames portions of *Dead Souls* which he had been meaning to preserve.

To allow the possibility of at least a partial mistake, admittedly, is to tamper with the myth which has become part of the Gogol folklore, that of a writer who got up from his deathbed in order to destroy in one wanton gesture the fruit of long years of creative labor, either as an act of penance, of renouncing literature at Father Matvej's behest, or as an ultimate recognition of his artistic and moral defeat. There is much in the poignant story of Gogol's last years to make this image credible if not necessarily compelling. Yet I submit that an intrusion of the accidental into this tale of anguish and frustration would have made the plot more rather than less Gogolian. The tragic

60. Barsukov, p. 534.

irony of a writer ground to death by what was to be his
liberating literary deed would have been compounded by the
grotesque absurdity of a mistake, the wanton quality of the
proceedings. Need I add that the notion of being tricked into a
self-destructive act by the Evil One lends to the situation an
uncannily Gogolian twist?

Whatever Gogol's initial intentions may have been, it is
obvious that in this literary suicide he enacted or prefigured the
actual one, and thus delivered himself a final coup de grâce. He
was now ready to die. His initial refusal to eat was a moral
decision rather than a physical symptom. Now, as a result of a
long fast, he contracted an "acute nervous fever" along with
typhus. Yet all he wanted was to be left alone, to be allowed to
die in peace. "Leave me be," he would say to friends and
physicians alike. "I am content."[61] "I know that I must die," he
declared one evening to Count Tolstoy.[62]

Though he was clearly beyond rescue, the doctors would not
leave him alone. Disregarding the dying man's wishes and the
obvious futility of the enterprise, they subjected him to treatment as painful as it was useless, such as placing him in a bath
of clear broth or—strangely symbolic detail!—sticking leeches
on his nose. Gogol's agony is rendered vividly, indeed with
somewhat morbid gusto, by Nabokov.[63] Rather than dwell on
it, I would like to mention an incident which it is difficult not to
call symbolic. It seems that Gogol's last intelligible words were:
"A ladder, quick, a ladder!"[64] To what was he reaching de
profundis? Was this upward gesture of a demon-ridden artist a
thrust toward the divine or toward the merely human?

Gogol died on February 21, 1852. He was forty-three years
old. Genuine grief over his untimely and bizarre death brought
together his former Moscow friends and allies who, in the last
decade of his life, had profound differences with him and with

61. Veresaev, *Gogol v zhizni,* p. 501.
62. Ibid., p. 500.
63. *Nikolai Gogol,* pp. 1-3.
64. Tarasenkov, *Poslednie dni zhizni N. V. Gogolja* in *Gogol v vospominanijakh sovremennikov,* p. 524.

each other—Aksakov, Pogodin, Shevyrëv, Samarin. On March
9, 1852, Pogodin wrote to Marja Ivanovna Gogol: "They say
that all of Moscow was at his funeral. Professors and students
carried the coffin all the way to the cemetery. Everyone was his
relative."[65]

Not unpredictably, it was Sergej Aksakov who spoke most
eloquently for Gogol's "relatives": "Gogol's entire life, his total
artistic endeavor, his unceasing ordeal, finally the destruction
by the artist of the work on which he labored so long and so
painfully, this terrible solemn night of the auto-da-fé, and then
his death, all this builds up to a grandiose, sombre poem whose
meaning will long remain undecipherable."[66]

In a letter to his son Ivan, Aksakov gave voice to a baffled
ambivalence toward the protagonist of that "sombre poem":

> I don't know whether anybody liked Gogol exclusively
> as a human being. I don't think so; it was, in fact impossible.
> How can you love one whose body and spirit are recovering
> from self-inflicted torture? We all knew that Gogol did not
> really care about anyone . . . I see Gogol as a saint . . . he is
> a true martyr of lofty thought, a martyr of our era, and at the
> same time a Christian martyr.[67]

The strange mixture of discomfort and reverence reflected in
the above yields, toward the end of Aksakov's memoir, a
curious admission. Though profoundly shocked by Gogol's
death, the author claims to have been less frightened by the
sight of his corpse than he normally was when faced by a dead
man. Was Aksakov implying here that Gogol was never truly
alive, that he always was more—and less—than human, half-
saint, half-zombie? Whatever the precise implications of this
postmortem, it was an appropriately unsettling and chilling
tribute to a haunting writer and an enigmatic human being.

65. *N. V. Gogol, Materilay i issledovanija, 1*, 188.
66. See Shenrok, *Materialy dlja biografii Gogolja*, pp. 9-10.
67. *Istorija moego znakomstva s Gogolem*, p. 222.

11

The Great Impersonator

No student of Gogol needs to be reminded of the fact that the haunting, uncanny quality of his prose finds a striking counterpart in the well advertised strangeness of the man behind it. "Queer," "strange," "enigmatic," adjectives such as these abound in the eyewitness testimony. "What an intelligent, queer, and sick creature!," exclaims Ivan Turgenev.[1] Aksakov, sympathetic and bewildered, speaks of the "unintelligible strangeness of his spirit."[2] A. O. Rosset writes to his sister, Alexandra Smirnova, who in Gogol's later years seems to have been his closest friend and confidante: "Gogol was one of the most undeciphered (*nerazgadannykh*) men I knew."[3] "Enigma" is the key term in Vjazemskij's poetic epitaph: "Your life was an enigma, so is today your death."[4] Gogol himself obviously seemed to share some of this bafflement. In a letter to Zhukovskij written in 1842, he looks to Part Two of *Dead Souls* as a moment of spiritual clarification or breakthrough that, at long last, would offer a solution to the "riddle of my existence."[5] Many of Gogol's contemporaries and not a few Gogol scholars saw the man who wrote *Dead Souls* as a bundle of contradictions. Shevyrëv described his external appearance

1. *Literary Reminiscences and Autobiographical Fragments* (New York, Farrar, Strauss and Cudahy, 1958), p. 161.
2. *Istorija moego znakomstva s Gogolem*, p. 17.
3. Quoted from P. N. Barsukov, *Zhizn' i trudy M. P. Pogodina, 2*, 547.
4. P. A. Vjazemskij, "Gogol" (1853), *Polnoe Sobranie Sochinenij* (St. Petersburg, 1887), *2*, 10-11.
5. *Polnoe Sobranie Sochinenij* (Complete Works), *12* (1952), 69.

as an odd mixture of sloppiness and dandyism.[6] A perceptive biographer, V. V. Kallash found in Gogol's correspondence an amazing coexistence of discordant, indeed opposite qualities—naïveté and cunning, meek submissiveness toward the powers-that-be and rugged intransigeance, a keen sense of reality and sentimental-elegiac dreaminess, childish faith and stodgy sanctimoniousness.[7] Konstantin Mochulskij, author of a highly empathetic study, *The Spiritual Path of Gogol,* is not far off the mark when he suggests that on the basis of the available evidence one could write two parallel, and widely disparate biographies of Gogol: almost any stage of Gogol's career, almost any incident in his life, is susceptible of either a favorable or a prejudicial interpretation. Mochulskij is quite justified in concluding: "We might as well recognize that these contradictions are inherent in Gogol's nature and forego all attempts at reconciliation or synthesis."[8] Doubtless, Gogol was a baffling, conflict-ridden, and profoundly disturbed man. Though it may not be too late for an illuminating retrospective diagnosis, attempts to assess Gogol's personality in psychiatric terms have been of limited value.

The fiftieth anniversary of Gogol's death, which occasioned a spate of memoirs and of critical or biographical reevaluations, featured at least three such post-factum diagnoses. The most thoughtful and plausible of them, Bazhenov's "Gogol's Illness and Death,"[9] describes Gogol as a depressive, most likely a manic-depressive. In a more ambitious and wide-ranging disquisition, drawing on both biographical and literary evidence, Chizh urges the view of Gogol as an all-around psychotic, complete with paranoia, delusions of grandeur, premature senility which presumably set in at the age of thirty, and

6. Quoted in Merezhkovskij, *Gogol: Tvorchestvo, zhizn' i religija,* (Gogol: Work, Life, and Religion), p. 133.
7. *N. V. Gogol v vospominanijakh sovremennikov i perepiske* (Moscow, 1924), p. 8.
8. *Dukhovnyj put' Gogolja,* p. 59.
9. "Bolezn' i smert' Gogolja," *Russkaja mysl', 1* (1902), 132-49; 52-71.

a plethora of other symptoms.[10] Some of Chizh's hypotheses may be valid, but he clearly weakens his case by what could be charitably termed ideological parochialism. At some point, Gogol's "reactionary" views are adduced as incontrovertible proof of his psychosis—a reasoning which assumes a more organic relationship between liberalism and sanity than can be conclusively demonstrated. The third psychiatrist, Troshin,[11] pronounced Chizh ludicrously wrong and gave Gogol, perhaps a bit too hastily, a clean bill of mental health. His symptoms, such as they were, were adjudged purely somatic. Gogol's life, to Troshin, is a "tug-of-war between physical frailty and genius." A layman may find all this just a bit confusing, though he will do well to remember that the above controversy represents a very early stage in the development of Russian psychiatry.

More recent attempts to approach Gogol's personality and work in psychological terms have been somewhat more provocative. I am not referring here primarily to the specific sexual symbolism that can be so easily read into some of Gogol's plots ("The Nose" and "Ivan Fedorovich Shponka and his Aunt," for example). I have in mind rather the ingenious and partly convincing discussions of Gogol's "retreat from love,"[12] of the manifold ways in which his vaunted fear of sex inflitrates his writings, through the theme of destructive passion which burns its victim to ashes ("Viy") or makes him betray his primary loyalties ("Taras Bulba"), or through his blindingly, unbelievably dazzling women who, be they witches or goddesses, are objects of awestruck worship rather than of quenchable desire.

That Gogol's sexuality was warped or stunted is more than likely. One of the few assumptions shared by the bulk of Gogol's biographers is that through all or most of his life he

10. "Bolezn' N. V. Gogolja," *Voprosy filosofii i psikhologii, 2-5* (Moscow 1903), *1*, (1904).

11. "Geni j i zdorov'e N. V. Gogol ja," *Voprosy filosofii i psikhologii 1* (Moscow, 1905), 37-82; *2* (1905), 187-249; *3* (1905), 333-83.

12. See Hugh McLean, "Gogol's Retreat from Love:—Toward an Interpretation of '*Mirgorod*,' " *American Contributions . . . Slavicists* (1958), pp. 225-44.

shunned physical contact with women. It is significant, indeed symbolic that Gogol's "first love" flamboyantly described in his notorious letter to his mother, written in the wake of the "Hanz Kuechelgarten" debacle,[13] should have been as mythical an affair as we have assumed it to be. It is no less revealing, perhaps, that the plot of this bit of "shameless fiction" (Nabokov) should have featured panicky flight from passion rather than its consummation. The same rhetoric of stepping back from danger, of heroically resisting a potentially destructive temptation recurs in several letters to Gogol's Nezhin friend, Danilevskij:

> I fully understand . . . your state of mind [a romantic infatuation Danilevskij had just reported], though, thanks to fate, I was spared this experience. I am saying "thanks to fate," for this flame would have promptly turned me into a heap of ashes . . . Fortunately, I have a strong will which saved me twice from an urge to look into the abyss.[14]

Whether this urge was half as strong as the above implies is a moot point. The fact remains that—whether because of the excess of "passion" that threatened to engulf him, or because of its dearth—Gogol steadfastly stayed away from the brink of sex.

This is not to say that he was incapable of a strong emotional involvement with a woman or that the thought of marriage never crossed his mind. Some biographers are under the impression that a few years before his death he proposed to Anna Velgorskaja, a devout and gentle lady whom he greatly admired, and was turned down. Yet, even if he did so—it is by no means certain—the chances of his being accepted appear to have been very slight. Countess Velgorskaja seems to have been genuinely interested in Gogol's work and in his ideas, but there is no indication that she was actively attracted to him.

13. See above, Chapter 2, p. 00.
14. N. V. Gogol, *Sochinenija* (St. Petersburg, 1857), 5, 165.

Moreover, her social standing was incomparably higher than Gogol's.

Gogol's friendship with Alexandra Smirnova is quite another matter. Shortly after his death, she wailed: "I have lost my most loyal, devoted, reliable friend."[15] In his often-quoted memoir Sergej Aksakov notes, with more than a touch of ambivalence, the striking affinity between the two: "It is difficult to describe what her presence does for Gogol. He behaves that way only in the happy moments of creativity. When she is around, Gogol is completely happy . . . they have a special world all to themselves . . . they have completely identical views, responses."[16] Some of Gogol's letters to her breathe an affection and tenderness which seems to verge on what the French call *amitié amoureuse*. And yet, at least on one occasion, Gogol found it possible to address this engaging woman as "my beautiful brother."[17] This, I submit, was more than a slip of the pen. For while half-submerged sexual attraction may well have been the undertow of this "special relationship," the overt emphasis for over a decade was on spiritual affinity, on the obsessive concern with the matters of the "soul." Increasingly, Gogol is cast—or casts himself—in the role of her confessor or spiritual guide, an eager foil for her escalating piety and remorse over her mundane, frivolous, dissipated youth. Aksakov's phrase "the penitent Magdalene" is telling if uncharacteristically harsh. It is fair to assume that even in her "penitent" stage, she was appealing or seductive enough to titillate a male ego. It is equally legitimate to surmise that this appeal was made reasonably safe as the dialogue between the anguished writer and the repentant socialite became a strenuous exercise in shared moral hypochondria.

It stands to reason that Gogol's apparent estrangement from an essential dimension of human existence contributed signifi-

15. *Zapiski, Dnevnik, Vospominanija, Pisma* (Moscow, Federacija, 1929), p. 132.
16. *Istorija moego znakomstva s Gogolem*, pp. 205-06.
17. *Polnoe Sobranie Sochinenij, 12*, 311.

cantly to that sense of nausea, that disgust with the "grossly" sensuous and physical which pervades so much of Gogol's work.[18] Moreover, it is altogether likely that some of the motifs or incidents which haunt Gogol's fiction can be traced back to this crippling flaw.

It occurs to me, at this point, that the problem of a possible connection between Gogol's strange personality and his grotesque art is susceptible of yet another treatment. Let me advance two tentative propositions: a) While the "Feudian" emphasis on Gogol's warped sexuality may well illuminate certain themes and emphases in his work, it might be more intriguing, and perhaps more essential, to try to establish a link between the core of his personality and the nature of his craft, more specifically his narrative manner. b) In our efforts to pin down what Aksakov called "the unintelligible strangeness of [Gogol's] spirit," we may get more assistance from existential psychology than from straightforward psychiatry or orthodox psychoanalysis in its familiar aspects. The view of the human psyche that lays special stress on such dichotomies as the real self versus the false, unauthentic self, and pays special attention to the devices of concealment and impersonation employed by a peculiarly frail ego as protection against the encroachments of feared reality[19] is likely to shed significant light on the strange case of Nikolaj Gogol.

18. In his useful book, *The Grotesque in English Literature* (Oxford, Clarendon Press, 1965), Arthur Clayborough identifies as an essential element of the negative attitude to life that often underlies grotesque imagery, a moral claustrophobia, a "rejection of the physical surroundings by which he [the artist] feels himself to be imprisoned" (p. 111).

19. For an important statement of this position, see R. D. Laing, *The Divided Self: A Study of Sanity and Madness* (London, Tavistock Publications, 1960). Some of Laing's formulations seem remarkably apposite. One of his test cases is described thus: "His ideal was never to give himself away to others, His personality was not true self-expression, but was largely a series of impersonations" (p. 74). At a later stage, Laing's discussion of the "false-self system" contains the following passage: "Anxiety creeps back more intensely than ever. The unrealness of perception extends to feelings of deadness of the shared world as a whole, to the body, in fact, to all that is and infiltrates even to the true self. Everything becomes suffused with nothingness" (p. 152).

A careful reading of Gogol's copious correspondence—a
revealing if not altogether attractive body of evidence—is
bound to make us wary of hasty diagnoses and tempting
simplifications. Thus, it would be misleading to describe Gogol
without qualification as a lonely, withdrawn man, in a word, an
isolate. There is ample evidence that he had a strong need for
friendship and intimacy, that he was capable of cordiality and
solicitude, that he often took an active, sometimes overactive,
interest in his fellow humans. Yet it is also a matter of
record—and a fact richly attested by Gogol's correspondence
—that most of his contemporaries who tried to be his friends
often found him tantalizingly elusive, devious, and distrustful,
that even those closest to him kept complaining of not being
able to reach him, of not knowing what made him tick. Aksakov
speaks of "the long and painful story of an imcomplete under-
standing between Gogol and the people who were closest to
him . . . who thought themselves his friends. . . . Not until
Gogol's death," he avers, "was their faith in his sincerity absolute or unquestioning."[20]

This was an understatement. The Moscow editor and historian, Mikhail Pogodin, a coarser and more impetuous man
than Aksakov, flatly accused Gogol of insincerity in a moment
of exasperation. The same charge, couched this time in political terms, was hurled at Gogol a few years later by Belinskij in
his famous diatribe.

Will this grave accusation stand up under closer scrutiny? I
do not think so. The notion of the later Gogol's ideological
hypocrisy has already been challenged by Nikolaj
Chernyshevskij who had as much reason to resent the tenor of
Selected Passages from Correspondence with Friends as did
Belinskij. And it seems to me that the tragic flaw in his personal
relations was not insincerity but a strange lack of spontaneity,
not a pretense of feelings which he did not have, but an
inability to "project" directly, to find a straightforward,

20. *Istorija moego znakomstva*, p. 110.

humanly credible vehicle for feelings he did experience, a
failure to achieve emotional communication with others and, I
suspect, with himself. Gogol alludes to this crippling defect in a
revealing letter to Shevyrev: "I never could speak frankly about
myself . . . but let me assure you: everything down to the last
movement will yet be revealed. There is much that I have not
been able to say, not because I don't want to say it, but I can't
say it because I have not yet found the words with which to say
it."[21]

In fact, as one wades through the volumes of Gogol's
copious correspondence, a paradoxical fact seems to emerge:
The more vital the emotion he is trying to convey, the more
stilted, ponderous, "dead" the mode of expression. Nearly
every time Gogol tries to "open up," to unburden himself, a
kind of stylistic rigor mortis sets in. A would-be confession
freezes into a cliché, undercutting credibility and blocking the
hoped-for response. An intimate chat is nipped in the bud as it
degenerates into a stodgy harangue, a sanctimonious homily.

This is apparent even in Gogol's peculiarly "unchildish"[22]
Nezhin letters. A schoolboy of nearly sixteen, he reacts to the
news about his father's death in a stilted and rhetorical letter.[23]
Nearly twenty years later he attempts to lay his soul bare to
Sergej Aksakov, Pogodin, and Shevyrëv.[24] A characteristic
failure of communication ensues. Writing from abroad, Gogol
makes a genuine attempt to take his Moscow friends into his

21. *Polnoe Sobranie Sochinenij, 12,* 213.

22. The point was made by Kallash in *N. V. Gogol v vospominanijakh
sovremennikov i perepiske.*

23. On April 23, 1825, Gogol writes to his mother: "Do not worry, dear-
est mummy. I endured this blow with the firmness of a true Christian. True,
I was at first terribly shaken by this news. I even wanted to take my life, but
God has prevented me from this, and toward the evening, I detected in my-
self only sadness which finally turned into a light, barely noticeable mel-
ancholy mixed with a feeling of awe toward our Maker. I bless you, my holy
Faith. Only in you do I find a source of comfort and consolation" *Sochinenija
N. V. Gogolja* [St. Petersburg, 1915], *9,* 9).

24. See especially Gogol's letter to Shevyrëv, Feb. 28, 1843.

confidence, to convey to them the nature of his moral crisis and prevail upon them to serve as his spiritual executors. What emerges instead is a tedious sermon and a pedantic, overbearing, tactless set of instructions which baffles and antagonizes his would-be confidants.

Finally, there is that crowning "misunderstanding," the debacle of *Selected Passages*. When, in an unprecedented act of moral exhibitionism, Gogol proceeded to share with the Russian reading public his hunger for salvation, his desperate reaching toward true Christian faith, he did not merely shock and horrify his erstwhile radical admirers, he also alienated most of his conservative readers, not so much by the tenor of his preaching, as by its governessy, lifeless ponderousness. Only in a few passages of this strange and much-abused book does live emotion break through the crust of sanctimonious rhetoric. When this happens, the feeling more often than not is one of anguish, of moral panic: "I am terrified, countrymen!"

Apollon Grigoriev, who in his less turgid moments could be very perceptive indeed, contributes a telling if somewhat cryptic, phrase: "Gogol was an altogether manufactured (*sdelannyj*) man."[25] Unfortunately, Grigoriev failed to amplify his tantalizing dictum. It is tempting to assume that he meant something akin to what I have suggested here—that Gogol was a thoroughly unspontaneous man who barricaded himself behind a set of contrivances, that out of an irrational fear of premature exposure, of rebuff and ridicule, he tended to hide his pathologically vulnerable self behind a screen of rhetoric, a crust of "moral make-up"[26] and thus, ironically, to insure the very misrepresentation which he was so anxious to prevent.

Is it permissible, at this point, to leap from *Wahrheit* to *Dichtung,* from the man's style of life to the style of his fiction? I believe it is, provided that we do not lose track of the fact that art, as distinguished from life, thrives on artifice, and that we

25. "I. S. Turgenev i ego dejatelnost': po povodu' Dvorjanskogo gnezda' " (1859), *Sobranie Sochinenij, 1,* 328.
26. Kallash, p. 8.

treat the link between the two realms as a mutually illuminating analogy rather than a one-way causal relationship.

Clearly, the basis for the analogy—such as it is—is the motif of the mask. Gogol's proclivity for the *skaz* technique and his adeptness at producing an illusion of oral narration, at mimicking the phraseological and intonational mannerisms of a "folksy" speaker, has been often commented on. Yet the skaz here is part of a larger phenomenon—the tendency to speak in somebody else's voice, the strategy of indirection and impersonation.

It all starts with the garrulous beekeeper Rudy Panko in *Evenings on a Farm near Dikanka* who obtrudes himself upon the narrative only intermittently. In Gogol's Ukrainian goblin tales, Panko had a definite function to perform. His folksiness, his dialect helped authenticate the proceedings by lending an additional regional flavor to the pseudo-folkloristic *Kunstmärchen*. Yet Gogol's proclivity for hiding behind a lowbrow narrator survived long after this particular motivation. The voice of the naïve villager, the small-town gossip, or the chronically befuddled St. Petersburg dweller is heard in the moronic raptures of the narrator of "The Tale of How Ivan Ivanovich Quarreled with Ivan Nikiforovich,"[27] the inane meanderings towards the end of "The Nose,"[28] in the misplaced hyperboles of the description of the governor's ball in *Dead Souls,* [29] and finally, in that masterpiece of inarticulateness, of hemming and hawing, of timid, status-conscious stammering which is the narrative texture of "The Overcoat."

There is nothing uniquely or even characteristically Gogolian about the very presence of a narrator mediating between the author and his audience. This is a frequent and time-honored literary device. What is more pertinent is the cat-and-mouse game which Gogol tends to play here with the point of view, the "now you see it, now you don't" quality of the

27. See above, Chapter 4, p. 70.
28. See above, Chapter 5, pp. 87-88.
29. See above, Chapter 8, p. 125.

narrative manner. As Viktor Vinogradov aptly pointed out, Gogol's prose is a verbal crazy quilt, a bizarre mosaic of various modes of discourse—literary, rhetorical, and collo- quial—which fails to project a psychologically coherent image of the narrator.[30] To put it somewhat differently, it is a dizzying succession of interlocking and mutually canceling verbal masks.

"Two Ivans" is a good case in point. It will not quite do to say simply that the tale is told by a babbling fool whose glaring inadequacy is shown up, in the final passage, by the much- quoted authorian sigh, "It's a dreary world, gentlemen!" Seen at closer range, the narrative texture proves to encompass at least three disparate modes. The comic skaz of a provincial chatterbox who raves about Ivan Ivanovich's "superb coat" and his alleged refinement and laments the rift between two "ornaments of Mirgorod" yields, if only for a short time, to a thoroughly literary mode as the narrator introduces, in a mock-heroic vein, the theme of Ivan Ivanovich's nocturnal sabotage.

Oh, if I were a painter, I would have depicted the charm of that night wondrously well! I would have depicted the whole of Mirgorod asleep; how the countless stars were looking steadily down upon the sleeping town; how the palpable stillness was broken by the everlasting barking of dogs . . . I would depict the black shadow of a bat across the white road flitting as it settled on the white chimneys of the houses. . . . But I could hardly have depicted Ivan Ivanovich as he went out that night with a saw in his hand. Oh, how many different emotions were written on his face![31]

In the next chapter, the first voice is heard again, rhapsodiz- ing the "wonderful city of Mirgorod" and the "splendid

30. *Etjudy o stile Gogolja* (Leningrad, Academia, 1926), p. 150.
31. *The Collected Tales and Plays of Nikolai Gogol,* p. 392.

puddle" in the middle of the city square. These eulogies are mercilessly undercut in the last movement of the story as a third voice, that of a despondent outsider ("Five years ago I was passing through the town of Mirgorod . . ."), delivers itself of a melancholy indictment of Mirgorod and the tedious world which it epitomizes.

So frequent and abrupt are the shifts in the point of view and the narrative tone that at times it becomes difficult to say who is telling the story. Nor is it any easier to answer the question, "Who in this polyphonic universe speaks for Nikolaj Gogol?" Certainly not the brilliantly mimicked and shrewdly debunked parochial. But is it the author's voice we hear in the lyrical effusions, the upward flights of eloquence such as, "Do you know the Ukrainian night?", or "And art not thou, my Russia, soaring along even like a spirited, never-to-be-outdistanced troika?" Perhaps. But I would prefer to speak here about a persona rather than a personality—a romantic poet, wacky, exuberant, dreamy, grandiloquent, now rapturous, now wistful, forever lovestruck by the beauty of a never-never land, forever intoxicated with the "music"—the cacophonies, the cadences, the sonorities—of the Russian language.

For in this lifeless, stagnant universe, language is the only active protagonist, the only dynamic force, both as a great impersonator of dismal reality and as a major avenue of escape from it. Where comic "sound gestures"[32] and inspired clowning reign supreme, as they do in "Ivan Fedorovich Shponka and His Aunt," in "Two Ivans," and, above all, in "The Overcoat," language effectively mimics and enacts its subject. The dislocation of speech—the logical incoherence, the orgy of non-sequiturs—serves as a verbal epitome of the subhuman inanity, or absurdity of the universe portrayed. Conversely, when in the triumphant finale of Part One of *Dead Souls,* Chichikov's troika and his grotesquely morbid schemes disappear into the

32. The phrase is drawn from Boris Eikhenbaum's "Kak sdelana 'Shinel' Gogolja," *Skvoz' literaturu, Voprosy poètiki, 4* (1924), 182.

"smoke and thunder" of Gogol's rolling eloquence, one can speak of a poetic sleight-of-hand whereby the dismal subject dissolves into, and is superseded by, dazzling verbal magic.

Here, it seems to me, lies the major difference between Gogol's "life" and his "work." In both realms, the motif of impersonation, the strategy of concealment was paramount. Yet what seems to have been a crucial flaw, in the man was for the artist a source of strength, richness, and infinits variety, an element of freedom rather than of constraint. This, I submit, is not surprising, for poetry, in the broader sense of the word, is self-transcendence as well as self-expression, or, to modify T. S. Eliot, an escape from, as well as a stylized vehicle for, personal emotions. For the man that Gogol apparently was, a flight into cliché was self-defeating, or more exactly a source as well as an acknowledgment of defeat, of a failure in dealing with his fellow humans. For Gogol the writer, the verbal mask was part and parcel of an intricate and exhilarating verbal play—a play with the manifold possibilities of the Russian literary idiom which this Ukrainian provincial, whose Russian grammar was not exactly flawless, enriched and enlivened beyond measure.

"Was unsterblich im Gesang soll Leben, muss im Leben untergehn," says Schiller.[33] Gogol's fate illustrates this dictum in a very special way. I do not wish to pretend to know what finally killed this strange, tortured man, what triggered his death which looks so much like a slow suicide. It is widely assumed that he broke down under the burden of some super-human moral effort, of a desperate straining toward an epi-phany, a Word that would "break the evil spell" (Remizov). Might we not speculate a bit further and suggest that Gogol may have been throttled by his mask, worn down by his futile attempts to break through it so as to overcome the emotional

33. "Ah, that what gains immortal life in song / In mortal life must perish" ("The Gods of Greece," *Schiller's Poems and Ballads,* tr. Lord Edward Lytton [London, 1887], p. 207).

numbness, and establish a meaningful dialogue with others and with his walled-off "real self"?

The man died in anguish and pain. The music of his prose, born from the anguish yet soaring beyond it, will endure as long as language.

Index